Subject Lessons

Subject Lessons

The Western Education of Colonial India

Sanjay Seth

Duke University Press
Durham and London
2007

© 2007 Duke University Press
All rights reserved.

Printed in the United States of America on acid-free paper ∞
Typeset in Trinité by Tseng Information Systems, Inc.
Library of Congress Cataloging-in-Publication Data
appear on the last printed page of this book.

To Raju and Nishad

Contents

Acknowledgments

This book has been long in the making, and I have many people and institutions to thank. I am grateful to the librarians and archivists of Indian Office Library and Records (incorporated into the British Library partway through my research), the National Archives of India, the Nehru Memorial Library and Museum, the Scottish National Library, the Gokhale Institute, the Cambridge South Asia Centre Library, the State Library of Victoria, and the Borchardt library of La Trobe University – especially its Inter-Library Loans section. The Australia Research Council provided small grants to facilitate research trips, as did La Trobe University, which also provided a supportive and congenial environment in which to write. The Japan Society for the Promotion of Science awarded me a year-long fellowship to work on this book; I am grateful to Professor Nariaki Nakazato and the Toyo Bunka Kenkyujo of Tokyo University for hosting me during a blissful year when I was able to work obsessively on the manuscript. Earlier versions of some of these chapters were presented at New Delhi, Princeton, Minneapolis, New York, Chicago, Santa Cruz, Berlin, Tokyo, Edinburgh, Melbourne, and Brisbane; my thanks to my audiences at these occasions, and to the organizers of these talks.

Many friends and colleagues have answered queries, provided references, and made helpful suggestions; my thanks to Shahid Amin, Robin Jeffrey, Francesca Orsini, John Fitzgerald, the late Ravinder Kumar, Pauline Nestor, Hilary McPhee, Joel Kahn, Barbara Cain, Angus McIntyre, Richard Delacy, Sudhir Chandra, Kama Maclean, Greg Bailey, the late Fred Hardy, Ashok Aklujkar, Dennis Altman, Joel Kahn, Robert Manne, and Kunal Chakrabarti. My thanks also to Sarbajeet Mukherjee for rendering research assistance in the National Library, Calcutta.

A number of colleagues read and commented on one or more chapters of this book. I am grateful to Ranajit Guha, Sumit Sarkar, Tanika Sarkar, Robin Archer, Leela Gandhi, Michael Dutton, Ian Hunter, Anita Ray, and Nariaki Nakazato for taking the trouble to do so, and for their comments and criticisms. I am grateful to Julia Adams and Reynolds Smith for editorial feedback and for shepherding this book through the publication process, and to Fred Kameny for his very professional copy editing.

Since my graduate student days Dipesh Chakrabarty has been a friend and interlocutor, and he has read, commented upon, and discussed this book with me over the years that it has taken to write it. It gives me pleasure to acknowledge my debt to him, and to thank him. Barry Hindess once again demonstrated that there is no more acute reader of an argument, with a keen eye for flaws and evasions; I hope that there are, thanks to his comments, fewer of these than there might have been. Akeel Bilgrami engaged me in long-distance debates during my year in Tokyo, and his comments have never failed to be stimulating and challenging. Rajyashree Pandey read the chapters through their successive drafts, and offered unconditional encouragement coupled with unconstrained criticism!

Many friends offered sustenance and hospitality while I was away from home: in India, Sudhir Chandra, Geetanjali Shree, Atul Joshi, Jayanti Pandey, Sara Rai, and Muhammad Aslam; in England, Terry Shakhanovsky, Robin Archer, Chris Macpherson, Greg Patching, and above all the Hardy family; and in Japan, Sonoe Matsui and her family. A community of friends in Melbourne provided occasions for ongoing *addas*; my thanks to Deborah Kessler, Pauline Nestor, and my fellow editors of *Postcolonial Studies*, Amanda Macdonald, Michele Grossman, and – especially – Leela Gandhi and Michael Dutton.

I am unusually blessed in that my siblings constitute not only my affective, but also my intellectual, community. I subjected Vanita Seth and Suman Seth to endless drafts of the manuscript, which they read with acuity and humor. It remains a source of great sadness to me that my mother, the person who would have derived the greatest pleasure from seeing this book in print, is not here to see it. My father has been a source of unqualified support and encouragement in this as in other endeavors. I owe him and my mother more than could ever be acknowledged.

Finally, and closest to home, Rajyashree and Nishad Pandey have provided me with a world which includes, but also extends well beyond, thinking and writing. I dedicate this to them.

Introduction

The colonial era is roughly coterminous with the rise of a knowledge that I will be calling "modern, western knowledge" – "modern" to denote its relatively recent emergence, "western" to indicate the cultural specificity of these historical origins. Along with guns and goods, this knowledge traveled to the colonies, and it was in part through this knowledge that the non-western world came to be conquered, represented, and ruled. But although it arrived from the outside, often at the point of a bayonet, this knowledge ceased to be merely the colonizer's knowledge. It found a home in its new locales. A number of agencies served to disseminate it, among them armies, railroads, trade, and the institutions and practices of colonial government.

In India the most direct and one of the most important of these agencies was western education. The 1830s witnessed a bitter dispute in the ranks of colonial officialdom over whether the British Indian government should patronize "Oriental" knowledges, or whether it should direct its attentions solely to promoting western knowledge, initially through the medium of English. Victory went to the "Anglicists," led by Thomas Babington Macaulay, and from 1835 India's colonial rulers became the agency for promoting "western education," that is, education which sought to disseminate modern, western knowledge through modern institutions and pedagogic processes. It was anticipated and desired by the victorious party that this would gradually supplant indigenous knowledges, which were condemned as (variously) "superstitious," "mythic," "primitive," and, more generally, untrue; or, as Macaulay characterized them, "medical doctrines which would disgrace an English farrier, astronomy which would move laughter in girls at an English boarding school, history abounding with kings thirty feet high and reigns thirty thousand years long, and geography made of seas of treacle and seas of butter."[1]

After 1835 India's colonial rulers spent the bulk of the state money allocated for educating their subjects on modern, western education. When in

1

1854 the authorities in Britain gave instructions for extending the provision of education beyond the élite classes of native society for which it had initially been intended, they made it clear that "the education which we desire to see extended in India is that which has for its object the diffusion of the improved arts, science, philosophy and literature of Europe; in short, European knowledge."[2] Schools were established to teach this knowledge, and in 1857 the universities of Calcutta, Bombay, and Madras were established, soon to be followed by universities in other parts of India.[3] The British thus undertook a task that lent its name to the title of a work by Charles Trevelyan, one of the architects of the decision of 1835: *The Education of the People of India*. While this effort was being made, from the early decades of the nineteenth century colonialism itself came to be seen as an essentially *pedagogic* enterprise. Those aspects of British rule which had long been hailed as the justification for foreign rule of another peoples – the Pax Britannica which created peace where once there had been disorder and brigandage, the "rule of law," the provision of public works, and so on – were now seen not only as goods in themselves but also as having an educative value. A textbook of 1897 told its audience of Indian schoolboys that the Penal Code, public works, railways, irrigation and civil works, schools, the post office and telegraph, and a free press were all forces working to educate India.[4] The ascription of pedagogic effects and benefits to almost all the practices and institutions of colonial rule became pervasive, so much so that sometimes it assumed burlesque forms: in 1913 a government enquiry declared, "The Committee regards the provision of proper latrine and urinal accommodation as not only necessary in the interests of . . . health . . . [and] sanitation . . . but also as having a distinctly educative value."[5] It became common to describe formal instruction or schooling as but an aspect or subset of this wider pedagogic mission.[6] Partly because it came to be seen in this way, western education was endowed with great significance, even though the sums expended upon it were minuscule, and the numbers directly affected by it a small proportion of the total population.[7]

There was also, for a long period, a keen awareness of the "exoticism" of western knowledge. The architects of the decision of 1835 were in no doubt as to the momentousness of the decision they had made. Charles Trevelyan wrote, "The decision which was come to is worthy of everlasting record. Although homely in its words, it will be mighty in its effects long after we are mouldering in the dust."[8] The *Pioneer*, an English-owned newspaper published from Allahabad, wrote that "the experiment [of Western education] going on in India is one which, in the immensity of its scope, the gravity of the issues depending on it, and the conditions under which it has to be carried on, has had no parallel in the world's history."[9] Schooling, not on the face of it the setting for high drama, was frequently treated in highly dramatic terms, and described in flowery language. Nor was this by any means confined to the British. Syed Mahmood wrote: "The origin, rise and progress of English education in India . . . constitute one of the most significant episodes, not only in the annals of India, but in the history of the civilised world."[10] Not to be outdone, a contributor to the nationalist *Modern Review* scaled new rhetorical heights: "The English education of India! It is one of the most momentous events the world has ever seen and most difficult problems the human brain has ever faced. How to transport the learning, method, and spirit of Western Europe to Middle Eastern Asia, among a subject race . . . and make it grow as native of the soil . . . It is a more difficult achievement than the annihilation of time and space by modern science."[11]

That sense of exoticism has long since faded. Today almost all serious, "respectable," and officially disseminated knowledge about the non-western world shares the presumptions and guiding categories of modern western knowledge. This is so whether the sites for the production of knowledge are located in the western world, or in the non-western world. And usually, this fact occasions little comment, let alone sustained reflection, because western knowledge is no longer seen as only one mode of knowing but as knowledge itself, compared to which all other traditions of reasoning are only Unreason, or earlier stages in the march toward Reason.

This book is a study of how western knowledge came to be disseminated in India, such that it came to assume its current status as the obvious, and almost the only, mode of knowing about India. The book is principally concerned not with the thinking and intentions of the colonizer but with how western education was received and consumed by the colonized. It is also, and simultaneously, an argument that the status of modern western knowledge – the assumption that it is not merely one mode of knowledge but is knowledge "as such," that it must be adequate to its Indian object because it is adequate to all objects – is questionable, and needs to be rethought. What follows thus has certain affinities with recent studies, some of them undertaken under the sign of postcolonial theory, that seek not to "apply" our modern western knowledge to the non-western world, but rather to make that knowledge itself a matter for investigation and problematizing.[12]

Subject to Pedagogy

New knowledges do not simply stuff the heads of existing people with new ideas; they serve to create new people, which is why "the history of knowledge constitutes a privileged point of view for the genealogy of the subject."[13] Knowledges position and construct knowers in different ways, and this was especially true of modern, western knowledge. Why "especially" so? Because modern knowledge helps initiate, and is a defining feature of, a deep transformation which creates a knowing subject who is set apart from, even set up against, the objects to be known.

This transformation has been characterized in a variety of ways, one of the more famous of which is Max Weber's notion of "disenchantment." According to Weber, modern western man's increasing capacity to "master" the world is attributable to a type of knowledge that approaches the world looking for laws and regularities rather than purposes and meanings. The efficacy of what might initially be a more-or-less methodological or technical postulate – that we act as if the world were rationally calculable – results in turning it into a natural stance. The world is disenchanted in the sense that no magic and no mysteries pervade the world nor yield up knowledge of it; and in that the world is external to us, it does not resonate with our longings and aspirations. We can find no support or vindication for our choices, values, and beliefs, for a disenchanted world does not provide us with our own reflection – it is blank, and cold. Our knowledge of it does not reveal its meaning: the only meanings we find "out there" are those which we have put there.[14]

This knowledge is fundamentally different from the premodern knowledge(s) of Europe, which were displaced by this new knowledge, and which, Charles Taylor writes, required "understanding the world in categories of meaning, as existing to embody or express an order of Ideas or archetypes, as manifesting the rhythm of divine life, or the foundational acts of the gods, or the will of God," and "seeing the world as a text, or the universe as a book."[15] Such knowledges presumed a very different relation between the knower and the known, between humans and their world; for one thing, they did not draw the line between the two so sharply. To simplify, they presumed that humans found meaning and purpose in the world; and as modern knowledge emerged and was defined through a critique of scholastic and other medieval knowledges, this was seen as the source and root of the errors of premodern knowledges. To find an order in the universe and seek to harmonize with it, or to find the correspondences so loved by the Renaissance, or to subscribe to theories of knowledge which attribute to man an "innate" disposition to assent to the good and the true – all these appeared, from an emergent, modern, and scientific perspective, as a confusing of man with his world, most clearly manifested in attributing to the world a meaning and purpose which in fact belongs to us, and which we have projected onto it. A conception of knowledge that posits a knowing subject and an object external to it is also one that makes policing this distinction the very basis of any valid knowledge. Any confusion between the knowing subject and the object must be guarded against; solipsism on the one hand, and "projecting" one's desires and purposes onto the world on the other, become the two cardinal sins to be avoided.

This was once a novel conception of knowledge, and the subject it presumed was not found ready-to-hand but rather had to be forged, had to be created through new pedagogic practices, and through the transformations and disciplines enforced by industrialization and capitalism, modern armies, and the modern novel – a process that was complex and difficult, and one that met with resistance. All the more so in the Indian subcontinent, where the knowledges in question were not autochthonous, and where the instruments for forging the new subject had not been slowly working away through the centuries of industrialization and the emergence of new disciplinary matrixes of family, prison, school, and factory, but were heavily dependent upon the violent and coercive agency of colonial rule.

As a study of western knowledge in colonial India, this is also a work about subjectivities. It is about how Western education in India posited and served to create – and sometimes failed to fully create – certain sorts of subjects.

Subject of History

This is in part a work of history, and it is also a work about writing history, and the possibility thereof. Why it should be about writing history is readily discernible, for this book is in a very precise sense a product of the history which it retells. It is a history of the western, rational type, approved of – and practised by – Macaulay, rather than, say, a Puranic history (Macaulay's "history abounding with kings thirty feet high and reigns thirty thousand years long"). As a history of western knowledge in India written from within that knowledge, a work such as this needs a reflexive moment; it needs to ask whether the ensuing circularity is an enabling hermeneutical circle or a disabling, self-referential one.

But what could it mean to ask about the "possibility" of history writing? Here I will try to explicate this question by returning to my brief description of Weber's account of "disenchantment," this time to complicate it by juxtaposing it with another account.

Part of the appeal of Weber's account is that in arguing that there are no meanings and purposes and values "in" the world, he does not conclude that meanings and values are superfluous. Weber's well-known insistence that the scientist seek to keep fact and values distinct is not born of a positivist denigration of the latter; indeed, in part Weber argues, in Kantian fashion, for a realm of objectivity in order to make room for values – as distinctly human products.[16] This yields, or can be made to yield, a historicism which is possibly more appealing now than it was in its own day. Just as individuals assign meaning and choose values, so different peoples at different times have shaped collective values and ways of being in the world. Scholars of the human sciences can, from texts, monuments, artworks and the like, reconstruct their world-picture or Weltanschauung – a favorite word of Weber's, as of a number of his contemporaries. Medieval men and women attributed their own actions and conceptions to transcendent beings; this was a part of their Weltanschauung, something the historian can reconstruct or piece together from their art, their philosophy, and so on. We moderns know better, although – the source of Weber's melancholy – the price of our superior (self-) knowledge may be that we are less at home in the world. In all cases, man is a meaning-endowing and culture-secreting being, and from the material and textual traces and remnants he leaves behind, we can piece together what sort of man he was.

In "The Age of the World Picture" Martin Heidegger seems at first glance to be offering an account similar to this one. Like Weber, he sees the more obvious manifestations of modernity – individualism, technology, and so on – as based upon something which is, however, more fundamental. This something "more fundamental" reads not entirely unlike Weber's distinction between a subject who has become central and a world of objects which is disenchanted, and Heidegger too talks of a world picture. But his account is in fact very different.

Heidegger also states that at the heart of modernity is the rise of an absolute subjectivity, such that the world appears to man as if it were "for" him. But this is not a new Weltanschauung, replacing the older one: the modern age is not distinguished from other ages by its peculiarly "modern" picture of the world, but rather by the very fact that it can conceive and grasp the world as picture.[17] Nor can the difference between the modern and the medieval and ancient worlds be understood in terms of different "cultural values" or "spiritual values," for there was nothing, writes Heidegger, like "culture" in the Middle Ages or "spiritual values" in the ancient world: "Only in the modern era have spirit and culture been deliberately experienced as fundamental modes of human comportment, and only in most recent times have 'values' been paraded as standards for such comportment."[18] The difference between our age and other ages (and other peoples, then and now) cannot be rendered in terms of different "outlooks," "views," "values," and "experiences," because such ways of thinking are already modern, are already products of a historical and intellectual transformation which places Man at the centre of things, which now exist for him and only exist inasmuch as they are pictured, valued or experienced.[19]

Unlike Weber and many others, who rightly urge that we recognize "our" way of understanding and engaging with our world as possibly specific to us rather than part of a "human condition," Heidegger goes further, questioning the very idea that man has always been a culture-secreting being, and that different men in different epochs "secreted" different values and meanings. To recognize, as Weber did, that others may have viewed the world differently is an advance over an ahistorical ascription of similarity, but under the seeming defamiliarization of this sort is still an unwarranted assumption, namely that always, everywhere, there is "Man," whose way of being in the world is to "view" it. One way of approaching Heidegger is thus to see him as radicalizing and going beyond such historicizing, and in so doing "explaining" its limitations. Historicizing approaches take a feature of the modern, Occidental world – namely that we are subjects whose values and world-picture become embodied in socially produced meaning – and read it into the world as such.

Pressing into service this aspect of Heidegger's thought, I will ask: Where Man has not become subject and the world has not become picture, is it still possible to write history? History writing is always the "history of" – that is, it has a subject whose past it recapitulates. For modern historiography, which is deeply imbued with humanist and anthropological premises, this subject is Man, conceived as a being who produces culture and meaning, and whose meanings can be deciphered from his texts and his monuments and other "traces" of his subjectivity. But if, as this book shall show, modern knowledge failed fully to produce a subject and to produce "the world as picture" in India, then how do we write history, and what is the status of the knowledge we produce when we do write it?

The Plan of This Book

These are questions of general, theoretical import. But how do these theoretical ambitions connect with a historical study of the diffusion of western education, and of the debates to which it gave rise? Moreover, what I am calling modern, western knowledge is internally highly differentiated – there are liberals and Marxists, Kantians and Hegelians, empiricists and idealists, and so on. Is it even possible to write about the dissemination of an object called "western knowledge"? And – a final question – if this book is a critique of aspects of modern western knowledge, do I write from a position outside this knowledge?

What makes it possible to speak of "modern western knowledge," notwithstanding the numerous camps within it, is that for all their differences, they share some "core presumptions," "categories," and "background assumptions" – terms that I will be using interchangeably. These are usually unstated, because they are (or have become) naturalized, and have assumed the status of axioms. Some prefer to call these core presumptions an "episteme" or "social imaginary," but whatever the nomenclature, in all cases what is being referred to is not any specific intellectual position, representation, or practice but the "foundational assumptions about what counts as an adequate representation or practice in the first place."[20] I seek to explicate these assumptions in the chapters that follow, and also to subject modern western knowledge to critical scrutiny, by showing that the presumptions that it takes to be axiomatic and universal are not in fact so, and were not so in India.

The character of this critical enterprise needs to be carefully specified. I do not argue that the presumptions characterizing western knowledge were falsified by the "reality" of India. Arguments of this sort – an example is the "nativist" contention that western knowledge is an "alien" imposition, and therefore an inadequate instrument by which to know India – suffer from a number of crippling defects. Critiques of this sort assume that knowledge is "of" an object external to it, and thus that acquiring knowledge is a matter of "mirroring" the "real";[21] in this view, if western knowledge is to be criticized, that is because it fails to provide an adequate account of its Indian object. In arguing so, this adherents of this view partake of a representational epistemology which, ironically, is that of the modern knowledge which they seek to call into question. And in judging western knowledge to be inadequate, they presuppose a correct or adequate understanding of the "reality" of India without being able to account for where such knowledge itself comes from, and what warrant we have for treating it as the standard by which to measure modern knowledge.

Here I do not seek to step "outside" western knowledge, measure it against the "reality" of India, and show it to be wanting. I seek instead to show that in the course of the dissemination of western knowledge in India, the debates and discourses to which it gave rise can be read as registering the fact (often experienced as a disquiet) that its "foundational assumptions" could not really be assumed. It is through an attentiveness to these disturbances on the surface of western knowledge in the course of its dissemination, rather than from a vantage point outside it, that one can locate and demonstrate how western knowledge was rendered problematic in India. Since knowledges do not merely cognize a world external to them but serve to constitute that world, I also remain attentive to the ways in which, in colonial India, western knowledge reshaped what it was thought to be merely describing.

This means that I write with and from within western knowledge. It also means that the enquiry into how this knowledge was disseminated, and the argument that its presumptions and axioms cannot always be taken as axiomatic, are not two separate exercises. It is not that I first provide a historical narrative of the arrival of western knowledge in India, and then seek to evaluate its truth claims, and its adequacy to its Indian object; it is precisely through the study of how the knowledge was disseminated that I show how its enabling epistemic presumptions were rendered problematic – or else served to remake its Indian object.

Chapters 1 and 2 follow a common intellectual strategy. Each documents a controversy and the discourse that it generated, and delves into the implicit (and sometimes explicit) presumptions which are shown to underlie and animate the debates. Chapter 1 surveys the century-long complaint that Indian students treated western education as a mere means to an end, and that they learned by rote, thereby defeating the purpose of an education predicated upon the idea that knowledge is only truly such when it has been "understood" rather than simply memorized. I interpret this complaint as articulating the anxiety that modern knowledge was not producing the modern subject which it presupposed, and ask whether we should conclude that this was because another subjectivity, corresponding to indigenous modes of relating to knowledge, was diverting and frustrating the impact of western education. This question turns upon whether the desire to read historical evidence in a fashion which does not naturalize the modern, western mode of being a subject (thereby treating it as the norm) is best served by reading "difference" into "subjectivity," or whether doing so only renders all forms of being human into different ways of being a subject, thereby dissolving the very difference to which this strategy seeks to remain sensitive.

Chapter 2 documents the widely expressed belief that western education, expected not only to transform Indian students' knowledge but also their character and morality, had indeed done so – but not for the better. Western-educated Indians were thought to have been plunged into the throes of a "moral crisis" as a result of their exposure to western knowledge, evidenced in their moral and intellectual "inconsistency." According to this view, the "inconsistent" beliefs and practices of educated Indians arose out of their immersion in two incommensurable worlds, each informed by different beliefs and its own moral code: the modern world of western knowledge and the institutions and practices of colonial civil society, and the world of traditional beliefs and institutions. I show that this diagnosis was enabled by a number of presuppositions that were and are modern presuppositions, encoded in modern, western knowledge; thus here the knowledge being disseminated in schools and universities was simultaneously put to use to characterize and explain an unexpected effect of this knowledge. How adequate was this knowledge to explaining its own effects? Could it comprehend and account for its own failures? What was the relation between western knowledge as a means for comprehending social change in India and western knowledge as one of the agents of that change?

We who live in an age gifted, or cursed, with the "historical sense" often think that everything has a history – that history simply "is," even if not all peoples developed a sense of historicity and the means by which to record and write it. In chapter 3 I argue the contrary: it is not that there is the fact of history, which among some peoples at certain times leads to history writing, but rather that the code and representational form which constitutes the modern practice of writing history gives us the history we think we had. If this argument, baldly summarized here, is valid – if history is not something which is always there, and which can be reconstructed well (as through modern protocols of history writing) or badly (as through myths and epics and legends), but something which is constituted and constructed through the codes which purport to simply re-present it – then we need to inquire more closely into the enabling presumptions of modern practices of history writing. We should not be surprised to discover that these presumptions are part and parcel of modern, western knowledge; history writing is itself, after all, a modern knowledge. However these presumptions include those which are discussed and shown to be problematic in the preceding chapters. Thus here I formulate and address a paradox: modern western knowledge provides many of the enabling assumptions of history writing, yet history writing finds these presumptions rendered problematic when it seeks to narrativize the emergence and dissemination of modern, western knowledge in India.

Whereas part I of this book seeks to interrogate the discourses to which the spread of education gave rise for their hidden presumptions, part II seeks to discern what place education acquired in the imagination of nationalists, and others, who both sought this education and criticized it. Western education was not only where the question of subjectivity came to be posed; it was also the site where collective identities were produced. Indeed, the impact of western education derived less from the transformations that it effected upon the relatively small numbers who were subject to pedagogy, and more from its having become the object of desire and contestation; less, for instance, because many nationalists were western-educated, and more because nationalism made western education an important part of its vision of what was required to bring into being an independent and modern nation. The role that western education came to play in the production of collective identities, and in particular the role that it played in the nationalist project to found a nation at once modern and yet different, provides the subject matter for part II of this book.

In the nineteenth century alarm was expressed over Muslim "backwardness," this backwardness being measured in terms of the failure of Muslims, by comparison with Hindus, to avail themselves of western education. Chapter 4 enquires into the epistemic conditions enabling this discourse, this time locating them not in unstated ontological and epistemological presumptions that characterize western knowledge but more specifically in the practices of colonial governmentality, and in intellectual disciplines closely associated with them. It was only when "population" became an object of knowledge and governance that "backwardness" could become a subject for investigation and concern. But measuring the backwardness of the Muslim entailed conceiving what it meant to be Muslim in a novel way, and thus a debate centering on western education and Muslims also created new ways of thinking – and being – Muslim.

Partha Chatterjee and others have shown that in the nineteenth century an emergent nationalism made the Indian woman the emblem and custodian of Indianness, at the same time as nationalists sought to imitate and acquire those "material" advantages of the West which were necessary to found an independent nation.[22] But if woman were to become the repository of an essential cultural identity which needed to be preserved, this did not mean that she was not herself to be subjected to change. At the same time that woman was made into an icon of Indian identity and culture, there began a concerted project to transform and "modernize" the middle-class woman and the Indian home. Female education was an important part of this project, and chapter 5 examines this and the tension which marked it. Because of the symbolic load which woman was required to bear, any signs that this project was failing not only testified to the continued backwardness of the Indian home, and thus of the would-be nation, but also, and more fundamentally, seemingly disqualified the educated nationalist élites' claims to being the modern vanguard of an ancient nation. Incapable of transforming their homes, how could they transform the nation they wished to lead?

Most books dealing with India's recent past find that the opposition between colonizer and nationalist was a decisive one, and many structure their investigations around it. For the most part that is not so of this book, and chapter 6 explains why. There were of course some important lines of division between nationalists and rulers over the subject of education. Many important nationalist figures, including Gandhi and Tagore, not only were trenchant critics of western education in India but sought to elaborate alternative visions of what education in India should be, and to give institutional expression to these visions, as did many lesser-known figures. This chapter seeks to remain attentive to the variety and richness of the nationalist imagination, while drawing attention to what is of central importance and yet nonetheless frequently overlooked: few nationalists doubted that what India needed was modern, western education, and hardly any advocated a return to "indigenous" knowledge practices, even as they urged that modern knowledge be disseminated through Indian languages rather than through the medium of English. That modern Western knowledge has come to be normalized, such that it is identified with knowledge as such, is as much the "gift" of nationalism as it is of colonialism.

Almost all the personages who figure in this book viewed western knowledge just as we tend to view it: as being in some sense intimately linked to modernity. The burden of my argument, however, is that while India was transformed, and western knowledge was an important agent in this transformation, this transformation did not principally occur because education "modernized" those Indians who were subject to it. Even as they engaged with modern institutions, engaged in modern practices, and acquired western knowledge, Indians often seemed to do so in ways that did not render them modern, and that did not accord with the core presumptions of this knowledge. The Epilogue of this book thus inquires into the relation between modern knowledge and modernity, and suggests that the homology we usually assume between the two needs to be rethought.

PART I

Subject to Pedagogy

CHAPTER ONE

Changing the Subject
Western Knowledge and the Question of Difference

Presiding over the "Anglicist" policy in education enunciated three years earlier, in 1838-39 the General Committee for Public Instruction in Bengal declared, "the ultimate object which we have in view is to infuse into the student, possessed of talents and leisure, a taste for literature and science," all of which would "hasten the regeneration of the country." The committee noted with satisfaction that western education was proving very popular with the middle classes, but also noted: "At present, education is for the most part appreciated only for the direct returns it yields."[1] As the "at present" indicates, the committee was hopeful that over time education would be appreciated for other reasons; and in the meantime, its instrumental value constituted a useful and even necessary inducement. But a few years later the same body observed that while many more students were entering and completing school, thus achieving their goal of attaining "the qualifications requisite to perform the mechanical duties of a writer [a clerk]," "our object to raise the character of the people by education and not by their purses is still far distant."[2]

The ensuing decades did not lessen the distance. The tendency to treat western education as a purely material or pecuniary asset came to be bemoaned with increasing frequency in subsequent years. In an exam answer at the Elphinstone Institution in 1850 a student wrote, "it is painful to write that the objects of the natives to send their children to the Government school are not the same as those of the Government. Their object is that their children may get a living for them."[3] Over half a century later India's eminent chemist Prafulla Chandra Ray, writing on "The Bengali Brain and Its Misuse," declared that a "diploma is judged by its monetary equivalent — as something which can be turned into cash."[4] These and numerous others observed, and usually lamented, that western education was treated as a means to an end, seldom valued in and for itself.

This chapter seeks to document in all its richness a discourse which spans over a century and which was generated from across all the usual cleavages demarcating opinion – the authors of it were British and Indian, loyalist and nationalist, humble and exalted, official and unofficial. What I call the "complaint concerning instrumentalism" and the closely associated "anxiety of cram" did not only voice the concern that there was a failure in the dissemination of western knowledge. When read carefully, this discourse can be shown to implicitly register and articulate the anxiety that western knowledge was failing to produce the subject who was the counterpart to this knowledge.

Contemporaries suggested that this failure was occurring because Indian students were appropriating the new knowledge much as they would have appropriated indigenous knowledges. I shall show that indigenous knowledges indeed posited and produced a different relation between knower and known, or between what we have become accustomed to see as the subject who knows and the object which is known; and the conclusion to be drawn, it would seem, is that cramming and instrumentalism testified to the (stubborn) presence of another subjectivity, an indigenous or premodern one. Such a conclusion would at once allow us to explain the failure being registered in the discourse of instrumentalism and cram, and moreover do so in a way which recognizes and remains sensitive to the different ways of relating to knowledge, tied to different ways of being in the world. But the category of "subjectivity" has a certain normativity built into it, and the question arises of whether it can be reworked to accommodate different ways of inhabiting the world, different ways of being a "self." Do such historicist emendations of our categories allow us to recognize difference, or do they unwittingly substantialize and universalize the difference to which they seek to attend?

"The Pinnacle of Bengali Ambition" . . .
The Complaint of Instrumentalism

It was frequently commented that education was not only regarded solely as a means to employment but more narrowly still: that it was treated (in the words of Viceroy Lord Irwin) as a "turnstile leading into the arena of Government service."[5] Western education was valued, according to an inspector for schools, because the natives had the idea that it would lead to "what is the highest pinnacle of Bengali ambition – employment under Government."[6] In the early years of the new education a middle school certificate was enough for a lowly position in government service, but very soon the requirements began to escalate, leading to the ditty,

> idil midil ki chodo aas
> leke khurpa khodo ghaas[7]

> Abandon the desire for middle school and the like,
> get a scythe and cut the grass.

A middle school certificate usually meant education to a certain standard in the vernacular. However, it was reported, such learning was not much valued, and it became progressively devalued once the acquisition of a government job of even lowly rank began to require more advanced qualifications, and hence education in English. Thus when the Despatch of 1854 sought to redress the earlier emphasis on education in English by urging that the "grant-in-aid" system be used to establish schools teaching modern knowledge in Indian languages, government officials reported that the middle classes were only interested in contributing to the establishment of English schools which might lead to government employment, and would "not lift a finger to aid in the establishment of a Vernacular School"; "they will be taught English or not taught at all."[8] This lack of enthusiasm for western learning conveyed in the vernacular, compared to the enthusiasm for western education in English, was seen to betoken a hardheaded calculation that only an English education would lead to a government job of the right sort of rank and income. The *Calcutta Review* noted that "for vernacular schools of an improved class there is little or no demand," "a knowledge of English . . . pays so much better than anything else, that it is the only thing much in demand."[9] Even as the middle classes wanted only education in English, the lower classes, who were not in a position to aspire to government jobs and hence to an education in English, were widely reported to prefer indigenous modes of learning to the vernacular schools provided by the government; an inspector of schools in Bengal reported, "Petty shop-keepers and traders are satisfied with what the Gooroomohashoy [the traditional village schoolteacher] teaches, [and] can see no use in their children learning Bengali, Geography, or the history of Bengal."[10] Muslim parents, as we shall see in chapter 4, were commonly thought to be resistant to sending their children to schools of the modern, western type, with many preferring to send their children to traditional schools that combined instruction in worldly matters with religious instruction.

A university degree – or indeed, even having sat for the matriculation exam for university entry and failed it[11] – was a mark of distinction, but only, according to the *Englishman*, because of its instrumental use, for the natives do not "attach the smallest value to . . . degrees, diplomas or certificates" issued by the University of Calcutta, "unless as passports to Government employment."[12] Indeed, the suspicion was widely voiced that the knowledge which secured one these qualifications was regarded with a certain skepticism, by pupil and teacher alike. Stories abounded of schoolmasters who told their pupils to give the "right" answer rather than the true answer – "you must learn these things so that you may be able to give satisfactory answers to the Superintendent when he comes," one teacher told his students, "but God only knows whether they are true or not."[13]

The alleged obsession with government employ could be explained in a number of ways.[14] For some it was a symptom of the Indian middle class's regrettable, even reprehensible, aversion to manual or commercial employment: that itself could be linked to the excessively impractical and "literary" character of the education imparted, which fitted students for nothing other than government employ.[15] For others, by contrast, the narrow and utilitarian character of the education that the colonizers gave their subjects made these subjects ill-qualified and ill-equipped to be anything other than underlings in the administration of the colonial state.[16] Others would point out that the desire to seek a regular income and a secure job – the chief attractions of government employ – were perfectly reasonable and explicable given an underdeveloped and distorted economy, which afforded few other opportunities. As a speaker to the Kapole Students Union told his audience, "[government] service is one of the best sources of earning a livelihood without any capital."[17]

Since an educated young man had the potential to acquire a secure job and a steady income, he was a very eligible marriage prospect. This meant that education could be translated ("cashed in") not only into an income, but also into a dowry: according to the Reverend Holmes, "It is a familiar fact that at each stage of his career a Bengali youth commands as bridegroom a price proportionate to the particular rung of the educational ladder on which he has succeeded in placing his foot. Should he have passed the matriculation, his father can command so much as his price . . . but if he have passed the B.A., up goes the price; whilst the M.A., B.L's are the prizes of the marriage market."[18]

Another dimension of the complaint I have labeled "instrumentalism" was that because education was seen only as a path to an income and perhaps a dowry, learning and even curiosity were seldom awakened. A "song of Calcutta University" published in the *Statesman* in 1904 captured both this lack of enthusiasm and an acknowledgment of the worldly benefits of education:

> Shall we sigh for the souls thou hast deadened?
> Shall we blame thee for brains thou hast sucked?
> Shall we ask how thy records were reddened?
> Or plead for the hosts that are plucked?
> Thy slaves are all dead to enjoyment,
> And sombre and barren their lives;-
> But thou leadest them on to employment
> And dowries and wives.[19]

Any intellectual awakening which did occur ceased, it was claimed, once the instrumental end was realized; nothing new was acquired, and that which had been acquired earlier was lost. Numerous commentators, Indian and British, complained that after completing their education, students declined to ever read or indeed even think.[20] According to one pamphleteer, "There are hardly any such things as students in the proper sense of the term in our country . . . people study for material gain . . . for situations in life . . . After getting into office they become like machines or worse still like fossils. They lose all interest in study."[21]

The most common explanation of this widely diagnosed condition was that instrumentalism flourished because Indians did not understand the character and significance of western education, including its transformative, regenerative powers. Education was what one acceded to because it was what the ruler required if one was to get ahead, not something embraced because one had come to value it or the knowledge that it produced. Instrumentalism was at once a sign that English education had been misunderstood and the particular form that this misunderstanding took: a subordination of learning to material concerns – jobs, marriage prospects and dowry – exogenous to education. Governor William Malcolm Hailey was adverting to something like this when opening the Punjab Educational Conference and Exhibition of 1926: "few of us would feel that education has exerted on the minds of the people at large that general stimulus, at once an awakening and a broadening of the mind, that we would have hoped to see. There is a general enthusiasm for the spread of schooling; yet paradoxically and unfortunately, people at large seem doubtful whether schooling in itself confers any lasting benefit on the scholar." In fact, Hailey went on, "one encounters the expression of a lurking feeling of regret that it should be necessary to adopt this somewhat mysterious device to hold one's own in the world; one finds even a feeling that the world would possibly be a better place if a man did not have to subject his children to a process which, for other purposes, seems to possess no very marked benefits of its own."[22]

There were of course those who pointed out that not all Indian students regarded education so instrumentally, or that to treat education as a passport to a job was hardly a uniquely Indian problem. The Indian student had his defenders, including British defenders. Many observers would note that instrumentalism was not unknown among British students, and Syed Bilgrami declared that the modern spirit of commercialism was responsible for transforming education into a commodity everywhere.[23] W. A. Potter, addressing the assembled graduates of Madras University in 1873, told them that "an ideal man who loves culture purely for its own sake and into whose mind there never enters . . . any idea of personal aggrandisement in the shape either of money or fame . . . is not, I venture to say, the type of ordinary graduate in any country."[24] But the critics would reply that while instrumentalism was not an exclusively Indian trait, in India it took on an exaggerated form. In England also, the Calcutta University Commission conceded, students tended to equate education with exams, and good performance in exams with worldly success: "But," the commission wrote, "we do not find that general closing of the ears and mind to everything that does not contribute to examination success."[25]

"Copying Machines" . . . The Anxiety of Cram

In 1902 the viceroy of India, Lord Curzon, told the convocation of Calcutta University, "The great fault of education as pursued in this country is, as we all know, that knowledge is cultivated by the memory instead of the mind, and that aids to the memory are mistaken for implements of the mind."[26] For more than fifty years on either side of this date, it was a constant lament that Indian students studied by "cramming," by which was meant not last-minute preparation but rather "getting a thing by rote, without understanding it or digesting its truth";[27] the technique was sometimes also referred to by students as "to by-heart it." The complaint begins very early, and it is made of primary schools as well as of universities, and of girls' education as well as boys'. It is not confined to British India, but is heard also in the princely states.[28] Perhaps most important, it is an observation and lament made by the British as well as by Indians, by colonial officials and also by nationalists. One complainant, the principal of Elphinstone College, spoke for many when he pithily declared, "Cram is the great canker of [Indian] education."[29]

Various explanations were advanced for why the "problem" of cram loomed so large, with remedies varying accordingly. The importance of exams in the Indian system of education were widely cited as a reason for cram. There were variations between provinces, but as an example, in Madras in 1896 there were three exams to be passed (primary, upper primary, and lower secondary) before the all-important matriculation exam. For half a century "aided" schools were assisted on the basis of a payment-by-results system, with results measured by success in exams; as was often observed,[30] the school had a powerful incentive to make passing exams the focus of all teaching. And then of course there were the examinations at university, which usually had to be passed in all subjects for the student to proceed to the next level. The excessive importance of exams meant – so ran the argument – that the entire system became distorted. The Hindi novelist and short-story writer Premchand told an educational conference in Gorakhpur that the "examination mentality is destroying education."[31] This argument came to be widely accepted; in a declaration on educational policy in 1904 the government observed that while external exams could not be entirely dispensed with, "their influence has been allowed to dominate the whole system of education in India," and announced that the number of exams leading up to university was to be reduced, and grants to schools no longer to be based on payment-by-results.[32] However, the problem remained; a decade later, in its next major statement on education, the government was still complaining that exams "encourage cram,"[33] and the link between exams and cramming continued to be made in subsequent years.

Although exams were widely held to be overemphasized at all levels of education, that was especially true at university level. The succession of exams; the need to pass in every subject to proceed to the next level; the high stakes for students whose families had made many sacrifices to get them this far – all conspired to make exams everything, and rote learning the be-all and end-all of university. The result, according to the Reverend Lal Behari Day, was that students "only take down the Professor's words, commit them to memory – often without understanding them – and reproduce them in the examination hall. A copying machine could do the same."[34] Numerous witnesses made it clear that cram was not a matter of lack of effort, but rather of the wrong sort of effort; it was to be condemned, but condemned above all because of its cost to the student. An Indian author of a pamphlet called *Our Young Men* bemoaned that these young men learned "every paragraph, every sentence, every phrase, every word in the text books . . . with a care and attention which . . . is simply painful."[35] The Calcutta University Commission rose to lyrical heights in describing the process: "It is impossible to peruse the evidence on the examination system as it exists today in Bengal without a feeling of profound sadness. The immensity of the efforts, disproportionate to the results; the painful anxiety of the candidates; the mechanical award of marks encouraging the least fruitful of efforts of the mind . . . the sterilising influence of the whole system on both teachers and taught and the consequent crying waste of the intelligence of the youth of Bengal."[36]

What greatly compounded the problem was that the first three universities in India – in Calcutta, Bombay, and Madras – were modeled after London University, then newly established. The university was merely a body affiliating colleges, conducting examinations, and conferring degrees; all teaching was done in the colleges, but the colleges were obliged to teach with a view to the "centrally" administered exams. The result, the editor of the *Dawn* opined, was that colleges in India were nothing like the colleges of Oxford or Cambridge but were rather "coaching agencies mis-named colleges";[37] and the vice-chancellor of Calcutta University, Sir Asutosh Mookerjee, adjudged that the institution of examination-only universities "necessarily produced the disastrous result that teaching was subordinated to examinations,"[38] which in turn led to cram.

That teaching and examination were done in English rather than the mother tongue of students was another reason widely given for the tendency of students to cram. Forced to learn in an unfamiliar language, students found their normal processes of study and thought rendered too difficult, and responded by committing things to memory. Numerous observers affirmed that the English of most students was simply not good enough to follow a lecture or write an essay. They either compensated by memorizing the text, or else teachers compensated for their poor English by dictating "word for word, what they wish them to learn," as the distinguished historian Jadunath Sarkar "confessed" he and most other college teachers did.[39]

The system of setting texts was often blamed for facilitating cram. The knowledge that exam questions would always be on or derived from a given source made it possible, even "rational," to memorize large chunks of the textbook. Schoolchildren, it was complained, "shut their eyes to everything which nature or books other than their text-books can supply";[40] they were "text-book gramaphones."[41] Attempts to alleviate the problem did not prove successful. Madras abolished the English textbook for the Matriculation exam but after fifteen years reintroduced it, declaring the experiment to have been a failure;[42] and in Calcutta a proposal to replace a single textbook with a number of required readings was met with the objection that it would only result in a further proliferation of "keys" or digests, "giving rise to a worse sort of cramming than the one we are trying to check."[43] Thus the problems created by textbooks were greatly compounded by the proliferation of "keys" and "made-easies," which relieved students of the need to study even the textbook, and provided model exam questions and answers besides. There was a flourishing market in these keys, which were "sold by every book-seller and advertised by every post."[44] The eminent lawyer and Liberal politician Tej Bahadur Sapru told the Calcutta University Commission that when he had been a student twenty-five years earlier it had been common for students to read a key in place of the textbook, and that according to his sons, now students at college, this continued to be so.[45]

Teachers were often held responsible for cramming. At college level a racialized education sector meant that Indian teachers, however able, were unlikely to advance far up a career ladder principally meant for Europeans.[46] This diminished the incentives for Indian teachers; conversely, European teachers occupied an exalted position irrespective of their abilities.[47] The college teacher at least had some status and a decent income; the schoolteacher had neither. "If we appraise the work of a village teacher only at three annas a day," a speaker told the Madras Educational Conference in 1896, "we should also be prepared to get a return of work proportionate to this starvation allowance."[48] The miserable pay and poor prospects of the school teacher meant, as witness after witness testified, that school teaching occupied an exceedingly poor position on the social scale.[49] On the eve of Independence, at the lower level of the educational ladder teachers were being paid rates at or below those earned by people in menial professions,[50] and most continued to be ill qualified and ill trained (or untrained) for teaching.[51] The headmaster of a high school in Bengal described the "typical" high school teacher: "Humble and unassuming in dress, deserving and craving for pity everywhere, he trudges along, a hopeless bundle of present woes and past miseries. When the first streak of light strikes the Eastern sky, he moves along the public road to serve as a domestic coach to a couple of young hopefuls and is generously paid five or six pieces of silver at the end of the month, comes home at about nine to attend to the multifarious domestic duties that await him. Dog-tired, he goes to school, sits in a ricketty chair, teaches a variety of subjects with occasional dozes . . . With the falling shades of the evening, he goes again to his coaching work." He went on to ask, "How can such a body of human beings who have no hope for the future, who are ever anxious to keep himself and his family out of the grip of dire starvation, stimulate young minds, kindle the Promethean spark, and show that life has its joys?"[52]

As with the charge of instrumentalism, there were voices which would defend the Indian student, and not simply on the grounds that the poor fellow had little choice but to cram. In a widely reported convocation address, Henry Maine questioned whether cramming necessarily led to superficial knowledge, and wondered whether the accusation of cram arose simply because "Natives of India learn with singular rapidity."[53] Maine's defense of cramming found few followers, but a more common response was to point out that cramming was not a vice limited to Indians. An Indian author quoted that unimpeachable English source, *Pall Mall* magazine, to the effect that English schoolboys and Oxbridge pupils passed their exams "by dint of cramming,"[54] and Viceroy Curzon, in a later avatar as chancellor of the University of Oxford, had occasion to defend Oxford students from the charge that they passed their exams by cramming with the same vigor with which he had earlier condemned Indian students.[55] But again, as with the complaint of instrumentalism, the reply was that even if the problem was not confined to India, it occurred in a particularly acute form there, and with especially unhappy consequences.[56]

The Subject of Knowledge

The two complaints were linked, and indeed they often occurred side by side in the same texts, as two sides of the same counterfeit coin. Sometimes it was suggested that because students had no real understanding or appreciation of the character and value of education, they regarded cram as an adequate way of acquiring it; or else, because cram was the only way they could get through the system, they were never really able to develop any understanding or appreciation of education, and were unable to regard it other than in instrumental terms. In either case, the discourse of cram and instrumentalism articulated the perception that western education could neither presume, nor had succeeded in creating, an Indian subject who could value and appropriate it in the terms which it required.

Does this mean that the British "aimed" to create a new (colonial) subject – for instance, a rational, enlightened, and even "expressive" subject? Not at all. Western education was not aimed simply at producing clerks to staff the lower ranks of the colonial administration, as was sometimes claimed (if it had been, it would have been wound up in the early 1870s, when British officials began to warn educated Indians that their numbers exceeded the proportion of positions the government was willing to make available to them), but neither was it aimed at producing Indian Emiles or Tom Paines. It is the way of posing the question that is unhelpful here; if posed in the language of intentionality the immediate response, not unnaturally – given that colonialism was an exploitative and oppressive system – is to deny any proposition that could be construed as ascribing good intentions to the colonizer. My argument is not about intention; my claim is not that the British sought to produce modern subjects, but rather that western, modern knowledge posits and presumes a subjectivity or type of selfhood, and that this is so irrespective of intentions. The introduction of modern, western knowledge implied not just the absorption of "facts" and theorems, the replacement of one set of ideas with another, but also a deportment, a stylistics, a whole series of "adjustments" in how human subjects inhabit the world (a great many of which are informal rather than formal, unstated rather than thematized). It does not necessarily follow that the production of such subjects was ever seriously "intended" – indeed, if one insists on imputing ill intentions to the rulers one could even, adapting an argument from Pierre Bourdieu, argue that "failure" was part of the intention, that the intention behind western education was to demonstrate the inability of most Indians to acquire it. However, because knowledge necessarily presupposes a corresponding subjectivity, what does follow is that any discourse about a failure in disseminating knowledge would also at some level register this fact, even if it did not explicitly thematize it. I read the discourse of cram and instrumentalism as registering, and on occasion thematizing, the perception that this subjectivity was lacking.

Thus instrumentalism and cram did not *simply* express the concern that western knowledge was being ineffectively diffused. In part they did not *even* signify the belief that knowledge was failing to be acquired, for inasmuch as the successful dissemination of knowledge was gauged by being able to perform certain functions – doing sums, passing exams – it sometimes had been acquired. But it turned out that even where this was so, sometimes the results had to be discounted. Hence an educationist complained that while Indian students in primary schools displayed an extraordinary facility at learning their times-tables, they had "no real comprehension of quite elementary number work when presented . . . in an ordinary, everyday, concrete way";[57] and another remarked that even where students could recite their lessons, they usually had no idea of the meaning, and indeed sometimes "they did not believe that the sentences could convey any meaning beyond being read."[58]

How and why could successful performance of designated tasks still constitute failure? Unlike the joke that intelligence is defined as that which is measured by an IQ test, the position taken here was that what was at issue was not a verifiable skill but rather a mode of relating to knowledge, so that even where students met the test measuring their acquisition of a skill (such as by passing their exams after cramming), the result could still be deemed a "failure" of education. It was a failure of education because mastery of the task had been achieved by means that sidestepped the transformation of the subject and the relation between subject and knowledge. What I draw attention to here is not that the complaint about cram and instrumentalism could be interpreted as "also" being about subjectivity; I am making the stronger claim that it made no sense unless it meant this, that only this meaning even makes intelligible the presumption that cramming and instrumentalism are a failure of knowledge rather than a form of it.

When the authors of the statements I have been documenting sought to explain *why* cramming and instrumentalism were a failure of knowledge rather than a form of it, they usually did so by distinguishing between understanding and "merely" memorizing, between learning how to "think" on the one hand and regurgitating on the other, between knowledge which is acquired by oneself and thus sustained by conviction and that which is accepted in deference to authority. Such a conception of knowledge has a lineage. The Reformation, the scientific revolution, and the Enlightenment all play a part in the emergence of the notion that only what is independently acquired, and sustained by personal conviction, counts as knowledge. By the latter part of the eighteenth century Kant would define Enlightenment in terms of the free and independent use of one's reason;[59] and Kant the pedagogue, in his "Announcement" of his winter courses for 1765–66, told prospective students that "the method of reflecting and concluding *for oneself* is the skill the student is really seeking."[60]

For some members of the Indian élite such a conception of knowledge had become part of their understanding, which is precisely why they were co-authors of the discourse of instrumentalism and cram. Sir Gooroo Dass

Banerjee, High Court judge and first Indian vice-chancellor of Calcutta University, was only one of the more distinguished of many in India who emphasized the critical difference between having a student understand something and "merely" rote-learn it, and between knowledge that had been made one's own and secondhand knowledge.[61] In his autobiography, the nationalist leader Bipan Chandra Pal explained that he had taken little interest in the "traditional" education he received as a young child, because the requirement that he learn Persian passages by heart did not "suit" his "impatient intellect, which was eager to know and understand."[62] A play in Hindi about a disenchanted young man, product of an Indian university, has him announce that he will dedicate his life to founding a "national" school where patriotism will be inculcated, all instruction will be in the vernacular, and rote learning will be abandoned in favor of teaching pupils how to think.[63] An American observer of the Indian scene used the same language as scores of Indians and Englishmen when he contrasted teaching students "to think and reason" with the prevailing "parrot-like memorizing."[64] Even at the lower reaches of the educational ladder the difference between successful education and failed education was expressed through contrasts of this sort; one educationist urged adoption of his proposed reforms of primary teaching on the grounds that "Dull routine" would "give way to freshness and change, for passivity we shall have activity, for constant repetition of meaningless sounds we shall have varied use of intelligent words, and for the stilted and insincere expression of somebody else's formal thoughts we shall have the direct and sincere, even if imperfect, expression of the boy's own simple thoughts."[65]

Lord Curzon's speech at the convocation of the University of Calcutta in 1902 – the same speech in which he declared, in a passage quoted earlier, that the great fault of education in India was its tendency to cultivate the memory instead of the mind – is a fine example. Curzon is at this point addressing himself to those young graduates who may go on to become teachers, and he continues:

> Knowledge is a very different thing from learning by rote, and in the same way education is a very different thing from instruction. Make your pupils, therefore, understand the meaning of books, instead of committing to memory the sentences and lines. Teach them what the Roman Empire did for the world, in preference to the names and the dates of the Caesars. Explain to them the meaning of government and administration and law, instead of making them repeat the names of

battles or the populations of towns. Educate them to reason and to understand reasoning, in preference to learning by heart the first three books of Euclid. Remember too, that knowledge is not a collection of neatly assorted facts like the specimens in glass cases in a museum. The pupil whose mind you merely stock in this fashion will no more learn what knowledge is than a man can hope to speak a foreign language by poring over a dictionary. What you have to do is not to stuff the mind of your pupil with the mere thoughts of others, excellent as they may be, but to teach him to use his own. One correct generalisation drawn with his own brain is worth a library full of second-hand knowledge.[66]

In this remarkable passage Curzon tries through a series of contrasts to convey the critical difference between rote learning and "real" learning. In one short passage he manages to make the following contrasts:

Knowledge/rote
education/instruction
meaning/memory
explanation/repetition
understanding, reasoning/learning by heart
own thoughts/others' thoughts
own generalisations/second-hand-knowledge

The first and fifth contrasts are different iterations of the distinction that Curzon is seeking to make: between genuine knowledge, the ability to understand the meaning of something through one's own reasoning processes, and committing something to one's memory. This difference, the last two contrasts indicate, is also the difference between having made knowledge one's own, and being "stuffed" with others' ideas and therefore in possession of only secondhand knowledge. The second and fourth contrasts refer to the different pedagogies corresponding to these two knowledges – one is inculcated through an education that explains, the other through an education that requires the student to repeat. Curzon also employs two metaphors to make his point: knowledge is not like a neat collection of specimens in a museum, and it cannot be acquired if conceived of thus any more than a language can be acquired simply by poring over a dictionary. The contrasts and repetitions weave in and out of each other as Curzon strives to make the same point from different angles and by use of different metaphors, and returns, again and again, to the distinction which he fears his student audience may not see:

a distinction in which good knowledge and failed knowledge map onto the distinction between autonomy and heteronomy, between an active subject and a passive one.

The Indian Heart

If the discourse of cram and instrumentalism expressed the anxiety that western education was not remaking subjects, we can now in fact go further. The discourse of cram and instrumentalism expressed the fear that not only was western education failing to remake colonial subjects, but Indian students and native practices were deflecting and "remaking" – that is, bending and distorting – education.

To return to the discourse of instrumentalism, attending to it carefully: the complaint is not, or not usually, that Indian students and their parents have only mundane and material desires and goals. The complaint is rather that while they do have other, nonmaterial desires and goals, they do not see western education as having anything to contribute to the fulfillment of these. An essayist in the *Modern Review* wrote, "The English learning is universally considered as an *Arthakari vidya* or learning that enables one to earn money."[67] Neither the essayist nor his audience assumed that earning money was the *only* goal of his fellow countrymen, but rather that "the English learning" pertained only to this goal. In a similar vein, it was a commonplace that for a Bengali, "English is the language of commerce, Bengali the language of the heart." Apart from again indicating the instrumental nature of the engagement with English and with western education, what this commonplace also registered was that the Bengali did, after all, have a heart. However, his western education did not address this; it addressed him only in his capacity as a householder, desirous of providing for his family and making his way in life. Education was failing to have the desired effects not only because it was inadequately understood and appreciated and hence used instrumentally; more than that, it was being compartmentalized or quarantined, put into the slot of "that which enables one to get ahead in life," instead of refashioning the understanding of what constitutes the good life. Such an attitude was cheerfully and pithily summed up by an unrepentant Muslim judicial official, who told an inspector of schools, "Men labour for Din [otherworldly purposes, salvation] or Duniya [this-worldly purposes]. For Din we have our own books, for Duniya 'Marshman's Guide to Civil Law in Urdu.' This is sure to lead us to a Principal Sadir Aminship [i.e. a promotion]."[68]

And what of cram? As we observed earlier, it was frequently noted that Indians had a "gift" for memorizing. The *Calcutta University Commission Report* observed, "There is clear evidence that the average student in Bengal has powers of memorization that would be regarded as exceptional in Europe . . . his main effort is devoted to memorization, and . . . such memorisation enables him to pass the university examination."[69] This capacity was seen to be closely connected with an indigenous pedagogy which, it was generally believed, had relied largely or exclusively on rote learning. The Indian student, many concluded, had drawn upon this, such that what was meant to be transformed had infected the agency of transformation. The report of the Bombay Board of Education for 1845 observed that the government-established vernacular schools were a "considerable improvement" over the indigenous schools they were intended to replace, but then noted: "we do not think that we are at liberty to assume that our vernacular establishments as at present conducted are capable of operating any effective permanent improvement on the native mind." Why was this so? A major reason was that the government schools had been infected by old methods, simply applying them to new materials: "The same inefficacious habit of committing everything which is put before them to memory exclusively prevails; catechisms of geography, of grammar, and the Government regulations are all treated in this manner, besides the complicated and needlessly long multiplication tables. And the people we are assured are much prepossessed in favour of these old practices."[70] Seventy years later the same point about the relation between the "old" and the "new" learning was still being made: "There were no radical changes, no new experiments in education . . . There was the same teaching of set and prescribed textbooks . . . the same emphasis on the study of words, the same taxing of the memory . . . The only marked difference was that the pale glow of religion which had cast a halo round education was swept away and it emerged definitely as a secular activity. It would not save your soul but it might secure you a job."[71]

WESTERN EDUCATION was to transform knowledge and the recipient of it, but indigenous practices had warped the system, and the Indian student had bent the system to his own strengths, finding loopholes which resulted in the pedagogic process being shaped by Indian students (and teachers), rather than the students reshaped by pedagogy. One could ask whether this result should be read as an example of "resistance" – the native fighting back, by subverting the practices and disciplines being foisted upon him. There is a sense in which one could see this as resistance, but it is a very specific sense of "resistance," one not closely tied to intentionality, and partly as a consequence of this, lacking heroic connotations. Wendy Brown notes that "resistance is by no means inherently subversive of power . . . it is only by recourse to a very non-Foucaultian moral evaluation of power as bad or as that which is to be overcome that it is possible to equate resistance with that which is good, progressive, or seeking an end to domination."[72] Just as I have insisted that western education posited the relation between knowledge and knower such that memory and mere mastery of authorities could not be regarded as a form of knowledge – without having the "positing" done by colonial officials who intended to produce modern Indian subjects – so one can say that it met with resistance in the form of the Indian student, who frequently failed to become such a subject. In both cases what is principally at issue are not intentions but rather the ways in which knowledge positions the recipient, and sometimes fails to do so. Thus are we able to recognize that the potentially transformative force of western education met an immovable object in the form of cramming and instrumentalism, and yet we avoid the absurdity of treating dowry-seeking crammers as heroic figures, resolutely fighting off British hegemony. And because we can write of resistance without presuming that Indian students were "seeking an end to domination," we shall observe in chapter 6 that those who *did* seek an end to (colonial) domination, such as nationalists, did not resist western education, which they instead saw as necessary to the emergence of a free and independent nation.

The question for the moment is this: If the Indian student was bending things his own way, was the failure to shape subjectivity occurring because another subjectivity was intervening – an indigenous one? Having shown that western knowledge presupposed a corresponding subjectivity, and that the discourse of instrumentalism and cramming registered its absence, we can now ask whether this insight testifies to the presence of another subjectivity, one connected to indigenous knowledges. For these knowledges, as I show below, posited a different relation between knowledge and the knower. The answer to this question turns on whether the "difference" at issue is one best registered by stretching the category of "subject" to accommodate diverse ways of relating to the world and our knowledge of it. But to arrive at the point where this question presents itself to us, first we need to address the indigenous knowledge practices that Indians were said to be drawing on as the source of their prodigious powers of rote.

Other Knowledges

Modern knowledge, for all its diversity, is conceived as unitary. It is distinguished according to its objects (the human sciences, further subdivided by discipline; and the natural sciences, similarly subdivided), rather than according to the persons for whom it is intended. One consequence of conceiving it thus is that the transmission of knowledge can be organized according to degree of difficulty: primary, secondary, tertiary, but in principle accessible to all. By contrast, in India knowledge was always in the plural, always took the form of so many knowledges and practices: esoteric and restricted knowledges accessible only to some social groups, "practical" and more widely available knowledges, varying according to caste and region and religion, and none of all this organized as an "educational system." Collectively this situation yielded a riotous variety of knowledge practices, from unstructured and occasional ones to more structured "institutions" such as *maktabs* and *madrassas* and *tols* and *pyal* "schools" and *patshalas* and others,[73] with knowledge passed on by *gurumahashoys* and *pandits* and *pantojis* and *maulvis* and *upadhyayas* and *acharyas*—only some among the variety of words for "teacher" or "learned man" in the subcontinent. Thus we cannot compare modern knowledge with indigenous knowledge, but rather have to specify to what we are choosing to refer among the various indigenous knowledges (and the practices in which they were embedded and those through which they were transmitted).

One type of knowledge with strictly coded and prescribed forms dictating how it was to be transmitted was knowledge of the Vedas, the sacred Hindu texts that go back some three thousand years and more. Knowledge of the Vedas was to be cultivated by those Brahmins whose task it was to recite from the relevant sacred sources at sacrificial occasions, and to preserve the Vedas through recitation.[74] (The Vedas had been orally composed and have been maintained, over an extraordinary time span, by oral transmission—Vedic texts are *srutis*, truths meant to be heard, which were not committed to writing till late in the day, and the tradition has injunctions against learning them from writing.) Each Brahmin family which cultivated Vedic knowledge had its own *sutra*, to be kept and passed on (but only to those considered authorized to receive it) through *svadhyaya*, oral transmission. The archaic Sanskrit in which the Vedas were composed was superseded by classical Sanskrit and then the various vernaculars, but they continue to be recited and transmitted in their original form. It was to become a common criticism that these Brahmins were in fact unlearned, for they did not understand what they recited. Even Indians who sought to defend indigenous traditions were sensitive to this charge, and either denied its truth or devised ingenious arguments to explain and excuse it.[75] But the criticism missed the point: the Vedas are *apauruseya*, of nonhuman origin, and the words *are* the meaning – that is, the meaning of the texts is imbricated with their sounds and the forms of their recitation. Hence how they were said was all-important, and the sacred texts include elaborate instructions on how they are to be recited – with what accents, where the tone is to fall, and so on. In *svadhyaya*, Frits Staal explains, "there is no sharp distinction between word and meaning."[76] This does not mean that they have no meaning, or that the meaning is unimportant, but rather that what the reciter and the Indologist understand by "meaning" might be two different things; and any approach predicated on the notion that words express or represent a meaning anterior to them will always find this to be "mere" memory.

It may be objected that this example is unilluminating, because this particular knowledge of the Vedas (there are others) is essentially liturgical. I have already noted that the subcontinent had knowledges rather than knowledge, so let us then consider other forms.

Also part of subcontinental knowledges are arts or sciences, such as (what we would call) grammars, logic, poetics, medicine, and astrology. These are certainly not liturgical; they involve intellectual operations like interpretation and classification. For instance, a philosophy was extracted from (or read into) the Vedas, producing Vedanta. Here "meaning" in a sense that we would recognize is very much present. But even here, we should notice two important differences when these knowledges are contrasted with modern ones, apart from the obvious differences of content.

First, memory learning was still an essential component of these knowledges.[77] The mode of transmitting knowledge invariably required committing vast amounts of material to memory (the texts memorized were usually composed in the form of verses, aphorisms, and other mnemonic forms, indicating they were composed to be memorized); and memory learning in the form of recitation and chanting was valorized by the traditions in which these knowledges were embedded, in the form of injunctions to memorize, prayers asking for the gift of memory, and rituals and initiation ceremonies.

The common "explanation" for the emphasis on memory learning is that books and manuscripts were scarce, in other words that memory learning was a "technique" necessitated by the shortcomings of technology. We are all familiar with Derrida's argument that western metaphysics privileges speech over writing; when it comes to historical understanding, however, we apparently assume that speech and memory are what you have to take recourse to in lieu of writing (else why does memory learning need "explaining" at all?). But this explanation does not account for premodern traditions of learning even in Europe, where (as in India) even after book manuscripts were made more widely available, memory training did not become redundant. In the high Middle Ages Thomas Aquinas had stored an extraordinary number of "texts" in his memory; Aquinas's capacity was exceptional, but the phenomenon was still common. Books themselves were for a long time conceived of as mnemonics, as "memorial cues and aids," and people often read books *in order to commit them to memory*.[78] In her important *The Book of Memory: A Study of Memory in Medieval Culture*, Mary Carruthers tells us that in medieval Europe *memoria* was not just a "technique," necessitated by the absence of the printing press, but an ethical practice, a discipline, and a way of developing character, judgment, and piety.[79] The knowledges of the subcontinent were very different from those of medieval Europe, but they shared this feature – that memory was an essential component of knowledge – implying a different relation between knower and known – not simply a technique necessitated by the absence of technology.

The second feature to note about knowledges of these higher arts is the extraordinary importance attached to forms or observances – to a stylistics and a deportment – as distinct from the content of learning. This feature is seen above all in the emphasis on absolute respect and devotion to the teacher. Texts which discuss how knowledge is to be transmitted devote at least as much attention to this aspect of it as to questions of method or "curriculum." Indeed, the question of how matters are best learned was in large part answered by the injunction to respect and obey the teacher. Lessons were to be commenced and concluded by having the student clasp the teacher's feet in his hands; and the injunction *acarya devo bhava*, "may your teacher be your god," was something every student knew.

We moderns have a ready-made explanation for this. Schooling, we will say, is not just about the transmission of knowledge but also about socialization, and about power. The child who is enjoined to treat his teacher with respect is receiving lessons in authority and order, over and above the knowledge he receives. If we are moderns who are capable of subjecting our own practices to the same critical scrutiny, we will add that the same is true of modern schooling; the discipline of the school bell, of standing in line and the like, instills the more abstract notions of order and authority which our societies require and continually reproduce.

Such an explanation of indigenous education would not be beside the point, but it would be grievously incomplete. Power and authority in India there were aplenty, no doubt; but the limit of this explanation is reached when we assume that modes of transmission are separable from the knowledge transmitted. We assume this for our knowledges, because a defining feature of modern knowledge is its formal character, the assumption that it is in principle conceivable outside of the current network of relations (and power) which characterizes the transmission of knowledge in most societies. Rationalization in the Weberian sense means precisely this: that knowledge is freed from substantive contexts and can be used "technically," to match means to ends. But the same is not true of the knowledges I am describing here. In "traditional" learning the content and the form are indistinguishable: absorbing the "information" or mastering the "skills" is not the content, with respect and awe for one's teacher the form, the process through which the knowledge happens to be transmitted; all are aspects of the same process. The knowledge transmitted was not a separable "thing," which happened to be transmitted through the *guru-shishya* relation; it could only be transmitted through that relation. This is not to say you *cannot* separate the two; some of these knowledges have now been wrenched from their contexts and have a new life as part of modern knowledge (for example, *ayurvedic* medicine), even if usually at the fringes of it. We sometimes think that this characteristic – that these knowledges can be reproduced in and through altogether different contexts – goes to "prove" that their contexts were so much window-dressing, contingent and inessential form rather than substantive content. In fact, of course, it proves nothing of the sort. We can treat machines and the knowledge which produces them as magical, and worship them – people do – and we do not thereby assume that this is their reality, and that scientific protocols and factories and laboratories are so much window-dressing, fetishes obscuring the enchantment which is the truth of these machines.

Let us finally consider one more form, or class, of knowledge practices. I have said that in the subcontinent knowledges were related to status, for the more ritualized and specialized knowledges were not available to all – not just "in fact," because of poverty and inequality, but "in principle." The knowledges described above fall into that category. But there were other knowledges which were suitable for almost all: for higher castes that might tarry briefly before proceeding to acquire knowledges corresponding to their status, for trading castes, for occupations connected with administering land and collecting revenue, and even, sometimes, for the children of tillers of the soil. The *patshala* and *pyal* schools (whether of the "basic" sort or the more specialized sort which taught account keeping, writing business letters, and other skills to children who were to go on to the hereditary profession of their caste) often transmitted a knowledge which, unlike that described above, had a practical value but little or no ritual status. Moreover, these schools often did so in a manner which was exceedingly effective. The British authorities were sometimes obliged to acknowledge as much, though they would usually add that this "success" was a form of failure. Almost all observers noted that in indigenous schools the boys memorized their times-tables with extraordinary facility. A senior official of the education department reported that the traditional or "native" system of math instruction, which entailed learning tables (including fractional tables) "up to an incredible standard," combined with the use of rules of thumb or formulae (*gurs*), "produce in the pupil a capacity for rapid and certain calculation which would quite nonplus an English schoolboy";[80] and an article in the *Calcutta Review* on arithmetic teaching in indigenous schools commented, "the method employed may not be as rational as ours, but the practical result is a much greater facility in simple calculations and account-keeping than is gained by the pupils of Government schools."[81]

Why, then, was this a shortcoming? Because the same students, asked to do anything out of the ordinary, could not apply their arithmetic, just as the students could sometimes read entire passages well, but on being asked what they meant, often could not explain them, and sometimes did not even know that the passages had a meaning beyond their recitation. That is, these students confused knowledge with its application, and had no knowledge outside its application. Our conception and practice of knowledge are very different. To be sure, we too have "applied knowledges," but each of these is an application of a knowledge which is always in principle independent of its uses. Indeed, the processes of rationalization mean that increasingly, knowledges and skills which could once only be acquired "on the job," and which had no existence outside their use or application, are now deemed to have a formal component, which is a knowledge like any other; their practical component now presupposes a mastery of the theory of which the practical component is the application. Nursing and tourism become university subjects, knowledges which have to be learned in such a way that the students can draw upon their stock of formal knowledge and "apply" it according to context – each person his or her own casuist. One can see why for the modern observer the Indian child's facility with arithmetic, however impressive, was deemed inadequate – to modern eyes a pedagogy which cannot produce the ability to apply a general knowledge to specific cases is a failed pedagogy.

Knowing and Being

From this description one thing at least should be very apparent, namely that comparing the different curriculums and pedagogies of indigenous schools with those of the modern type is to miss the point, because indigenous practices were not the same thing with a different content. As Tim Mitchell observes (in the context of a discussion of the sort of learning which occurs in the great mosque of al-Azhar), in cases such as this the very category of education "is a misnomer, a misapprehending of the kinds of practice in which the life of the community . . . was lived. It is to take a dominant practice of the late nineteenth and twentieth century and project it back onto a world in which it did not exist, resulting in unhelpful observations about the limited nature of its 'curriculum.' "[82] If we categorize these knowledges as a form of "education," we are condemned to reproduce Macaulay's understanding, seeing in these knowledges only inferior versions of modern knowledge and pedagogy. It is only if we grant that these knowledges corresponded to different ways of constituting the relation between knower and known, different ways of *being* and not just learning, that we can begin to grasp them in their specificity.

If it is true that indigenous education corresponded to what I here provisionally label a different way of being and not just knowing, this helps to explain why "indigenous education" continued for quite some time to be popular (often disconcertingly so, for educational officials), especially among those (lower) classes which did not see themselves as being in a position to tap into the instrumental benefits of western education. The Indian Education (Hunter) Commission noted that "the schoolmaster of an old fashioned indigenous school is much respected"; and even the "shouting and confusion" in class which the commission saw as characteristic of indigenous schools, "form part of the peculiar charm which parents appreciate in the indigenous system."[83] The institution of the indigenous "schoolteacher" was, many observers attested, one which ordinary folk were reluctant to regard as superseded. A speaker at the Madras Educational Conference of 1898 sought to explain why this might have been so: "[The *pyal* school teacher] begins the school with the rising sun, and the din of the school house, which is like music to the parents' ears, is over only with the setting sun. He makes the pupils cite correctly or incorrectly stanzas from standard authors, entertains them with stories of perennial interest from the great epics of the Mahabharata or Ramayana . . . When the Dussera [festival] comes once a year it delights the heart of many a proud mother to see her son decked out in all the colours of the rainbow, and march with banners flying and music playing, and perform the kolatum dance." By contrast, the teacher of the government vernacular school "goes to school after the sun has risen high and closes it before the sun sets. He does not allow the pupils to cry out at the top of their voice, and the absence of the accustomed din of the school house goes much against him. He does not pay court to every villager. He scorns the Dussera festivities."[84]

No doubt this description does not speak for all parents whose children attended a *pyal* school or *patshala*; I am not claiming any "representative" status for the passages excerpted above. Nor am I "romanticizing" the *pyal* schools: untouchable castes were not permitted access to these institutions, and more generally, the life of the communities in question was also characterized by considerable inequality and brutality. What I am pointing to in drawing attention to how "indigenous schooling" differed from modern schooling is this: if and only if we assume (as we often unthinkingly do) that both these were types of schooling, *then* we are bound to rush to our normal judgments about the inadequacies of "indigenous education," and to assume that whatever the failings of modern education may have been, and may still be, it is incomparably superior to its Indian predecessor and competitor. But if the comparison is not of like with like, then judgments become less obvious and more complicated.

This was perhaps why even those whose western education had been preceded by a few years of "traditional education" – and there were many such in the nineteenth century and into the twentieth[85] – were of two minds about this "premodern education." One might expect that those who had been graced by "understanding" rather than repetition, and who had gone on to inhabit the modern institutions of law courts, councils, and universities, might be unambiguous in rejecting a pedagogy which stifled their subjectivity; that having experienced two kinds of education, they would, in J. S. Mill's terms, emphatically opt to be "Socrates dissatisfied" rather than a "pig satisfied." In fact, reactions were sometimes more complex.

An interesting example – again, I do not claim any representative status for it – is that of S. N. Chaturvedi, an official in the Provincial Educational Service of the United Provinces. Chaturvedi was the author of two books, and in *The History of Rural Education in the United Provinces of Agra and Oudh* (1840–1926) he describes his own experiences of indigenous education.[86] After some basic instruction from a *maulvi* at home Chaturvedi attended a *patshala* in his village, then a *mahajani patshala* in Allahabad where he learned bookkeeping, arithmetic, and the *mahajani* (bankers') script, and then a Sanskrit *patshala* where he learned Sanskrit vocabulary, verses, and grammar, and a few verses of the Vedas, before he moved on to the English schools which "had caught" his "fancy," subsequent to which he took a degree from Allahabad University and a teacher's diploma from London. Chaturvedi is an official of the new educational system (he is receiving the patronage of an eminent Englishman, Sir Philip Hartog, who has written the foreword to his book, and he dedicates it to the director of public instruction of the United Provinces). He intersperses the description of his indigenous education with a condemnation of its narrowness, its lack of practicality, and the great reliance on memory learning. But these criticisms are belied by the tone of his description, his detailed account of the daily routine, of a teacher whose "stern looks and authoritative voice were generally sufficient to keep us little urchins in order,"[87] and of the festivities that the schoolchildren indulged in on the Nag Panchami day, as well as by his reproduction in full of some of the couplets and aphorisms that the pupils learned, and his summation of the attributes that the education instilled: "Respect for authority, devotion to learning for its own sake, humility, an almost ascetic attitude towards life, and great regard for spiritual values were the outstanding traits of the products, of these schools."[88] At the point where the lyricism of the description threatens to overwhelm the narrative, Chaturvedi draws back thus: "these very virtues were their defects . . . The respect for authority was so much emphasized that the pupil could not think or act for himself . . . Humility was so much encouraged that all courage to differ or resist was completely killed."[89] To those concerned with "national advancement" all this made the people look too much toward the past. From the point of view of the individual, however, "in spite of the disadvantages they suffered owing to the causes described above, the more educated of them obtained a capacity of intellectual enjoyment and material contentment which made their lives bright, cheerful and happy. Even those who could obtain only the necessary rudiments of the three R's shared in these advantages."[90]

This is, at the very least, a rather ambiguous condemnation. When it

comes to evaluating his childhood experiences under the category "education," the (modern) criteria built into this category lead Chaturvedi to the
standard oppositions (thinking versus remembering, one's own knowledge
versus secondhand knowledge) and compel a negative judgment. But the
terms of his description overflow "education" and clearly become a description of a way of life – and as they do so, the description itself assumes an
altogether softer and more benign hue.

Subjectivity and Difference

Documenting the discourse of what I have labeled "cram" and "instrumentalism," I have argued that this discourse did more than signify a widespread
feeling that knowledge was being unsuccessfully disseminated: it is best read
as signifying that the dissemination of western knowledge required, but had
not produced, a corresponding form of knowing subject. I have gone on to
ask whether this meant that there was another subjectivity present, one frustrating the emergence of the desired one.

It would seem that I have answered this question very emphatically. Cramming, as we have seen, was widely attributed to the survival and adaptation
of indigenous knowledge practices. These other knowledges and associated
forms of learning corresponded, I have argued, to a subjectivity or selfhood
different from that presumed by modern knowledge and pedagogy. The obvious implication – "obvious" only because I have carefully been leading the
way to it – is that the failure to produce the modern subject testified to the
resilience of an existing one, the one it was to have displaced, the "native"
subject presumed by the indigenous learning practices described above.

I will embrace this conclusion, though in a very provisional way, suggesting that it is indeed necessary to think this thought, but only to then
problematize and surpass it. I will conclude by arguing that it is necessary
to entertain the idea of a "different subjectivity," but that we cannot end
the argument there, for the "different" in "different subjectivity" is simultaneously enabled and obscured by the concept of "subjectivity."

Built into the discourse of cram and instrumentalism is a certain ambiguity or imprecision. In some cases cram and instrumentalism are seen as
failures of pedagogy: too much rote learning, and the wrong sort of understanding of the value and purpose of western knowledge. That this concern
is tied to and presumes a certain conception of the subject is something that
we, as readers and interpreters of this discourse, unearth in it. In other cases

(such as in Curzon's convocation speech, discussed earlier) the failure of pedagogy is explicitly connected to subjectivity, and even dimly registers that the
absence in question is not a complete lack, but something indicating the
presence of another way of relating to knowledge. The second understanding
is unquestionably the deeper one, but upon closer examination it turns out
to be not that different from the first: the absence of the desired subjectivity
is understood as the presence of another, but this "other" turns out to be an
inadequate or, more accurately, unrealized version of the first. The subject
who loses himself in the world by cramming, for instance, is clearly different from the subject who stands apart from the world and makes it his own;
but he also turns out to be a (potentially) modern subject who has simply
failed to emancipate himself from his background. Why this ambiguity or
imprecision?

Because within the categories in which this question is posed, "different
sort of subject" and "failing to fully become a subject" are in principle in-
separable. All forms of subjectivity turn out to be variations upon – and more
precisely, partially realized versions of – a single subjectivity: a "different"
subject is always one who has failed to "fully" become a subject. Facetiously:
in this categorical frame there are only acorns, oaks, and acorns on the way
to becoming oaks; a chestnut will always appear as an acorn which for some
reason is suffering from arrested development. My point is not simply that
the notion of subjectivity has a teleology built into it, such that all forms of
subjectivity culminate in modern forms of selfhood, nor, by implication, that
subjectivity has a certain normativity built into it. The point I am seeking to
make incorporates both of these, but also goes beyond them. To clarify, let
me use an example.

The term "slave" is for us moderns a social category, meaning that we
understand "slave" to signify a free man en-slaved, rather than, as for the
Greeks, understanding it to denote a form of selfhood. Our idea of human
selfhood or subjectivity has, in other words, a certain notion of "freedom"
already built into it. Words like freedom make us think of Rousseau and Kant
and the French and American revolutions, and of "fuller" conceptions of freedom – not just freedom as non-enslavement but as autonomy, as choosing
our ends, and the means toward them. These associations are of course apt,
and are part of what I have been invoking in insisting that modern knowledge presumes a form of subjectivity – active rather than passive, and so on.
But the "first" sense of freedom – first in the sense of being both logically
prior and historically earlier – is freedom in the sense of not being merged

into the background, lost into nature like animals and slaves, nomos rather than physis. The Greeks did not think that all men possessed this freedom, and thus it was not built into their conception of what it means to be a human self.[91]

My point is this. When it comes to the modern self – the self who is heir to the bourgeois revolutions and to Kantian philosophy – we, being intelligent products of a historicist age, can acknowledge that the free, autonomous chooser possessed of rights is not the only type of human that there has been. With a certain effort and a certain vigilance we can try to desist from reading all other forms of selfhood as leading toward and culminating in this one, and thus as being incomplete forms of this one. Doing so is our way of staying sensitive to difference. But our notion of self or subject is not thereby rendered, as we imagine, into an empty form into which any content can be poured; it already has a certain content inscribed into its very form. When we "think" difference we do so in the manner of Weber, as described in the Introduction; we picture other humans who in turn picture the world in ways very different from our own. The subject who threatens to merge into the world appears, to be sure, as very different from us, but his difference lies in his adopting a stance toward the world that is one of merging. The subject who attributes his agency to supernatural powers is again very different from us; but his difference lies in his attributing his own beliefs and capacities to another. Yet like us, he too pictures the world, he too endows it with meanings (meanings different from ours); and that being so, we are inescapably led back to seeing his sense of self as a version of ours, lacking only in self-consciousness (all subjects endow the world with meaning, but we modern subjects know that this is what we do). If we nonetheless declare that this subject's way of looking at the world is "as valid" as ours, our intention is belied by the mode in which it is thought. Our commitment to difference remains embedded in intentions, while our categories, the grammar of our thought, lead us always into teleology and normativity. The best we can do is to be vigilant; but it is an unequal struggle, for we struggle to express one thing, while our conceptual language leads us to express another.

It seems to me necessary to entertain the thought that cramming and instrumentalism testified to the presence of another subjectivity, and to travel this route of argument. Without doing so – if we did not "stretch" the category "subject" so that we could imagine different kinds of subjects – the questions of cramming and instrumentalism would remain ones of pedagogy and technique, and "difference" would appear only in its racist form, as the ques-

tion of the stubbornly unintelligent Indian. We cannot dispense with historicizing, because the alternative is a universalism in which there is only ever
one norm, and all difference is a deviation from it, or a journey toward it. But
nor, I end by suggesting, should we be content with it. I do not wish to end
this chapter with a resounding demonstration that the absence of modern
subjectivity, to which the discourse of cram and instrumentalism testified,
was the consequence of another subjectivity, an indigenous one. Instead I
suggest that we need to search for ways by which we can "think" this difference without substantializing it into another "subjectivity," and thereby
bringing it under a category which erases with one hand the difference which
it writes with the other. We need to search for forms of thought which allow
us to recognize that there have been and are ways of thinking the world other
than modern, occidental ones; but also ways of thinking difference without
invoking the Subject and without setting into motion an anthropology which
ceaselessly transforms human beings into Man.

CHAPTER TWO

Diagnosing Moral Crisis
Western Knowledge and Its Indian Object

Nineteenth-century discussions of education presupposed that education was not simply about the transmission of knowledge, but also about the shaping of character. The elementary education provided for the poorer classes, for which the English state undertook responsibility in 1870, was intended to inculcate the virtues of industry, thrift, and self-discipline in the lower classes. For the upper classes the public school was thought to instill manly independence and leadership. When the British Indian government undertook some responsibility for educating its Indian subjects, there was a similar expectation that this would lead "to the introduction among them of useful knowledge *and* to the improvement of their moral character."[1] With the subsequent decision of 1835 that government patronage was to be limited to western education, this emphasis was affirmed; if education had a beneficial effect upon character, then instruction in western, rational knowledge was surely likely to lead to the greatest improvement in the Indian character.

It was generally assumed that the western-educated native would be honest and upright, and thus more reliable and diligent in the service of government than his corrupt predecessor; and that a sign of his intellectual and moral superiority would be his recognition of the virtues of British rule, and his secure attachment to the continuation of that rule. Christian missionaries also hoped to improve the native by means of the schools that they provided, by weaning him from evil customs and mistaken beliefs, and equipping him with the means to make his way in the world without falling prey to its temptations. They hoped to effect the greatest improvement of all by making him a Christian.

However in 1913 a major government statement on educational policy observed that "the most thoughtful minds in India lament the tendency of the

existing system of education to develop the intellectual at the expense of the
moral and religious faculties," and went so far as to declare the tendency "unquestionably the most important educational problem of the time."[2] This
claim marked the climax of the discourse on the "moral decline" and "moral
crisis" of the educated Indian – a discourse expressing the fear that the improvement consequent upon education had not in fact occurred, but rather
that educated Indians had become less moral, less pious, and less disciplined
than before. This discourse was coterminous with the beginnings of western education, and had been gaining in intensity since the last quarter of
the nineteenth century. By the early years of the new century "moral crisis"
was a matter of almost obsessive debate; an Englishman observed that it was
the subject of mention in "every discussion on Indian education,"[3] while an
Indian educator complained that the subject of the "moral decline" of the
educated Indian, and the commonly proposed remedies of moral or religious
education, had become a "pest of the platform."[4]

Western knowledge was disseminated through schools and universities
because it was presumed superior to the indigenous knowledges it replaced.
In this chapter I examine how the same knowledge being disseminated in
schools and universities was also pressed into service to characterize and explain the moral decline of the educated Indian. How adequate was this knowledge to explaining its own, unexpected effects? Could it comprehend and
account for its own failures? And more generally, what was the relation between western knowledge as a means for comprehending social changes in
India and western knowledge as one of the agents of that change?

"Unhinged and Unsettled"

The warning that educated Indians were in danger of being plunged into a
moral crisis was first raised, principally by missionaries, in the years following the earliest government patronage of western education. The policy of
not permitting religious instruction in government schools and colleges –
so much at odds with the situation in Britain, where state involvement in
education was to be accompanied by bitter debates over the religious character of education, and over whether secular or religious bodies were to control
it – was pursued because of a strong feeling in official ranks that any inter-
ference with the religious beliefs of their Indian subjects might endanger
British rule and East India Company profits. It became one of the goals of the
missionaries' agitation in India to persuade the government in India or the

authorities back home to overturn what they called a "godless" educational policy. One of their chief arguments was that the resolutely secular education offered in government schools and colleges was bound to lead to impiety and skepticism.[5]

Missionaries did not object to the provision of secular learning as such. The historic controversies which had marked the advance of secular knowledges in the Christian West were never played out in colonial India. Missionaries and government officials alike shared the belief that modern science was a solvent of Indian religious beliefs, which in their view mingled a false theology with fantastical and nonsensical explanations of the world and its functioning. Inasmuch as western learning undermined native understandings of how the world worked, it could not but also call into question their faith in their religion. Those who had played a leading role in the decision of 1835 to limit government patronage to western education, including Thomas Macaulay and Charles Trevelyan, had insisted that government-provided education must not allow any religious instruction and must not be associated with any attempts at conversion. Nonetheless, they and many others anticipated that this education would be conducive to the Christianization of India. Macaulay wrote in 1836, "No Hindoo, who has received an English education, ever remains sincerely attached to his own religion . . . It is my firm belief that, if our plans of education are followed up, there will not be a single idolater among the respectable classes in Bengal thirty years hence."[6] Sharing in this conviction, missionaries made the provision of education one of their chief tasks in India, in the hope that western education would prove corrosive of Hindu beliefs and would thus prepare the minds of educated Hindus for a later receptiveness to the word of God.[7]

The Scottish Church missionary Alexander Duff revealingly described how he came to the important discovery that the "truths of modern literature and science" could play an important, if largely negative or destructive, role in promoting Christianity. In his monumental *India and Indian Missions*, he recounts how, soon after the opening of his General Assembly Institution in Calcutta in 1830, he was conducting a junior class in which he asked, "What is rain?" A student replied that it came from the trunk of the elephant of the god Indra. Pressed for his source, the student cited his guru, whose authority in turn was a *Shastra*, a Hindu text. Instead of directly contradicting the student, Duff describes how he led his students through the everyday example of rice boiling in a pot—the rising of steam, condensation, the re-formation of water—at each point explaining the process and gaining the assent of students for the explanation. Assent is spontaneously given – heat causes the evaporation of water in the form of steam, etc. – until suddenly one boy, "as if . . . finding that he had . . . gone too far," manifests alarm and exclaims, "Ah! What have I been thinking? *If your account be the true one, what becomes of our Shastra?*" The explanation, Duff writes, introduced the first doubt, the first suspicion, regarding the truth of the Hindu faith, and thus constituted the first step in "a mental struggle, which, though painfully protracted . . . only terminated in the case of some, with the entire overthrow of Hinduism."[8] If this encounter with western scientific knowledge was a revelation for his student, the incident was also, Duff declares, something of a revelation for him: "It now seemed as if geography, general history, and natural philosophy, – from their direct effect in destroying Hinduism, – had been divested of their secularity, and stamped with an impress of sacredness. In this view of the case, the teaching of these branches seemed no longer an indirect, secondary, ambiguous part of missionary labour, – but, in a sense, as direct, primary, and indubitable as the teaching of religion itself."[9]

In Duff's school what had been destroyed could be replaced, since the corrosive or "destructive" effects of western learning only paved the way for teaching the true word of God. But where, as in government schools, this was not permitted, missionaries contended that only destruction occurred, and that the result would be skepticism, impiety, and immorality among the educated classes in India. In the first half of the nineteenth century they would frequently point to the controversy surrounding Hindu College as proof of their contention. Established in 1817 by some of the leading Brahmins in Calcutta as a nondenominational center for the teaching of the new, European knowledge, in the 1830s Hindu College was to briefly become home to a rationalist and skeptical "movement," led by a young and charismatic teacher, Henry Derozio. Although it never comprised more than a handful of students, "Young Bengal" scandalized Calcutta society by its mocking of established convention and religious beliefs, and its espousal of agnosticism and atheism.[10] The commotion caused in respectable Calcutta society led to the dismissal of Derozio from the college staff and to denunciations of the immoral and "skeptical" effects of western education, which missionaries denounced as secular or "godless." Duff, for instance, very often presented his institution as an alternative model to that provided by Hindu College, and even as a measure to "reclaim" Hindu College students who had gone astray, but "whose education and worldly circumstances invest them with such mighty influence among their fellow-country-men."[11]

While Hindu College provided missionaries with a useful example of the dangers of secular education, and an opportunity to extol the virtues of their own schools and colleges, there was nonetheless a very real sense in which government-provided secular education was seen as an ally in their struggle, even if one much inferior to the desired alternative of Bible-teaching government schools. Duff approvingly quoted the editor of the *Inquirer* newspaper, a former student at Hindu College and a convert to Christianity, to the effect that "the Hindu college . . . has . . . destroyed many a native's belief in Hinduism . . . No missionary ever taught us to forsake the religion of our fathers; it was Government that did us this service."[12] Another Scottish Church missionary, James Bryce, wrote that even if government education did not make Christians of its students, "it at least *un-Hinduizes* them,"[13] and added indulgently, " 'Young Bengal' . . . are indulging the very silly, but not perhaps unnatural pride, that their 'little learning' is carrying them beyond . . . priestcraft, as they designate all religious belief whatever. Teach them to drink a little deeper of the stream, and they may bend submissive to the apostles of the Cross."[14]

However, the relative confidence of this earlier period – the expectation that western education would eventually lead to weaning more and more of the educated classes from their own religion and winning them over to Christianity, even if indirectly, after detours through the reformed Hinduism of the Arya Samaj or the Hindu-Christian eclecticism of the Brahmo Samaj – began to give way to concern in the latter part of the nineteenth century. The concern was fueled, above all else, by the sense that the hoped-for transition to Christianity was not in the offing. For most of those who became dissatisfied with existing forms of Hinduism, the reformed versions which they embraced proved to be not stopping-places on a longer journey toward Christianity but rather the terminus. Moreover, from the latter decades of the nineteenth century the Arya Samaj in the north of India became more aggressively anti-Christian and even began to make efforts to reconvert Hindus who had converted to Islam or Christianity, while in the south the Hindu Preaching and Tract Societies similarly sought to combat missionary influence.[15] The missionary critique of "godless education" continued, but with a new sense of urgency; the dire predictions that had been made were now held to have come true, and the educated Indian was said to have fallen prey to impiety and immorality. Lurid pictures were painted of the mental and moral state of educated Indians. The headmaster of Bishop Corries Grammar School in Madras warned the government that "in the present transition state, brought about by European knowledge and science," the students and graduates of government colleges "threw off all restraints"; indulging in the vices of "pride, discontent, drunkenness," they "defile the flesh, despise dominion."[16] The Reverend M. A. Sherring wrote, "The educated classes in all directions are revolting from ancient superstitions . . . The landmarks of ancient Brahmanical thought are being abandoned one after the other, and nothing positive is taking their place . . . Mental distraction and disorder have taken the place of mental stagnation, and at present the intellectual condition of the educated classes is that of chaos and doubt."[17]

By the last quarter of the nineteenth century the government also began to voice concerns about the morality of educated Indians. The *Report of the Indian Education [Hunter] Commission* of 1883 found that there had been a deterioration in the morality and manners of college students, and recommended the preparation of a "moral text-book" for teaching morality and manners; it also recommended that in all government colleges, and all private colleges in receipt of government aid, a senior professor or the principal give a regular course of lectures on "the duties of a man and citizen."[18] These recommendations were not accepted by the Government of India, but the existence of a "problem" was affirmed a few years later in a government circular which acknowledged that a western, secular education "has in some measure resulted in the growth of tendencies unfavourable to discipline and favourable to irreverence in the rising generation," and had "cut loose the rising generation from many of the moral and social bonds of their forefathers."[19]

The problem of moral decline, and the search for some form of moral training and disciplining which would remedy it, now became a regular feature of governmental discussions. The issue was discussed at the Simla Conference of educationists, convened in September 1901 by Viceroy Curzon as the prelude to his far-reaching educational reforms,[20] and the suggestions made there were incorporated into the text of a Government of India Resolution on Indian Educational Policy issued in 1904.[21] In 1905 the mass campaign against the colonial government's decision to partition Bengal began, and the "indiscipline" of Indians, especially educated ones, became a favourite topic. This was all the more so since students played a very prominent role in the Swadeshi movement, and a boycott of official educational institutions was an important feature of the agitation. Valentine Chirol's series of articles in the *Times*, revised and immediately collected into a book titled *Indian Unrest* (1910), was widely quoted and very influential. "The estrangement of . . . the young Hindu who has passed or is passing through our schools and colleges," Chirol wrote, is "the most alarming phenomenon of the present day . . . of all the problems with which British statesmanship is confronted in India none is more difficult and more urgent than the educational problem."[22] In Chirol's analysis the source of the Hindu student's disaffection was not western education per se but the imperfect assimilation of this education. It had been imperfectly assimilated, according to Chirol, because in India education had been divorced from religion. This separation was something of an experiment even in Europe, which relied upon "a highly-developed code of ethics and an inherited sense of social and civic duty to supply the place of religious sanctions"; but it was an absurdity in India, where "morality apart from religion is an almost impossible conception."[23] Thus according to Chirol, the complete exclusion of religious teaching from schools and colleges had been a mistake; it had alienated some Indians from their values and traditions, and that in turn had unleashed a counter-reaction. Chirol asked rhetorically, "Did not the incipient revolt against all the traditions of Hinduism that followed the introduction of western education help to engender the wholesale reaction against western influences which underlies the present unrest?"[24]

Complaints about "indiscipline" and "moral decline" were clearly expressions of alarm at the rise of criticism and agitation from the ranks of educated Indians. However, the authorities were at pains to insist that their diagnosis was not simply a way of pathologizing and belittling the phenomenon of nationalist unrest. They sought to show that the problem of moral decline was a much wider one, of which unrest was only a manifestation; and that the existence of a problem was also attested to by Indians. The director of public instruction for Bengal, for instance, reported: "there is a strong feeling amongst parents and teachers of whatever creed or caste that the divorce of education and religion, contrary as it is to the whole of the Indian tradition . . . has not been good for the youth of the country and has resulted in a large measure of moral deterioration."[25] Governor Sir George Clarke of Bombay told a conference, "it is widely admitted by thoughtful Indians that there are some signs of the weakening of parental influence, of the loss of reverence for authority, of a decadence of manners and of growing moral laxity. The restraining forces of ancient India have lost some of their power; the restraining forces of the west are inoperative in India. There has been a certain moral loss without any corresponding gain."[26]

Ruling circles, Anglo-India hands in England, and the unofficial English community in India were now all receptive to the claim that the educated Indian was undergoing a moral crisis, and that some form or another of moral education was the required antidote. Proposals for moral textbooks of various types abounded,[27] and many were already in use, such as Todd's *Student Manual*, Murdoch's *Indian Student's Manual* and his *My Duties*, Roper Lethbridge's *A Moral Reader from English and Oriental Sources*, John Sime's *Man and His Duties: A Moral Reader*, Norton's *Courtesy Reader*, Waldegraves's *Handbook of Moral Lessons*, as well as many readers in the vernaculars, such as (to give but one example) Lala Narain Das's *Shikshamani*, published from Jullundar in 1905 for use in girls' *patshalas*, with thirty short chapters on duties to God, parents, and so on. Such moral readers for junior grades often contained elevating stories drawn from Indian sources, and biographies of great men – though the efficacy of these, as of moral textbooks intended for senior students, was widely doubted.[28] The Sanatan Dharma series produced by Annie Besant's Central Hindu School and College, for the purpose of "organizing and systematizing Hindu religious and moral instruction throughout India,"[29] was in use in schools in the princely state of Mysore, as well as some Hindu schools in British India.

Even the hitherto taboo question of allowing religious instruction was discussed at the highest levels of government after 1910. In the course of internal discussions Viceroy Minto wrote, "For various reasons British administrators have kept clear of moral and religious teaching, and it is consequently ceasing to exist, with the terrible results we now have to recognise."[30] The education member of the Government of India thought that for political reasons it would be disastrous to formally renounce the policy of "religious neutrality" in schooling, but also thought that "by degrees we shall drift quietly into a system in which religious and moral instruction will play a not inconsiderable part."[31] And in fact Punjab and the United Provinces were by now already permitting religious instruction to be imparted in government schools, where the parents of pupils requested it and took the initiative. Thus the government had even begun to overcome its long-standing aversion to allowing religious teaching in government schools, though to the chagrin of missionaries, it was not the propagation of Christianity that was countenanced but rather the instruction of children in their own faith. The question of moral decline continued to occupy the Government – officialdom returned to the issue after the First World War[32] – and thus for some forty years the bureaucracy wrestled with the problem and explored ways of addressing it through some form or other of moral and religious education.

The accusations were of course widely disputed. Government itself did not speak with one voice; for instance, when in 1887 the Government of India issued a circular diagnosing the problem and asking provincial governments to suggest measures to tackle it, a number of these responded by contesting the diagnosis, or the precise terms of it. An official in the Bombay Department of Public Instruction wrote, "I must decline to believe that our present system is producing a generation of irreverent and insubordinate youth."[33] The official response on behalf of the Bombay government, presented by its secretary, did not go so far as to dispute that there was a problem, but attributed it to the occurrence everywhere of a one-sided and materialistic transition, producing similar effects: "The morality of the rising generations of Englishmen... does not present such uniform or so satisfactory features as to enable Englishmen to parade it for the example of Asiatics."[34] The response from Madras was similarly lukewarm, and later a senior British official in the Madras Department of Education declared that in "integrity and truthfulness," educated Hindus in his presidency stood "immeasurably above the men of the past generation."[35] The idea of the moral decline of the educated Indian was similarly the subject of frequent refutation at university convocation ceremonies.[36]

Educated Indians, as one might expect, frequently contested the diagnosis of a moral decline. Justice Telang, one of the few Indian members appointed to the Hunter Commission, disputed its analysis of the issue and dissented from its recommendations urging "moral education."[37] Others protested that western education, far from leading to immorality, had "made better men and better citizens."[38] Indian students were far more religious, according to the distinguished lawyer Tej Bahadur Sapru, than one was "entitled to expect from young men of their age."[39] Some, like Brajendranath Seal, professor at Calcutta University, simply responded with derision to "the hunt after orgies of secret vices or indulgences among a class so staid and generally abstemious as the Bengali youth of our colleges."[40]

But the numerous denials only testified to the ubiquitousness of the complaint, and to the fact that a wider public – including Indian members of it – participated in producing the discourse, as well as in contesting it. Members of the Brahmo Samaj, who regarded themselves as having abandoned idolatry and achieved a rationalist deism in their eclectic mix of Hinduism and Christianity, lamented the fate of their fellow countrymen who had failed to follow their path. A public meeting of the Brahmo Samaj in 1861 adopted a statement telling the "British Nation" that the "sublime principles and truths of Western Science" it had introduced to India had served to "emancipate the native mind from the horrors of Hinduism," but "he has just learnt to disbelieve all that his creed would have taught him, without finding aught that would close up the hiatus. The mind hence becomes unsettled in its doctrines."[41] The Brahmo Samaj leader Keshab Chunder Sen warned that India was undergoing a tremendous revolution, in the course of which some educated Indians "run into the wildest vagaries of infidelity and scepticism and habits of dissipation. It is sad to reflect that the number of enlightened sceptics is growing in our midst . . . [men] who laugh at religion and morality . . . Their number may soon assume fearful proportions";[42] "In times of transition . . . we always find that men for a while become reckless. The old faith is gone, and no new faith is established in its place. Society is unhinged and unsettled."[43] Even Bipan Chandra Pal, a radical (the word used at the time was "extremist") nationalist, commiserated with those who, having been exposed to western education in the first decades following its introduction, had become alienated from their own traditions, but who had lacked the fortitude to defy Hindu tradition and become Brahmos like him.[44]

Those who had established or were proposing denominational and "national" schools and colleges found that the discourse of moral decline could be pressed into service for their own ends. Madan Mohan Malaviya, nationalist and a moving force behind the plans for a Hindu University, wrote: "one of the strongest arguments in favour of a denominational University is that it will be able to make up an acknowledged deficiency in the present system of education; that it will be able, to use the words of the Government of India, to 'supply religious and ethical instruction to complete the educational training of . . . scholars' and thus to lay the surest foundation for the formation of their character."[45] At a public meeting held in Calcutta in 1911 to publicize and seek support for a Hindu University, Surendranath Banerjea was even more blunt: "We hear a great deal about moral education these days. The Government universities have failed to grapple with the question. The Hindu University will solve it."[46]

Indian educationalists, not to be suspected of a generalized opposition to western education, sometimes testified to its moral ill effects. In 1905 a memorial to the viceroy signed by 378 Indians and British, including a large number of headmasters and other teachers, expressed concern that in schools little attention was paid to the "moral culture" of their boys, who consequently did not always display the desired "robust moral tone."[47] At the same time the princely government of Mysore decided to introduce moral and religious instruction into schools and colleges, citing as its reasons the increase in disrespect, vanity, and aggression among students.[48]

Diagnosing Moral Decline

The observation of moral decline always came with an explanation. The symptoms of decline, and the evidence for it, lay in impiety, dissolute behaviour,
bad manners, conceit, immorality, and a decline in respect for elders and for
"authority" more generally; these were usually gathered together under the
rubric of "inconsistency." The etiology of this intellectual and moral inconsistency and confusion was traced back to an incomplete (or stalled) transition, which left the educated Indian caught between two worlds and two
moral codes, unable to choose consistently between them. The "inconsisten-
cies" which no doubt also marked the life of Indian peasants – and which
presumably are a feature of social life everywhere, for there is no society where
people's diverse ideas and practices seamlessly interlace with one another –
were not seen to generate equivalent difficulties, and did not become the subject of a discourse of moral decline, because the peasant was not seen to be
straddling different cultural worlds, and thus liable to being stranded between them.

That the educated Indian was given to intellectual inconsistency was a
commonplace. Writing in 1913, Sir Bampfylde Fuller observed that educated
natives "give eager intellectual assent" to ideals inspired by English literature, science, and romantic love; and yet, he observed, they "live their lives
unchanged."[49] "An Englishman," he concluded, "is constantly disconcerted
by the extraordinary contradictions which he observes between the words
and the actions of an educated Indian, who seems untouched by inconsis-
tencies which appear to him scandalous."[50] A few years later William Archer
wrote, "Indians have an amazing capacity for learning, and for ignoring the
consequences of what they learn,"[51] an inconsistency that he attributed to a
native aptitude for western learning, combined with a continued reverence
for authoritative texts and gurus. Educated Indians also frequently noted,
and sometimes bemoaned, their inconsistency. A contributor to the *Modern
Review* wrote:

> We have a divorce between college and life. We read in our text-books
> that men are born equal and free, that the stars do not influence human
> life . . . We give intellectual assent to these propositions, we prove
> them – in our answer papers, – so satisfactorily as to secure first class
> marks. But we do not translate them into action, we do not apply them
> to our life and society. Every Hindu (and Mussalman) graduate regu-

lates his marriages and very often his journeys by astrology, which, in the answer-paper, he has proved to be an exploded science. Even social reformers, who have celebrated widow-marriages in their families in the teeth of social opposition, still believe in their descent from mythical ancestors . . . The Principal of a College (now no more) where chemistry was compulsory . . . believes that he cured a case of cholera in his family by making the patient drink the washings of the butcher's knife in the temple of Kalighat. The v-c of a learned University kept a Senate meeting waiting for half an hour, because he had scalded his fingers in cooking his own meals in the absence of any other member of the sub-caste of Brahmans to which he belonged . . . In hardly any college can *all* the Hindu members of the staff be induced to take even light refreshments together, and yet they are not sanskritists, not orthodox Pandits, but Masters of modern European subjects and even Masters of Science or Kantian philosophy.[52]

This intellectual and moral confusion was attributed to the need of the educated Indian to negotiate two distinct worlds, cultural domains characterized and governed by radically different conceptions of how the world worked, what a man's place in it was, and what constituted moral behaviour. Other observations and complaints – the much-lamented unpunctuality of the educated Indian, and his alleged inability to identify his interests with the institution of which he was a part, despite his acknowledged capacity to identify with, and sacrifice his interests to, the joint family – were similarly interpreted as arising out of his carrying the values, practices, and rituals of the joint family and caste into the world of the law court, office, and university. According to this explanation, the educated Indian had lost faith in the governing presumptions and beliefs of traditional Indian society, without yet being in a position to embrace the mores and presumptions governing modern, western life. We have already encountered this line of reasoning: have heard Governor Sir George Clarke explaining that the "restraining forces" of ancient India had lost their force among the educated, while the restraining forces of the West had not taken their place, resulting in a net "moral loss"; and Keshab Chunder Sen and other Brahmos attributing moral decline to the Hindu's being "emancipated" from his own creed without having found another to take its place. Many other voices joined in characterizing and explaining the moral crisis of the educated Hindu in similar terms. The *Pioneer* observed: "we have introduced [the educated Bengali] to a literature which at every page proves the foolishness of his old beliefs," but have "given the native no new religion whereon to found a new morality"; the result was that whereas "of old he had a moral code he felt he had to obey because he feared the displeasure of the gods by whom he believed it had been promulgated," now "the Hindu Pantheon has fallen, and with it all the Bengali ever had of morality."[53] A contributor to the *Educational Review* similarly attributed "the slackness of discipline, want of self control and decay of the reverential spirit in the life of the student" to the fact that "the old bonds of moral and religious sanctions are loosening and the new ones have not yet got sufficient grip."[54] The author of a history of education, denying that Bengali graduates were more immoral than graduates of other countries, nonetheless conceded that their education "loosened the hold on them of the conventions and decencies of Indian society, while it did not or could not provide regulating principles of equal authority or usefulness."[55] And a witness explained to the Hartog Commission, "We Indians are at present at a stage of transition and we do not know where we are. The old religious beliefs, the old traditions, the old culture is fast slipping away from our sight and we have yet to find and assimilate a culture which we can call our own."[56]

ONE OF THE chief symptoms of moral crisis was "inconsistency," usually thought to arise from an incomplete "transition." In some instances educated Indians were thought to hold inconsistent ideas; in others, there was thought to be an inconsistency between on the one hand their ideas and beliefs and on the other their actions and practices; and in other instances still, the actions and practices that they engaged in were held to be inconsistent with one another. But while it is clear enough what it means to declare that ideas or beliefs are inconsistent or contradictory, what could it mean to say that an idea is inconsistent with a practice, or that two actions or practices are inconsistent with each other? This makes sense on the presumption that every action and practice can be traced back to the idea or belief animating it, and to then find *these* to be inconsistent with one another; that is, it makes sense on the presumption that actions and practices are underpinned by and are expressions of ideas, beliefs, and values. In the discourse of moral decline, morality, even when it was something "done," was seen as something that was "held" in the form of beliefs and convictions, usually having their basis in religious belief and commitments. The moral confusion of the educated Indian could thus be seen not only in his openly professing values which were not consonant with, or were antithetical to, each other, but also in his engaging in practices which (in the view of the authors of the discourse of moral decline) were animated by ideas and convictions which were at odds with one another. Thus an important presumption underlying the explanation by inconsistency was that it accorded centrality to consciousness and the "mind"; all actions, social practices, and institutions were seen to be expressions and manifestations of ideas and beliefs. As Marx put it in *Capital I*, "what distinguishes the worst architect from the best of bees is this, that the architect raises his structure in imagination before he erects it in reality."[57]

In the passage quoted above, Marx points to this uniquely human faculty as one that serves to differentiate men from animals, whose activities are not objectifications of their thoughts. But historically this faculty also served – as indeed it did for Marx and Engels – to exorcise the gods. Gods are not another source and origin of practices and institutions, because now gods are themselves seen as the manifestations and creations of men; gods exist in men's consciousness. When in the nineteenth and twentieth centuries Feuerbach, Marx, Tylor, Frazer, Muller, Durkheim, Weber, and others wrote about religion and magic, they presumed – irrespective of their own religious convictions – that the religion of their subjects was to be understood first by seeing it as an emanation of their (or their society's) fears, thoughts, aspirations, and desires. The privileging of consciousness thus turns out to be connected to another, "anthropological," presumption: the consciousness that is privileged is that of Man. Every act, practice, and institution is the manifestation of an idea or belief, and the only source and origin of ideas and beliefs is Man.

If it is assumed that Man is the source of ideas and representations, and hence that the social world is to be explained by reference to men – that there is nothing "more" needed to understand social phenomena – it is also assumed that there is nothing "less," that once you have traced practices back to ideas, and ideas back to men, there is no further regress possible. The presumption that Man is source and origin is thus connected to another presumption, namely that he is singular and indivisible. He is not for instance regarded, as he is in the thinking of some societies, as divisible into the "forces" or components which constitute him.

As my references to figures as diverse as Marx, Tylor, Frazer, Muller, Durkheim, Weber, and others indicate, the presumptions to which I am drawing attention were not those of any particular intellectual current or school, but rather those of modern thought as it came to be constituted from the early modern period onward. There are of course many important differences between Marxists and Weberians, between Tylor and Durkheim, and so on;

these differences have constituted the stuff of intellectual debate in the West (and not only in the West) for a long time. But there are also shared presumptions, which we often overlook, in part precisely because being shared by the diverse intellectual currents which compose our intellectual life, they have become naturalized, and have come to appear not as presumptions made by a particular mode of thinking but as the very preconditions of any sort of thinking.

The presumptions to which I am drawing attention are similar to Kant's and Durkheim's "categories." Arguing against skepticism and empiricism, Kant sought to show that certain intuitions and categories are not derived from experience but are the precondition for experience and knowledge. Drawing directly (but loosely) upon Kant, Durkheim (also rejecting empiricism) argued that a priori mental conceptions are what make it possible to have experience and knowledge. However, whereas for Kant these categories are transcendentally necessary and hence universal, Durkheim traces the "necessity" of the categories to their social and religious origins. In the process these categories are rendered historical and variable, although, notwithstanding some readings of Durkheim, they are not thereby "relativized." Durkheim's categories are still "necessary and universal," but their content "varies incessantly" from society to society.[58] The presumptions underlying the characterization of moral crisis – the privileging of consciousness, the anthropological view of Man as the source and origin of all ideas and practices and institutions, and the idea that Man and his consciousness are indivisible – are, I suggest, analogous to categories in the Kantian or Durkheimian sense. They are not "hypotheses" or explanations, but fundamental categories which make hypotheses and explanations possible (in this case, the explanation of moral crisis in terms of inconsistency and transition).

Below I suggest, however, that when pressed into service in characterizing and explaining the moral crisis of the educated Indian, these categories reveal that they are inadequate to their object; and that, pace Kant and Durkheim, these categories are in fact not universal and necessary but specifically modern. They are modern in a twofold sense. First, a number of the presumptions to which I have drawn attention only assume their self-evident and axiomatic status in modern times. Second, taken collectively, they signify a tectonic shift from the world to the subject. If Cartesianism and empiricism effected a split between a perceiving, knowing subject and an object known, philosophy after Kant has accorded to the subject an increasingly "active" role. The categories are not ways of recognizing and naming a world which is in fact ordered in those ways, but rather something which we impose upon the world, which apply to experience because they serve to constitute it.

Diagnosing the Diagnosis

The view that religion is principally a matter of belief, and that religions vary according to what is believed, is the product of a very specific European and Christian history. This is one in which deism and the "discovery" of "natural religion" play a large part, because the presumption that there was a natural religion underpinning all religions is what gave rise to the view of religions as systems of belief. Peter Harrison argues that in England in the course of the seventeenth and eighteenth centuries " 'religion' was constructed along essentially rationalist lines, for it was created in the image of the prevailing rationalist methods of investigation . . . inquiry into the religion of a people became a matter of asking what was believed."[59] If religion was conceived as a matter concerning belief, it is this, conversely, which made it possible to invent the category "religion," as the species of which different religious beliefs are the genus. It is in the course of the history of Christianity and debates around it in Enlightenment and post-Enlightenment Europe that "religion" and "belief" emerge as mutually constitutive categories. Thus the very notion of "religion" is itself "a Christian theological category,"[60] "a modern invention which the West, during the last two hundred years or so, has exported to the rest of the world."[61]

We can see this process of "exportation" at work in the eighteenth century, when European observers tried to characterize the religion of the "Gentoos," and did so by interpreting Hinduism, in modern and Christian (often specifically Protestant) terms, as "a set of hard and fast doctrinal presuppositions."[62] In some readings Hinduism was even found to be a more-or-less monotheistic creed, with the profusion of Hindu gods representing different aspects of one God. That many Hindus had reified these aspects of the one God into different deities to be propitiated was seen as a consequence of the vulgarization of this intricate creed by the unlettered masses. The distinction between a high or classical Hinduism and a "primitive" popular Hinduism became a common distinction in European writings from very early on,[63] and it was to have a long life. This was so not only among the Orientalists, who were not much interested in popular Hinduism, but also in a later, "ethnological" literature. Studies such as W. Crooke's *The Popular Religion and Folk-lore of Northern India* (2nd edn, 1896), Henry Whitehead's *The Village Gods of South*

India (1921), and L. S. S. O'Malley's *Popular Hinduism: The Religion of the Masses* (1935), to cite but a few, drew a distinction between a primitive, even "animist" popular Hinduism, swarming with gods and spirits and idols, and a more philosophical and genuinely spiritual Hinduism, for which the multitude of gods were different facets of a singular supreme Being.[64] These accounts usually arranged religions on an evolutionary scale, with primitive forms of animism and fetishism giving way to "higher" forms. What was unusual about India in this view was that its primitive forms were not displaced but rather continued to survive, so that different kinds and "levels" of religious development coexisted, making India a valuable laboratory for studying religion and religious "evolution."

Some Hindus also came to reinterpret and redefine their religion in ways influenced by western accounts and critiques of it. In the course of the nineteenth century movements of religious reform such as the Brahmo Samaj and the Arya Samaj sought to reform or redefine Hinduism (often by claiming that popular, "superstitious" forms represented a degradation of an original Hinduism, or "survivals" of the religious beliefs of the pre-Aryan inhabitants of India). The result was that the riotous pantheon of gods was downgraded, and Hinduism emerged, like other "proper" religions, as a philosophy and a set of coherent beliefs to which its adherents subscribed. But for the vast majority of Hindus, then and even today – as ethnologists continually discover[65] – their religious practice was not an expression of their religious beliefs. This continued to be true as well of a great many western-educated Hindus, as Max Muller found when he quizzed Indians about their religion on their arrival in Oxford, only to discover that "they hardly understood what we mean by religion. Religion, as a mere belief, apart from ceremonies and customs, is to them but one, and by no means the most important, concern of life, and they often wonder why we should take so deep an interest in mere dogma, or as they express it, make such a fuss about religion."[66]

Hindus did not in fact "believe" in their religion, and it was not beliefs that constituted Hinduism. Indeed, Hindus do not even "believe" that their numerous gods exist; they know them to coexist with humans. Whatever the validity of seeing these gods as "projections," or as "symbols," or, in Durkheim's words, as "exist[ing] only because they are represented as such in minds,"[67] these interpretations are far removed from the Hindu understanding, in which gods and humans coexist as persons. It is of course true of many religious people that they do not simply "believe" in their gods or spirits, but know them to exist. There is an inherent paradox in seeking to characterize a society of this sort in the rationalist categories of modern thought, a paradox that we will attend to more closely in chapter 3. For present purposes, however, it is sufficient to note that what is at issue is not simply the polite skepticism of the social scientist versus the devotion of the religious. Hindus did not "know" their gods to exist in some *supernatural* realm, they knew that their gods existed because they formed part of the *everyday* world of humans. Ashis Nandy writes, "Deities in everyday Hinduism . . . are not entities outside everyday life, nor do they preside over life from outside; they constitute a significant part of it . . . Gods are above and beyond humans but they are, paradoxically, not outside the human fraternity."[68] There is no sharp separation between a sacred realm inhabited by gods and a mundane one of men; as C. J. Fuller observes, popular Hinduism is "premised on the lack of any absolute divide between them. . . . human beings can be divine forms under many and various conditions, and the claim to divinity is unsensational, even banal, in a way that it could never be in a monotheistic religion lacking 330 million deities."[69]

The numerous deities of Hinduism are co-present with humans, and highly visible; they exist as spirits, as ghosts, and in the form of those numerous idols that so offended the sensibility of their rulers. "Sympathetic" observers, as well as those Hindus who sought to defend the honor of their religion by denying that idolatry was an integral element of it, often suggested that these representations were a popular corruption. Others suggested that they were allegorical devices made necessary to render the "supreme being" of Hinduism "intelligible to the vulgar."[70] The first explanation drew upon the distinction between a vulgar, debased religion and a high, pure one, mentioned earlier. The second explanation additionally drew upon a Christian understanding and defense of idols. Christianity has been hostile to the worship of "graven images," but it nonetheless finds a legitimate place for religious images. St. Thomas Aquinas, for instance, wrote that there was a "threefold reason for the institution of images in the Church: first, for the instruction of the unlettered, who might learn from them as from books; second, so that the mystery of the Incarnation and the examples of the saints might remain more firmly in our memory by being daily represented to our eyes; and third, to excite the emotions which are more effectively aroused by things seen than by things heard."[71]

But the analogy suggested by the comparison does not hold: whereas in the Christian tradition images were very clearly representations of an original, for most Hindus idols or *murtis* (images, forms) are not in fact "representations" of gods that reside elsewhere.[72] At the very least, the idol or image or *murti*, once its eyes have been pierced and appropriate ceremonies observed,[73] partakes of the *shakti* (power) of the god; for most Hindus, it *is* a god. As Diana Eck explains, "the *murti* is more than a likeness; it is the deity itself taken 'form.' The uses of the word *murti* in the Upanishads and the Bhagavad Gita suggest that the form *is* its essence. The flame is the *murti* of the fire . . . or the year is the *murti* of time . . . the *murti* is a body-taking, a manifestation, and is not different from the reality itself."[74]

Thus the profusion of icons in Hinduism is also a profusion of gods; they are ever present, part of the world of humans. To render this by saying that "Hindus believe that there are numerous gods," as the sociologist of religion must do (since modern social science cannot treat gods as real beings, as actors in the world), is not only and obviously to deny the self-understandings of the subjects of one's study. It is also, and less obviously, to translate their self-understandings into our categories – to claim that the gods "actually" reside in human consciousness, and are thus a matter of beliefs.[75] But inasmuch as Hindus did not inhabit a world in which the existence of their gods was dependent upon human belief in them, a key presumption of the whole discourse of moral crisis becomes deeply problematic. How could western-educated Hindus have been torn between their traditional religious beliefs and the ideas that they encountered as a consequence of their exposure to western education, if their Hinduism was not a matter of beliefs in the first place?

With *murtis* our commonsensical distinction between an original and its image, sign and referent, reality and its representation, does not hold. Other religious objects can also be both themselves and not themselves; such logical and ontological leaps are an everyday part of Hindu practice. Fuller gives some commonly known examples. In Bengali Vaishnavism the saint Chaitanya is at once revered as the founder of the Gaudiya Vaishnava devotionalist order, as an incarnation of Krishna, as Krishna himself, as Krishna's perfect devotee Radha, and as the combined Radha-Krishna. The Ganges is at once an "image" of the goddess Ganga and Ganga herself; the cow is an "image" of Lakshmi and Lakshmi herself. Other religious objects can include all others and simultaneously be infinitely replicable; the holy city of Kashi (Benares) is said to include all other *tirthas* (pilgrimage sites) within it, so that by going to Kashi one can also make a pilgrimage to all *tirthas*; conversely, going to any holy site is to visit Kashi.[76]

Examples like these could be almost endlessly multiplied, and confronted with similar phenomena, observers sometimes concluded that Indians were simply lacking an elementary grasp of logic. The principal of the Inter-denominational Women's Christian College in Madras attributed Indian inconsistency to the absence of any tradition of Aristotelian logic, and thus to knowledge of the law of noncontradiction: "The mind of the South Indian student works paratactically rather than hypotactically; opinions formed on different grounds remain side by side within their consciousness without mental contact, and there is little effort at combination."[77] In Hegel's view Hindu ontology displayed a cavalier disregard for the categories of logic: he told the students attending his lectures on religion, "there is here no category of being. [Hindus] have no category for what we call the independence of things, for what we articulate by the phrase 'there are' or 'there is.' "[78] In more sympathetic and sensitive readings, this inability to "fix" things, to identify them and keep them distinguished from one another, is sometimes captured by words such as "fluidity."[79] The "fluidity" in question here is, however, perhaps not so much a fluidity of Hinduism (especially given that the same society and religion, viewed from the perspective of caste, is frequently found to be extraordinarily "rigid" and "inflexible"); rather, it may be the ethnologist's way of registering and staying sensitive to the imperfect fit between her categories and their object, an object which viscously slides and spills across the organizing distinctions of thought.

The profusion of gods in India, embodied in the innumerable idols which they inhabit, thus indicates not only that Hindus did not "believe" in their gods but also that the logical distinctions which we assume to be fundamental to thought were here conspicuous by their absence. Some concluded from this that the Hindus possessed no logic; others that this was a world of "fluid" categories. By contrast Lucien Lévy-Bruhl, studying the evidence on societies which similarly seemed prone to fundamental category mistakes, thought he discerned an alternative logic at work. Lévy-Bruhl rejected the explanation that "primitives" attributed mystical and anthropomorphic qualities to natural phenomena ("animism"), on the grounds that such an explanation attributed to the native a fundamental distinction between nature and the supernatural, between matter and the mystic, and between the observing subject and the object, which was not his.[80] The "superstition" of the native was in fact quite different from the superstitions which continue to exist even in "civilized" societies: "The superstitious man, and frequently also the religious man, among us, believes in a twofold order of reality, the one visible, palpable, and subordinate to the essential laws of motion; the other invisible, intangible, 'spiritual' forming a mystic sphere which encompasses the first. But the primitive's mentality does not recognize two distinct worlds in contact with each other, and more or less interpenetrating. To him there is but one. Every reality, like every influence, is mystic, and consequently every perception is also mystic."[81] As a consequence, "in the collective representations of primitive mentality, objects, beings, phenomena can be, though in a way incomprehensible to us, both themselves and something other than themselves ... The ubiquity or multipresence of existing beings, the identity of one with many, of the same and of another, of the individual and the species – in short, everything that would scandalize and reduce to despair thought which is subject to the law of contradiction, is implicitly admitted by this prelogical mentality."[82]

The use of unfortunate terms such as "primitive," "mystical," and "prelogical" notwithstanding, we could conclude, as Rodney Needham does, that Lévy-Bruhl's insights allow us to conceive the "strangeness" of other mentalities not as "mere errors, as detected by a finally superior rationality of which we were the fortunate possessors," but as evidence that "other civilizations present us with *alternative* categories and modes of thought."[83] That would be an advance over declaring Hinduism to be possessed of no logic at all, or registering its "difference" by means of terms such as "fluidity." However, Lévy-Bruhl's explanation still presupposes an active subject who organizes and experiences the world through the categories of mind – the work from which I have been quoting is titled *Les fonctions mentales dans les sociétés inférieures*. Lévy-Bruhl takes us "beyond" Durkheim in allowing us to recognize that these categories may vary quite radically, but the categories in question are still those which humans "impose" upon the world, in the sense that they are what is necessary for them to be able to experience and understand their world.

By contrast, Timothy Mitchell, rereading Pierre Bourdieu's account of the housing of the Kabyle people, seeks to avoid reducing different understandings to mental categories and the operations of the mind. Presented with understandings that see in material objects homologies and attractions, and forces and potentials that require balancing and tending, we are apt to read these relations as "representations" and "symbols." Mitchell resists such readings:

There is nothing symbolic in this world. Gall is not associated with wormwood because it symbolizes bitterness. It occurs itself as the trace of bitterness. The grain does not represent fertility, and therefore the woman. It is itself fertile, and duplicates in itself the swelling of a pregnant woman's belly. Neither the grain nor the woman is merely a sign signifying the other and neither, it follows, has the status of the original, the "real" referent or meaning of which the other would be merely the sign. These associations, in consequence, should not be explained in terms of any symbolic or cultural "code," the separate realm to which we imagine such origins to belong . . . resemblances and differences do not form a separate realm of meaning, a code apart from things themselves; hence this very notion of a "thing" does not occur. For the same reason, there is not "nature" – in our own sense of the great referent, the signified in terms of which such a code is distinguished.[84]

The relations in question "are not the relations between an object and its meaning, as we would say, or between a symbol and the idea for which it stands."[85]

The "primitives" studied by Lévy-Bruhl and the Berber-speaking Kabyle of Algeria discussed by Mitchell are of course societies very different from that of India. I draw attention to them not to suggest a strict analogy, but rather to suggest that where we see an apparent absence of logic, or a "symbolism" run riot, we may in fact be observing a different logic at work,[86] or an ontology which is not accessible to knowledge or experience only through the categories of a collective mind. The latter point is one to which I shall return. But for now, let us conclude by noting that even the idea of a unified self as the source and site of ideas and of consciousness, seemingly so undeniable, was a category not at all self-evident to every Hindu. It has often been observed that the Hindu philosophical tradition has a "weak" conception of selfhood.[87] (The Buddhist doctrines of *anatman*, or not-self, and dependent origination go considerably further, denying that there is a reality corresponding to the grammatical subject of verbs, and suggesting that the personality is not a permanent self or subject but rather a temporary constellation composed of five forces or *skandas*.)[88] Persons are not indivisible, bounded units but are "dividual" or divisible, in the sense that they are themselves composed of substances and essences. These are absorbed and passed on through various exchanges: in McKim Marriot's description, "To exist, dividual persons absorb heterogenous material influences. They must also give out from themselves particles of their own coded substances – essences, residues, or other active influences – that may then reproduce in others something of the nature of the persons in whom they have originated. Persons engage in transfers of bodily substance-codes through parentage, through marriage, and through services and other kinds of interpersonal contacts. They transfer coded food substances by way of trade, payments, alms, feasts or other prestations."[89] In all this "the assumption of the easy, proper separability of action from actor, of code from substance . . . that pervades both Western philosophy and Western common sense . . . is generally absent."[90] E. Valentine Daniel, in his study of personhood among Tamil Hindus, describes how the Tamil villager seeks to find an equilibrium between his own substance and the substance of village, house, sexual partner, and so on. Again, each person himself is assumed to be composed of substances which are exchanged, altered, and conducive (or not) to good health and prosperity, and this militates against the easy-going and "natural" presumption that while society, group, and family can all be decomposed into individual persons, the person or self is not subject to further division.

The gap or mismatch between the categories employed to diagnose "moral decline" and the moral and religious life of Hindus would seem to extend even to the self. Far from being the unified, indivisible seat of consciousness and source of moral ideas and actions presumed by our categories, the Hindu self appears as a "leaky" one, with porous boundaries.[91]

What Counts as an Explanation?

It may be objected that all I have done is demonstrate how social actors made sense of their situation in ways not consonant with the explanations offered of their predicament, but that this in no way invalidates the explanations. Not only are explanations within the social sciences often expected to be at odds with those offered by the subjects of study, but it is sometimes considered a sign of their superior quality that they go "behind" or "beneath" the self-understandings of their subjects to explain what is "really" going on. Sometimes this is thought to be because there are systematic and more or less insurmountable reasons why social actors are condemned to misunderstand their own situation; society is opaque to its constituents, and necessarily so. In Durkheim's words, "social life should be explained, not by the notions of those who participate in it, but by more profound causes which are unperceived by consciousness."[92] For others, there are systemic factors leading social actors to misread their own circumstances, but this opacity is not insurmountable. The correct reading, once presented to those whose own situation is opaque to them, renders the situation intelligible, and can emancipate social actors (or patients) from their misunderstanding.[93] In either case, to demonstrate as I have done that the self-understandings of social actors are at odds with the categories employed in the explanation of moral crisis does not in any way negate this explanation.

Inasmuch as the tools of analysis – what I have labeled presumptions or categories – are here drawn from the modern western intellectual tradition and applied to understand colonial India, what is at issue is how well the fundamental assumptions of modern western thought "traveled" when relocated in colonial India. This is a question to which we shall return repeatedly, for it is one of the central questions animating this book. But for present purposes, whatever the general merits of the proposition that the social scientist can disregard or at least "bracket" the self-understandings of those being studied, in the case of a diagnosis of moral crisis these self-understandings are critical to the explanation being offered. For irrespective of whether the subjects of this explanation would have recognized or embraced the categories, these categories had to be part of the world they inhabited if the phenomenon of moral crisis was even to be visible, let alone become the subject of speculation and explanation.

Let me explain what I mean by way of an example. When Freud discusses the dreams of historical figures, he is operating in the manner prescribed by Durkheim. That some of these people from times past regarded their dreams as revelations, and thus that their own conceptions are at odds with those of the analyst, can be discarded or bracketed, and the dream can be analyzed. However, where Freud engages in psychoanalytic practice, with the aim of analyzing dreams to identify a neurosis, it is necessary for the patient to accept, as a minimum, that dreams reveal the workings of his or her mind, rather than revelations of the gods, if the analysis is to serve any therapeutic purpose. Analogously, *if the subjects of the discourse of moral decline did not privilege consciousness, then consciousness could not have been the battleground upon which their contending beliefs met; if their "religion" was not something "believed" and their morality something "held," they could not have been torn by conflicting beliefs and moralities; and if they did not have a unified self, they could not have suffered from a divided one.* In short, if the subjects of this explanation did not inhabit a world where categories of consciousness, mind, and the indivisible self pertained, they could not have experienced a moral crisis, and there would be nothing to explain in the first place.

Could we then draw the opposite conclusion – not that there was a moral crisis which was then explained in terms of inconsistency and transition, but rather that the categories presumed and employed by the explanation made visible or "produced" the very crisis which was to be explained? Were "inconsistency" and "crisis" built into the categories of explanation, rather than being a feature of the life of the educated Indian – which would render comprehensible why so many educated Indians remained blithely unaware that they were "torn" and in the throes of crisis?

This will not do either, because there *were* those who testified to having emerged from a moral crisis, or who testified that some of their fellow countrymen were undergoing one. Many examples of this were provided earlier in this chapter, such as Keshab Chunder Sen declaring that India was undergoing a transition in which "the old faith is gone, and no new faith is established in its place"; or a witness before the Hartog Commission explaining, "We Indians are at present at a stage of transition and we do not know where we are. The old religious beliefs, the old traditions, the old culture is fast slipping away from our sight and we have yet to find and assimilate a culture which we can call our own." Thus it cannot be that the explanation of moral crisis conjured up a phenomenon that did not exist. Our demonstration – that the categories in which this crisis was explained did not correspond to the world inhabited by those whom it sought to explain – cannot be dismissed as irrelevant on the grounds that the categories of explanation do not have to accord with the self-understandings of those being explained. But at the same time, we have to be able to account for why some educated Indians *did* explain themselves in these ways. Our question now becomes: Why did some Indians find the categories underlying the explanation of moral crisis adequate for explaining and making sense of their experience, or that of others, while a great many educated Indians did not?

Compartments of the "Mind"

In his *When A Great Tradition Modernizes* (1972), Milton Singer studied a small sample of nineteen industrialist leaders based in Madras, men whose occupation made them very much a part of the modern, but other aspects of whose lives, he found, continued to be marked by "traditional" patterns and practices.[94] Singer found that "the industrial leaders not only did not experience soul-shattering conflicts between their religious and social traditions and their industrial careers, but in fact adapted the two spheres."[95] They did so by

a *compartmentalization* of two spheres of conduct and belief that would
otherwise collide . . . The physical setting for the traditional religious
sphere is the home, where many of the traditional ritual observances of
Sanskritic Hinduism are performed. The physical setting for modern
practices is the office and factory; there English is used, Western dress
is worn, contacts with different castes and communities are frequent,
and the instruments and concepts of modern science and technology
engage the attention. Each of the leaders passes daily from one context to the other and symbolizes the passage by changing from Indian
dhoti to Western shirt and trousers and from his Indian language to
English . . . The home is categorized as the domain of one's family, caste,
religion, and language community; the norms appropriate to these
groups are in operation here. The office and factory, on the other hand,
are categorized as a domain that includes nonrelatives, other castes and
communities, and even foreigners; the norms of behaviour there will
accordingly be very different from those prevailing in the home.[96]

"By compartmentalizing their lives in this way," Singer writes, "they are
able to function both as good Hindus and as good industrialists."[97] Whereas
the discourse of moral crisis purported to find that trafficking between the
world of universities and offices and the world of home and religious ritual
produced people who were troubled and even torn, Singer concludes that the
"coexistence of the traditional and the modern in India have not produced
the 'schism in the soul' predicted by classical [modernization] theory."[98] He
does so, however, by employing the same categories of understanding and
analysis as those used by the producers of the discourse of moral crisis. Thus
he uses the verb "categorized," indicating that it is the agent who assigns the
norms of belief and action to different spheres; and he explains that the industrialist divides his norms into two compartments of his mind, applying
each to the relevant sphere of social action, rather as a bilingual speaker keeps
two languages in her head, using whichever is appropriate according to context. The same categories which inform the analysis of moral inconsistency
are here employed to yield a diametrically opposed result.

In *Provincializing Europe*, Dipesh Chakrabarty discusses a Bengali text written by Bhabanicharan Bandyopadhyaya, a Bengali Brahmin and magazine
editor. *Kalikata kamalalaya* (1823) stages a debate between a Brahmin living
and working in Calcutta and a newcomer from the countryside. The newcomer gives voice to many of the anxieties of the time, for example that

making a living in the emergent "civil society" of colonial Calcutta entailed neglecting ritual observances appropriate to a high-caste Hindu: that it entailed the mixing of languages, clothes, food, and so on. The resident of Calcutta concedes that there are those of whom this is true, but adds that good Hindus manage to straddle two worlds: that of obligations and rituals to the gods and one's male ancestors, and that of (necessary) engagement with colonial civil society in the course of pursuing worldly interests such as wealth and power. They do so by seeking to erect and maintain boundaries between these domains – for instance, they continue to perform their ritual duties (adjusting the times when making one's livelihood requires this), and they do not stay at work longer than necessary. There is nothing here, according to Chakrabarty, "that suggests any attraction to the idea that the time of the household should keep pace with the time of the civil-political society. The themes of discipline, routine, punctuality . . . are absent from KK [Kalikata Kamalalaya]. If anything, there was an emphasis to the contrary. In the world KK depicted, the householder never spent more time at office than was minimally needed and concentrated on ministering to the needs of gods and ancestors. The self, in its highest form, was visualized as part of the male lineage, kula, and was thus more tied to a mytho-religious practice of time than to the temporality of secular history."[99] The Brahmin who successfully negotiates the world of colonial civil and political society and the Hindu world of ritual and caste obligations (and the protagonist of KK concedes that there are those who do not successfully do so) is not riven by conflict and inconsistency – though here, as in Singer's account, there is a palpable tension around the allocation of time, since the limited number of hours in the day means that compromises must be made. The protagonist of KK explains to his interlocutor (in Chakrabarty's words) "that in spite of the new structuring of the day required by colonial civil society, the true Hindu strove to maintain a critical symbolic boundary between the three spheres of involvement and action (karma) that defined life. These spheres were: daivakarma (action to do with the realm of the gods), pitrikarma (action pertaining to one's male ancestors), and vishaykarma (actions undertaken in pursuit of worldly interests such as wealth, livelihood, fame, and secular power)."[100] The practices belonging to colonial civil society belong to vishaykarma, and "the city-dweller's aim was to prevent [these practices and the words and ideas associated with them] from polluting the ritually purer domains in which one transacted with gods and ancestors (daivakarma and pitrikarma)."[101]

At first glance this may seem very similar to Singer's account: the successful Brahmin is one who manages to "compartmentalize," to straddle two domains requiring different values and practices without being torn or conflicted. However, in Chakrabarty's reading of this text there is nothing to suggest that it is the Brahmin who assigns or "categorizes," as if the continued existence of these different realms were conjured up by and maintained in the mind, or by "culture" as a sort of sedimented, collective mind. Rather, the good Brahmin is one who maintains categorical distinctions which are not of his making, but which precede his activities and understandings; they are what endow human activities with their boundaries and meanings, what make a meaningful human life possible. *Daivakarma, pitrikarma,* and *vishay-karma* are not logical categories, features of the human mind, but rather ontological ones: they are not what humans use to categorize and organize experience; they are what make meaningful and ethical experience possible in the first place.

In chapter 1 we saw that the Indian student was accused of treating western education instrumentally, as something only pertaining to worldly success. This "decision" by the student was usually seen as unfortunate, even reprehensible; here, as in Singer's reading, the presumption was that students did the categorizing and assigning. If we attend to the evidence carefully, though, we will notice that the guilty parties often explained their actions by referring to existing realms similar to those employed by the protagonist of KK. They distinguished between "arthakari vidya" – knowledge pertaining to *artha* (worldly affairs) – and knowledges pertaining to *dharma* (ethical and lawful life) and *kama* (pleasure); or, as with the Muslim judicial official quoted in chapter 1, between knowledge pertaining to *duniya* (worldly matters) and that pertaining to *din* (religious matters). Here again, as in KK, these different domains can be seen – and were seen by those who explained their actions in these terms – not as ways of dividing up human realms and actions but as existing categories to which human actions, to be ethical, had to conform. The judgment that western knowledge belonged to the realm of *artha* or *duniya* (rather than *dharma* or *kama* or *din*) was made by the student; but it was not the student who divided the world conceptually into these domains. To the student, as with Kant or Durkheim, these categories were the precondition for having meaningful experience, and also for living an ethical life. But for the student, if not for Kant or Durkheim, these distinctions were part of an existent order, part of the furniture of the world that had to be acknowledged and adapted to, rather than categories of the "mind" or of Reason, by means of which humans organize and order their world.

We have seen that the categories of our modern, western thought, even where they were not adequate to their object, sometimes did become so. Some Indians did come to endorse and contribute to the discourse of moral inconsistency and crisis. Therefore it is perfectly possible, even plausible (the plausibility of this does not rest upon our wholly endorsing Singer's methods or his conclusions) that the world described in KK should have yielded to the world described by Singer, one in which educated and "modern" Indians, now possessed of mind and consciousness and an indivisible self, could experience conflict – or devise ways to avoid it. Such changes have undoubtedly occurred; we are now better placed to specify the nature of the "transition."

Diagnosing Moral Crisis: A Second Opinion

The discourse of moral decline arose because it was felt by many that the knowledge disseminated through schools and universities had produced an unexpected effect: educated Indians had been plunged into a moral crisis, no longer fully able to believe in the moral code derived from their own religion and worldview, without yet being in a position to embrace the rationality and morality corresponding to the new world of colonial civil society. I have argued that this characterization and explanation presumed categories that were not adequate to their object; a great many educated Indians who were described as being in the throes of a moral crisis were themselves quite unaware that they were. Others, however, had come to subscribe to this explanation and to characterize their own experience in terms of it. Why was this so, and what was the nature of the difference between the two groups?

As we saw at the beginning of this chapter, Duff, Macaulay, and others anticipated that the introduction of western education would lead Hindus to forsake their religion, and eventually to become Christians. They were wrong; a few conversions aside, most educated Hindus did not abandon their religion (this was precisely what led missionaries to add their voice to the discourse of moral crisis, a "crisis" which functioned, in part, as an explanation of why the desired conversions had not occurred). The prediction was mistaken for many of the reasons we have been discussing: it assumed that religion was a matter of belief, and that belief in Hinduism would be undermined when its tenets were challenged by other ones. However, that some educated Hindus did convert, and in doing so gave explanations that supported Macaulay's and Duff's reasoning (recall, for instance, the Indian Christian who declared that the western knowledge imbibed at Hindu College had been instrumental in leading Hindus like him away from their religion) might suggest that this explanation or prediction, and the presumptions that were embedded in it, came to be true (for some). Change did occur, a crisis was experienced, and inconsistency was one of the manifestations of this crisis.

However, in the light of the preceding discussion, we would now offer an explanation in terms very different from those employed in the discourse of moral crisis. We would now say that a conflict of beliefs and ensuing inconsistency and crisis were not the "cause" of religious conversion but rather were a way of describing and making sense of this conversion. Conflict and crisis could only be experienced where the categories through which we experience the world came to be seen as ones that human consciousness imposes upon the world, rather than distinctions to which humans adapt themselves. It is not that there were conflicts in their mind that led some to become Christians; it is rather that once they had become Christians and had come to see their religion as something consisting of beliefs and values, they retrospectively made sense of their conversion in these terms. The explanation is a way of making sense of and narrating a change (and making sense of change by narrating it), and doing so in the terms and categories of one's changed position, explaining both how one could once have been wrong and why one is now right. Here to "explain" is not the same thing as to locate a "cause"; and the explanation is something integral to the transformation being characterized, rather than external to it.

An example may help to make the point. In his rereading of Freud's analysis of the Wolf Man (in which Freud traces the patient's neurosis back to an episode when the patient saw his parents having sex), Slavoj Žižek locates this trauma within the "real" rather than the symbolic. One could say that this real event was the "cause" of the subsequent neurosis. However, at the age of two the episode was not a trauma for the child at all; it only became so later, when the child entered the symbolic order and could not fit this scene into it: "the trauma has no existence of its own prior to symbolization," and therefore it would be a mistake to "obliterate this retrospective character of the trauma and 'substantialize' it into a positive entity, one that can be isolated as a cause preceding its symbolic effects." There is thus a peculiarity about invoking the trauma as an explanation for the neurosis, which Žižek characterizes as "the paradox of trauma qua cause, which does not pre-exist its effects but is itself retroactively 'posited' by them," and which involves "a kind of temporal loop."[102] I do not offer this illustration as a strict analogy (we obviously cannot fit the social phenomenon in question into the Lacanian categories of the real and symbolic); it is the form of the argument that is relevant. Žižek suggests that with the Wolf Man the very idea of cause only makes sense inasmuch as it is retrospectively posited; the question of whether it was "really" a cause ("really" meaning antecedent to its effects, not retrospectively posited by them) is unanswerable, because it is meaningless.

The explanation of moral crisis in terms of inconsistency and transition, I submit, is of this sort. Only those for whom the categories of mind, belief, the indivisible self, and the like had become meaningful could characterize their experience (or that of others) in terms of crisis and inconsistency. They would have had to experience the world through categories of the mind, in the form described by Kant and Durkheim, rather than as described by the protagonist of KK. Conversely, those for whom these categories did not make sense – for whom the categories which made experience possible and gave it its characteristic forms were ontological ones, such that knowledge and experience were "of" these distinctions rather than "through" them – could not even see or experience the effect which was to be explained. The conceptual vocabulary that would allow them to even experience, let alone describe, a crisis in "the mind" was not available.

This, let us note, is not the same as simply saying that the explanation of moral crisis was "sometimes" accurate, that the explanation seemed to hold for some educated Indians but not others. It does say that, but it goes further, clarifying what it means to say that some Indians experienced a crisis – namely that they now inhabited a world and lived a life in which religion and morality were beliefs held, and in which the dissonance between beliefs rooted in a Hindu life-world and those of the modern, "rational" world of colonial civil society could be perceived and experienced as contrary pulls and as conflict. The question of *why* – of why some Indians experienced this and others did not – has not dissolved, because we have not dismissed moral crisis as false, as a mere specter produced by a faulty explanation. But we have so formulated the question that it does not simply involve identifying which sociological factors led some to succumb to crisis and others not, as if the fact of crisis were separate from and anterior to the explanation of it. We are rather asking, Why did some cross over into that realm where they could experience crisis and (which is the same thing) have the language with which to perceive and articulate it?

The factors that historians normally cite when explaining fundamental changes in India, and the "transition" from one form of society and way of life to another, may all continue to be relevant: the rise of the market and an impersonal cash nexus, the erosion of traditional communities, and so on.[103] The account we are now offering does not displace these historical explanations but rather reconceives what we mean by "explaining a phenomenon." We now see these social phenomena and social changes not as acting upon social actors so as to change the ways they thought and believed and the values they embraced, but as bringing into being conceptions of "belief" and "values."

As a result we must see the categories of our western, modern social science not simply as ways of explaining change but as constitutive of it. The modern western knowledge introduced and disseminated through western education, and through the bureaucratic operations of the office and the impersonal cash nexus of the market, was not just a way of knowing India but also a force in reshaping it. And the knowledge which traveled to India was most at home in its new locale – that is to say, was best able to fulfill its function of "understanding" and "explaining" India – where it had the effect of reshaping the object that it sought to know.

CHAPTER THREE

Which Past? Whose History?

History writing in a form that we would recognize as such arrived in India with the British. From the moment that the British became territorial rulers of Bengal down to the moment they were forced to relinquish their Indian possessions, they wrote histories of India, beginning in the latter eighteenth century with Alexander Dow's *The History of Hindostan* and continuing in the nineteenth with Mark Wilks's *Historical Sketches of the South of India*, John Malcolm's *Sketch of the Political History of India*, James Mill's *The History of British India*, Duff's *History of the Mahrattas*, Mountstuart Elphinstone's *The History of India*, and W. W. Hunter's *A Brief History of the Indian Peoples* and in the twentieth with V. A. Smith's *Oxford History of India* and the multiauthor and multivolume *Cambridge History of India*. It was from such works, and from the teaching of history in schools and colleges, "that the Bengali intellectual learnt to rethink his own past according to a post-Enlightenment, rationalist view of history."[1] The history textbooks which proliferated in schools and universities, Ranajit Guha goes on to observe, played an especially important role: "It was these text-books which, more than anything else, helped history to establish itself as a normal knowledge – normal in a Kuhnian sense – within a culture still largely anchored to the Puranic tradition."[2]

Histories of India by British authors were very soon followed by Indian ones. At first these histories tended to accept the narrative of Britain's improving mission in India, but soon historiography became the site of contestation, as nationalists sought to write histories that would do justice to the past of their people. These were not, however, Puranic histories of colonialism but histories in the rationalist, post-Enlightenment mode.[3] Whether the histories written by Indians were loyalist or nationalist in their content, they took for their form the modern and western mode of history writing.

The same is true of this book. A history of sorts, it tells of western education, the chief vehicle for the dissemination of western knowledge, from within that knowledge. The Introduction observed that at some point it would be necessary to problematize this fact, to render history writing into an object of enquiry rather to presume its adequacy to its subject matter. What does it mean to write a history of western education and knowledge from within that knowledge? When we write a history of those who inhabited "a culture still largely anchored to the Puranic tradition," and who therefore would not necessarily recognize their past in the rationalist histories that we write of them, what is the status of the knowledge that has been produced?

Most historians assume that there is an object called "history," and that their task is to re-present it more or less objectively, to the degree that its surviving documents allow us to do so. To be sure, nowadays only innocents aspire to write history "as it really was." Most historians will concede that history writing is influenced by the historical circumstances of its production, and will acknowledge that because history is written, it is shaped by the resources of a linguistic community and the narrative conventions characterizing it. Nonetheless, the modern historical enterprise presumes that an object called "history" exists, and that because it does it can be objectively represented, even if only through a "qualified objectivity";[4] and on these grounds it is assumed that "real" history writing is qualitatively different from, say, epic and myth. If we too assumed that rationalist historiography is the privileged medium by which to recount all pasts, there would be no reason to enquire into the implications of writing a history of western education from within western knowledge. In posing and pursuing this question, I therefore engage those modes of thinking about history with a similar skepticism toward the presumption that rationalist historiography affords objective knowledge, and that it is the only true mode of representing the past.

Since there are a number of steps in the argument of this chapter, a brief sketch may be helpful. I begin by examining those writing within the hermeneutical tradition, who characterize encounters with past texts as engagements with the intellectual tradition from which we reason, rather than as a mode of gaining "objective" knowledge about the past. In outlining and endorsing their position, I also suggest that while it provides a better way of understanding what we do when we write history, it is corrosive of the idea that history writing as a discipline is possessed of its own object, namely "history" or "the past." If, as Hans-Georg Gadamer argues, all understanding in the human sciences is hermeneutical and also historical – that is, grounded and enabled by the inescapably temporal nature of Being – then it is difficult to see what the specific object of *historiographical* enquiry could be.

Historiography, I go on to argue, is not the objective retelling of a self-evident object, the past, but neither is it a reflex or expression of human temporality; it is instead a "code," one that creates its object. Drawing upon Foucault, Certeau, and Lévi-Strauss, I suggest that the central element in this code is humanism-anthropology. It is not because man is a meaning producing being, who leaves behind traces of himself, that it is possible to engage in history writing: the re-creation of the sort of man this was through an examination of his traces. Rather, it is historiography that helps to secure this humanist-anthropological presumption. Moreover, the presumption that Man is a culture secreting and meaning producing being – for instance, that gods are to be explained with reference to men rather than men with reference to gods – is not a universal, "transcendental presupposition" but rather a specifically modern presumption. Writing the history of those who did not share this presumption – who thought, for instance, that the affairs of men were best understood by reference to the designs of their Creator, not that their God was understood and explained as a creation of these men – is thus an anachronistic enterprise. Where, as in Europe, this view yielded to the humanist presumption underlying history writing, the anachronism in question can be a productive one. In this case the practice of history does not yield objective knowledge of the past, for we are "translating" the world and the self-understandings of our subjects into our modern terms; but it can yield an understanding of how their world gave way to ours, and thus of how we are both connected to and different from the objects of our historical enquiries.

The value that this has when practiced in a hermeneutic rather than objectivist mode only applies, however, inasmuch as the code of history is applied to the past out of which the code itself emerges; when applied to Indian pasts, it is neither an objective way of knowing what happened nor even a dialogue which enables better self-understanding. Here the code of history is not an outgrowth of earlier intellectual traditions but an external imposition; and because it does not arise out of the past that it retells, the hermeneutic "payload" of an anachronistic engagement with the past is lost. I conclude, therefore, by considering what the status of history writing is in this case, and specifically what the status is of a history of western education like that undertaken in this book.

History and Hermeneutics

In a commonly told story, the successes of the mathematical and physical sciences led to the extension of their methods to the emergent sciences of man to found a "science of society." Such a science would be based upon knowledge of the universal and invariant features of the human mind, and of the laws presumed to govern the functioning of society, just as they governed the natural world. This bred a reaction which, while willing to concede the fecundity of this approach when applied to nature, denied that it was equally applicable to the human sciences or, as many of those making this argument came to call them, the *Geisteswissenschaften*. It was claimed that the knowledge produced in the human sciences was different from that of the natural sciences, and required methods which recognized this difference. It was variously argued that the human sciences required an ideothetic rather than a nomothetic method; that they produced understanding rather than explanation; that the knowledge gained was of particulars, rather than generalizable laws and predictions based upon them; and that the human sciences were concerned with meanings, not causes. Many of these arguments were made with special reference to the domain of history. It was often claimed that knowledge of human affairs was inescapably historical in a way that knowledge of nature was not, with this having implications for the method of enquiry to be pursued, as well as for the character and status of the knowledge produced.

By the latter part of the nineteenth century Wilhelm Dilthey could declare that the successes of the "historical school" had emancipated the human sciences from their bondage to the natural sciences, but that they had done so without adequately specifying their own philosophical foundations. Much of Dilthey's large corpus was thus devoted to trying to develop the "philosophical foundations of the human studies."[5]

According to Dilthey, in the human sciences the objects to be known are products of human consciousness, as objectified in texts and other works of men; and the knowledge in question takes the form of understanding and interpreting, rather than coming to know causal processes and laws.[6] Dilthey borrows the term "objective mind" from Hegel to designate the object of the human sciences: "the manifold forms in which what individuals hold in common have objectified themselves in the world of the senses. In this objective mind the past is a permanently enduring present for us. Its realm extends from the style of life and the forms of social intercourse to the system of purposes which society has created for itself and to custom, law, state, religion, art, science and philosophy."[7] The knowledge sought by the human sciences is still conceived in terms of correct or adequate cognition, that is, in terms of consciousness grasping its object – Dilthey affirms that he works within the philosophical tradition of Descartes, Locke, Hume, and Kant – but Dilthey also registers an important difference: "no real blood flows in the veins of the knowing subject constructed by Locke, Hume and Kant; it is only the diluted juice of reason, a mere process of thought. . . . However, my historical and psychological studies of man as a whole led me to explain cognition and its concepts in terms of the powers of man as a willing, feeling and imagining being . . . The questions we all ask of philosophy cannot be answered by rigid *a priori* conditions of knowledge but only by a history which starts from the totality of our nature and sketches its development."[8]

Dilthey does not just historicize the object to be known: he goes considerably further by historicizing the subject who knows. This step took him beyond the Cartesian and Kantian legacy within which he was working, because epistemological certainty was rendered problematic the moment the subject was not a transcendental subject but rather one situated in a time and place. In his "Drafts for a Critique of Historical Reason," Dilthey put it as follows: "On the one hand, the knowing subject creates this mind-constructed world and, on the other, strives to know it objectively. How, then, does the mental construction of the mind-constructed world make knowledge of mind-constructed reality possible? This is the problem of what I have called the Critique of Historical Reason."[9]

This was a problem that Dilthey posed sharply and with which he struggled, but it was one he never surmounted. He is often approvingly quoted as having written that Man "understands history because he himself is a historical being."[10] But this statement, as Hans-Georg Gadamer points out, far from constituting a solution, simply restates the problem and underlines the gravity of it: "Is not the fact that consciousness is historically conditioned inevitably an insuperable barrier to its reaching perfect fulfilment in historical knowledge?"[11] For Hegel this problem was overcome because absolute knowledge gathers all of history up into it. But while Dilthey borrowed "objective mind" and much else besides from Hegel, this was a step he was unwilling to take; he and the entire generation who sought to provide philosophical grounding for history and the human sciences were united in rejecting Hegel's speculative philosophy, which in Dilthey's words "leaves the temporal, empirical and historical relations behind."[12] Dilthey sought instead to ground historical knowledge in "life experience," and as Gadamer notes, "if life is the inexhaustible, creative reality that Dilthey conceives, then must not the constant development of the meaningful context of history exclude any knowledge attaining to objectivity?"[13]

In the terms in which Dilthey posed the problem, it could not be solved. For while Dilthey went beyond his Kantian and Cartesian legacy in posing the problem, he nonetheless "remained committed, in some fundamental sense, to their nonhistorical ideal of interpretation, that is, to apodictic certitude and universal validity."[14] Any solution to the problem that Dilthey poses – namely, how can we achieve objective knowledge given that our knowledge is historically conditioned? – requires rethinking historicity, rethinking the requirement of objective Truth, or both. This task is undertaken by Gadamer, who continues the "hermeneutical" enquiry of Dilthey and his predecessors, by means of a detour through Heidegger.

Ontology and "Effective History"

For Gadamer the Enlightenment search for certitude is misconceived, in part because there is no Archimedean point from where we can survey and know the world without being influenced by our own location in it: "It is true that all understanding of the texts of philosophy requires the recognition of the knowledge that they contain. Without this we would understand nothing at all. But this does not mean that we in any way step outside the historical conditions in which we find ourselves and in which we understand . . . The standpoint that is beyond any standpoint, a standpoint from which we could conceive its true identity, is a pure illusion."[15] It therefore follows that "the idea of an absolute reason is impossible for historical humanity."[16]

According to Gadamer, this does not mean that interpretation and knowledge are arbitrary – that if objectivity is impossible, only pure and arbitrary subjectivism is left. It is this misconception that makes us cling to the search for pure objectivity, but in fact the choice is not between an unachievable objective certitude and an understanding that is wholly contingent upon our individual predilections. For the key element of our historical situatedness is that it is *collective*. Our prejudgments and preconceptions are not arbitrary individual ones, but those of our community and our intellectual tradition: "Long before we understand ourselves through the process of self-examination, we understand ourselves in a self-evident way in the family, society and state in which we live. The focus of subjectivity is a distorting mirror. The self-awareness of the individual is only a flickering in the closed circuits of historical life."[17]

The preconceptions through which we conceive of and approach the object that we seek to understand are those of our tradition, but "tradition" conceived not, in Enlightenment terms, as the antithesis of Reason (as blind obedience to authority); rather, tradition is something which survives because it is continually being renewed, affirmed, and also cultivated and changed.[18] This conception leads to Gadamer's famous rehabilitation of prejudice. Instead of seeking apodictic truth, for which our historicity will prove an insuperable problem, we must accept the inescapability of our location within traditions, and hence of prejudice: "What is necessary is a fundamental rehabilitation of the concept of prejudice and a recognition of the fact that there are legitimate prejudices, if we want to do justice to man's finite, historical mode of being."[19] This need not mean that we are imprisoned within our prejudices – we need, Gadamer writes, to distinguish between legitimate prejudices and those which reason needs to overcome – but it does mean that we cannot somehow erase or bracket them and encounter the object of understanding as if they did not exist.[20] Conversely, the "object" of our understanding – say, a text from the past – is itself never a "pure" object, for it comes to us with accretions of meaning, as always already interpreted. Understanding is therefore not an encounter between a disembodied consciousness which seeks to know a pure object, but an encounter between a subject and an object, both of which come with their own pre-understandings and accretions, their own historical "horizon." Understanding consists of a genuine dialogue or conversation (a favored metaphor of Gadamer) which aims at a fusion of horizons. Where this aim can be met (and it cannot always be met, because sometimes we will not be able to accept the truth of the horizon the object brings in its train), the resulting "fusion," as Georgia Warnke points out, is very like a Hegelian synthesis: "In the consensus or synthesis that results the truth of one's own position and that of the object are both preserved in a new stage of the tradition and cancelled as adequate positions on their own."[21]

Gadamer takes the step that Dilthey found himself unable to take, namely to recognize that the historicity of the enquiring subject renders objective knowledge impossible. Gadamer thus redescribes what happens in the human sciences as a dialogue between the tradition out of which we reason and the objects by which we are addressed. But it is not that Gadamer simply urges us to now regard as a virtue what previously appeared as a vice, namely the impossibility of any objective grounding for knowledge, and the apparent inescapability of subjectiveness in our judgments. He claims not merely that our historical situatedness is a fact with important epistemological implications, but that our historicity is itself grounded in the ontological structure of what it means to be human. He does this by drawing upon the thought of Martin Heidegger.

Gadamer draws upon the fundamental ontology of *Being and Time* to rethink our historicity not as an inescapable limit to our knowledge but as its enabling condition. As Ricoeur describes it, the idea that hermeneutics is concerned with providing an epistemological grounding for the human sciences is displaced by Heidegger and then Gadamer, as they "attempt to dig beneath the epistemological enterprise in order to disclose its ontological condition."[22] For Heidegger, history as historians understand it, as objective events and processes of the past, is merely the ontic manifestation of a more fundamental ontological condition that provides its ground, namely the temporalizing modes of human being. The abstract time of world history presumed by the historian is moreover the least authentic of the modes of human temporality, for it is rooted in the forgetting of human finitude. It is these modes, unified in the three ekstases of future, past, and present, that constitute our historicity, not as an objective past that affects us but as the "happening" that we ourselves are: "The historical is not only something from which one gets information, and about which there are books; it is much more what we ourselves are, that which we bear."[23]

Gadamer writes that after Heidegger the phrase "we study history only insofar as we are ourselves historical" no longer means, as it did for Dilthey, that there is a resemblance between knower and known (a resemblance which can lead only to a grounding of history in intuitive and psychological terms); it now means "that the historicalness of human There-being [*Dasein*] in its expectancy and its forgetting is the condition of our being able to represent the past."[24] As Gadamer summarizes it, "the hermeneutic importance of temporal distance could be [properly] understood only as a result of the ontological direction that Heidegger gave to understanding as an 'existential' and of his temporal interpretation of the mode of being of There-being. Time is no longer primarily a gulf to be bridged, because it separates, but is actually the supportive ground of the process in which the present is rooted. Hence temporal distance is not something that must be overcome . . . the important thing is to recognize the distance in time as a positive and productive possibility of understanding. It is not a yawning abyss, but is filled with the continuity of custom and tradition."[25]

What Gadamer terms "effective history" – the fact that our historicity is present as the enabling condition of enquiry in the human sciences, taking the form of a conversation between tradition and ourselves – is not a method but a description of what all understanding necessarily involves. The famous "hermeneutic circle" is now described not as a method to be followed but as "an ontological structural element in [all] understanding," [26] and the hermeneutic enterprise, thus redefined with the aid of Heidegger, is proposed not as "a new discipline ancillary to the human sciences" but as that which allows us to "understand ourselves better and recognise that in all understanding, whether we are expressly aware of it or not, the power of effective-history is at work." [27] All historical enquiries, even naïvely objectivist ones that are unaware of their own historicity and that aim to present things "as they really happened," are in fact consequences of this ontological and existential condition. Understanding becomes superior when this fact is brought to self-consciousness. For then one no longer seeks an epistemological certainty which is quite simply unattainable, nor does one strive through empathy or other methods to recreate the past and bracket the present, a procedure equally impossible once one realizes that any event or aspect of the past appears before us as always already interpreted. Effective history, grounded in the reality that the texts of the past come to us already interpreted and that we encounter them through our tradition, is always operative; it is not so much a limit to our knowledge which cannot be surpassed, but is the very basis of understanding. It does not mean that we are trapped within our tradition, but rather that the engagement with texts of the past is a search for a fusion of horizons, where the object comes to be differently understood and the interpreting subject works within his tradition in a manner which opens it to amendment and transformation.

This argument rests upon the claim that because of the fact of human temporality and historicity, all intellectual enquiry (Gadamer partly exempts the natural sciences) is subject to "effective history." This, we should note, is not the same as providing a new, non-objectivist epistemological "grounding" for the discipline and practice of modern *historiography*. Indeed, to argue that all the human sciences are equally subject to effective history is potentially to deprive history writing of *any* specific object; if all consciousness is "historical consciousness" then it is difficult to see what place exists for a discipline specifically addressed to an object called "history." Gadamer himself is somewhat ambiguous on this matter: he sometimes writes of "historical research," as if the ontological argument has specific epistemological implications for historiography, a historiography which would be an improved version of the existing discipline. But he also, and more consistently, suggests that what a recognition of human historicity leads to is not better knowledge of the "historical object" but rather self-knowledge: "The effective historical consciousness knows that which shows itself as the object of investigation is not an "object" which the progress of research will somehow eventually unveil *in seinem Ansichseins* [in its being as it is in itself]. Rather, with a historical phenomenon – a picture, a text, a political or social event – one is able to see one's own self in the other, in the sense that through it one learns to comprehend oneself better."[28]

Historicity and Temporality

Even if the temporal and finite mode of human being provides the foundation for our historicity, there are many ways by which people have constituted and represented their past to themselves, of which historiography, as we have come to understand it in the modern West, is only one. Historicity is also registered and represented in myth, legend, epic, and the like. Is there any reason for regarding history writing as more representative of our historicity than these? Does the analytic of finitude do more than establish the irreducibly temporal character of Dasein – does it in some way also serve to "ground" historiography, once the objectivist position that history is simply "there," waiting to be written about, has been rejected? The question, in other words, is whether the historicality of Dasein has any implications for historiography, and in particular whether it can be made to give us any ground for preferring one mode of thinking and recounting the past over any other.

In division 2, part V, of *Being and Time* (especially S 75–77) Heidegger shows that historiography's objectifying notion of the past derives from an inadequately grounded concept of time, or more precisely from an exclusive focus on only one of the three modes of human temporality. In Ricoeur's words, "The structures of fallenness, of everydayness, of anonymity, that stem from the analytic of Dasein are sufficient, Heidegger believes, to account for this misunderstanding by which we ascribe a history to things."[29] But it does not thereby follow that a proper ontology will lead to an alternative conception of historiography. In *Being and Time* Heidegger *does* seem to indicate that his analysis of finitude and the historicality of Dasein have implications for historical science or "historiology." He argues that historical science is enabled by the historicity of Dasein, which is itself "rooted in temporality";[30] and thus "the Interpretation of Dasein's historicality will prove, at bottom, just a more concrete working out of temporality."[31] Heidegger seems to be signaling that a proper appreciation of the historicality of Dasein, rooted in an appreciation of its temporality and specifically in its "authentic Being-towards-death – that is to say, the finitude of temporality,"[32] will put historiology on a better footing, and more generally will yield dividends for the theory of the human sciences. However, what these might be is not a question that Heidegger pursues in *Being and Time*. And as early as the Davos debate with Cassirer, Heidegger was already seeking to refute what he would later call "anthropological" readings of *Being and Time*, and denying that one could extract from it an alternative philosophy of the human sciences.[33] The writings after the *kehre*, or "turning," explicitly move away from such themes (it is telling that Gadamer's use of Heidegger's thought for his own project relies almost exclusively on *Being and Time*), and there is ample reason to believe that the later Heidegger would have regarded attempts to derive a rationale for historiography from his analysis of temporality as fundamentally misconceived.

Paul Ricoeur writes that while moving "behind" epistemological questions to their ontological "ground" is important and illuminating, "With Heidegger we can move backwards to the ground but any return from ontology to the epistemological question about the status of the human sciences is impossible."[34] As his use of "impossible" indicates, in Ricoeur's view it is not that the epistemological consequences of Heidegger's ontology have not been followed through, but that Heidegger's philosophy is inhospitable to epistemological questions, tending to dissolve rather than solve them. With regard to history, Ricoeur writes, "The only way of justifying the ontological priority of historicality over historiography would be, it seems to me, to show convincingly how the latter proceeds from the former. Here we run into the greatest difficulty for any thinking about time that refers every derivative form of temporality to one primordial form, the mortal temporality of Care. This poses a major obstacle to any historical thinking. I cannot see how the repetition of possibilities inherited by each of us as a result of being thrown into the world can measure up to the scope of the historical past."[35] At the end of Ricoeur's monumental three-volume study *Time and Narrative*, he concludes that "temporality cannot be spoken of in the direct discourse of phenomenology, but rather requires the mediation of the indirect discourse of narration."[36] For instance, the basis of both individual and collective identities – what allows us to speak of a person or community as being the same entity across all the changes that it undergoes, and what thus allows us to

think of "it" as having a "history" – is narrative: "subjects recognize themselves in the stories they tell about themselves."[37] He gives as an example
the Jews: "it was in telling these narratives taken to be testimony about the
founding events of its history that biblical Israel became the historical community that bears this name. The relation is circular – the historical community called the Jewish people has drawn its identity from the reception of
those texts that it had produced."[38] I am sympathetic to this argument, but
it is clear that here there is no object belonging to history which might provide the subject matter for historiography; rather, historical and other narratives constitute the object, thus making it available for historical enquiry.
For Ricoeur as with Gadamer, an insistence upon the "historicity" of human
beings serves not to produce a new, ontologically grounded version of the
discipline of historiography, but rather to undermine the possibility of any
distinctively historiographical enterprise.

Why should historiography as we practice it be in any way privileged as
the mode by which humans understand their historicity, and represent it to
themselves? If the ontological argument demonstrates, in Gadamer's words
quoted above, that "time is no longer primarily a gulf to be bridged, because
it separates, but is actually the supportive ground of the process in which
the present is rooted," and that "temporal distance is not something that
must be overcome," then do not other modes of representing the past, such
as those which treat the past as an ever-present resource, ready to hand as
a guide to the present, not meet this description better? And to the degree
that this analysis is grounded in Heidegger's ontology of the temporal finitude of Dasein, where the most authentic past is one that can be retrieved for
repetition in an authentic future,[39] are not these other modes of narrating
the past in fact *more* "authentic," and true to the temporality of Dasein, than
historiography? In short, the ontological grounding of human historicity in
temporality may undermine an objectivist understanding of history, but it is
difficult to see what "productive" implications it has for the specific practices
by which humans have represented their past to themselves; and even more
difficult to see how it could ground modern, rationalist historiography, even
an alternative, nonobjectivist version of this historiography.

The Code of History

The objectivist presumption that history simply "is" and that historiography
is the best way of representing the past will not do, even in its modulated,

post-Rankean formulations. It is not that history simply happens, and that historiography is the attempt to recreate what has happened through a rigorous method, as objectivist historiography imagines. But neither is historiography the reflex of our historicity, grounded in the temporality of Dasein. It is an intellectual and cultural construct, one particular way of constructing and construing the past; at once a tradition of reasoning, a way of being, and a certain practice of subjectivity. The desire to write history is specific to certain people (societies, classes) and not others. It is connected to some phenomena – the emergence of the modern state, "progress," scientific rationality – and not others, against which it usually defines itself (magic, gods). Paul Veyne writes that "the problem of the birth of historiography is not distinct from that of knowing why it was born in a particular form."[40] That is, the emergence of history writing as a specific mode of relating to and constituting the past is not derivative of some deep underlying reality, and certainly not of human temporality: "History is a bookish, not an existential notion; it is the organization by the intelligence of data relating to a temporality that is not that of Dasein."[41] Lévi-Strauss similarly argues that historiography is a code which organizes and constitutes its object, through chronology.[42]

If history writing constitutes its object, then how does it do so? If it is a code, what is it that it encodes?

Various answers to these questions have been given, including Lévi-Strauss's famous claim that the code of history is chronology, and the claim that historiography codes or effects an absolute divide between a dead past and the present.[43] Both features are important and defining ones of the code of history, but above all else, historiography encodes the humanism or anthropology that became a defining feature of western thought from the early modern period. It does so, first of all, inasmuch as its subject is Man. This seems unremarkable – who else could the object of history be, if not Man? That this seems obvious only indicates how much we are heirs to the transformation which made anthropological assumptions the axioms of our intellectual practice and the bedrock of our culture. Tracing the semantic and epistemic changes underlying the emergence of the concept of history, Reinhardt Koselleck however notes that before the Enlightenment "there was no history for which humanity might have been the subject"[44] but rather histories in the plural, of specific institutions and communities. The emergence of historiography thus corresponds to the emergence of a "collective singular" – Man – as the object of history. Of course, history continues to be written in the plural. Histories of an earlier sort – of kings and kingdoms and so on – continue to be written, and because the emergence of historiography coincides with another Enlightenment innovation, the invention of the idea of society,[45] in addition to these earlier histories we also gain histories of societies and of nations. That histories of various kinds continue to be written helps to disguise the change which has occurred, and allows us to imagine that history writing is continuous with earlier modes of thinking and writing about the past, distinguished principally by its more rigorous method, in particular its fidelity to sources. In fact modern historiography and the modern historical sense are something altogether new, for although histories in the plural continue to be written, these are now all subplots of a larger narrative, the one History of Man, and as such are to be related to each other as different moments in a larger narrative enclosed within a singular time frame.

That historiography emerges as the study of the past of Man also means that nature no longer has a history. Voltaire's essay on "Histoire" in the Encyclopaedia, for example, declares that "natural history" is in fact a part of physics, not history. More generally, "historia naturalis" has ceased to belong to the domain of history.[46] Gods are also expelled from the domain of history, and not because of secularization: historiography can coexist with religion, and indeed even, as in Ranke's case, with the conviction that a divine Providence animates history. But God or gods can no longer be historical actors, because the subject of history is man, and only man. It is this anthropological-humanist presumption that disqualifies many of the other forms by which peoples have conceived and narrated their past – these are now declared to not be history writing at all, and indeed the emergent discipline defines itself against them. It also means not only that God ceases to be a historical actor, but he is himself to be explained, as a creature of men.

This last is one of the more dramatic implications of an epistemic and cultural shift, which among its other effects saw the ways in which European men and women related their past (and related to the past) replaced by this new "code," or "bookish notion." "The task of the modern era," Ludwig Feuerbach wrote, is "the humanization of God – the transformation and dissolution of theology into anthropology."[47] The modern era has been steadily discharging that task. Once, to understand men you had to understand God; now, to understand the gods of men you have to understand the men, because their gods are the fantastical creation of their minds. Once the purposes and the acts of gods explained the world of men; now gods are themselves signs of men, traces from which historians, anthropologists, and sociologists can recreate the meanings and purposes with which these men endowed their

world. Thus it is not only that the subject of history is Man, but that this subject is a Subject – a meaning-producing and purpose-endowing being who
objectifies himself in the world, and through whose objectifications we can
recreate what sort of men these were, and what sort of world they had created
and inhabited.

To be sure, there are important differences in how all this is formulated.
In some cases the signs which give us information about their makers are
understood as "objective spirit"; in others, collectively they constitute a "culture"; in others still, these are the signs which make up the social text. In
some versions that men are authors means that their productions are more or
less transparent to them, or will become so once Man produces the conditions
of his life and his own nature under conditions of freedom; in others, we are
the products of our own productions, but these productions operate in ways
which are opaque to us and partly beyond our control and determination.
Different disciplines constituted on the basis of these founding presumptions also operationalize or mobilize them in different ways. In ethnology
and anthropology, for instance, culture is often treated as a text which, to
quote James Clifford, has a "generalized author [which] goes under a variety
of names: the native point of view, 'the Trobrianders,' 'the Neuer.' "[48] From
the text one can "read backwards" and gain knowledge about its author.

In historiography, the specific form in which anthropological assumptions are encoded can be clearly seen in the fetishistic concern with the primary source, the text, or text analogue, which after Ranke was seen to define
historiography when it became institutionalized as a discipline. Paying attention to primary sources is the essence of historiography not principally because it is more "rigorous" than earlier methods, but because primary sources
are, according to an idea now naturalized, remnants that objectify the meanings and purposes of historical actors, from which we can piece together
the past. Thus, Marc Bloch wrote, "it is men that history seeks to grasp,"[49]
through "a knowledge of their tracks. Whether it is the bones immured in
the Syrian fortifications, a word or form whose use reveals a custom, a narrative written by the witness of some scene . . . what do we really mean by
document, if it is not a 'track.' "[50] For documents to exist as such it is precisely
necessary that they be seen as "survivals," as "tracks," as "traces." Only when
we see the score of a Beethoven symphony as something surviving from the
past that might be mined for information about music, court culture, and
many other things besides – rather than as wrapping paper – does it become
a document. That is precisely why even documents of dubious value for the

direct information which they contain – forgeries are an extreme instance – are nonetheless of historical value, since they can, as traces, be made to yield other sorts of information.[51]

A "Transcendental Presupposition"

Historiography thus "encodes" anthropological presumptions with specific reference to the object that it constructs and of which it purports to offer knowledge, namely the human past. Historiography is by no means the only site where this epistemic and cultural transformation, one which marks the birth of modern, western knowledge and culture, came to be effected. The transformation in question is very much wider. One after another, modern writers of diverse philosophical affiliations, working from within different disciplines – Vico, Herder, Tylor, Cassirer, Geertz, Dilthey, Greenblatt and the "New Historicists," and numerous others – testify that behind most things lurks Man; that art and literature, religion and morality and myth, law and custom, and common sense are all "products," "expressions," or "traces" of "societies" or "peoples" or "cultures." I have designated this shift, in shorthand, as anthropology-humanism. As observed, what precise form these presumptions take varies, across authors and also across disciplines. The differences are important, but underlying them is a more basic commonality, a shared epistemological space. Max Weber characterized it thus: "The transcendental presupposition of every cultural science . . . is that we are cultural beings, endowed with the capacity and the will to take a deliberate attitude towards the world and to lend it significance."[52]

I cite Weber not only because "transcendental presupposition" is a particularly apt formulation, but also because Weber recognizes that the adoption of this presupposition marks a cultural and epistemic transformation. This is precisely the transformation which we discussed in the Introduction, a shift from seeing the world as a text, imbued with meaning and purpose, of which men, as creatures made in God's image and endowed with grace and reason, are privileged readers, to the view of the world as a social text of which men are the authors. In Weber's account this presupposition arises with the "disenchantment of the world," as modern men and women in the Occident recognize that they are cultural beings who endow the world with significance precisely because, and in proportion to the extent to which, they are forced to recognize the absence of meanings already in the world, waiting to be "discovered": "The fate of an epoch which has eaten of the tree of knowledge is that it must know that we cannot learn the *meaning* of the world from the results of its analysis, be it ever so perfect; it must rather be in a position to create this meaning itself."[53] This has not always been presumed, and thus this disenchanted outlook has a history, consisting in the specific form that rationalization took in Occidental religions, culminating in Protestantism and the social and scientific developments with which it was associated.

But if the realization that we endow meaning upon the world has a history, in what sense is this a *transcendental* presupposition? That is, if it is borne of the specific history of the modern West, how can it be said to be a presupposition of universal import? For example, if in the past men and women in Europe saw God as the source of reality and of meaning, whereas we disenchanted moderns do not, then by what warrant do we privilege our presupposition, and conclude that their God has to be understood and explained as meanings with which they endowed their world, rather than as that which gave them life and the world meaning? And by what right to we do so for the nonwestern world, which may not have undergone the same processes of rationalization, culminating in the disenchantment of the world?

The answer, according to Weber, is that while we moderns have come to see the world as disenchanted because of a very specific (Occidental) history, humans have always been the producers of meanings and purposes, even when they have not realized it. David Kolb writes, "In Weber's eyes, modernity is an explicit recognition of what the self and society have been all along. Modern identity is not just another in a sequence of historic constructions; it is the unveiling of what has been at the root of these constructions."[54] From this perspective, it is enchantment, as intellectual "error," that needs "explaining"; the disenchantment of the world, while it has a history, is the truth finally uncovered. Like other moderns, Weber sees modernity as a privileged vantage point that finally makes comprehensible all the history that preceded it—a point to which we shall return in the Epilogue.

Weber's analysis of disenchantment is deeply indebted to Nietzsche. When Nietzsche has a madman announce the death of God, and when he announces the advent of nihilism and the destruction of values, he too is announcing that belief in a transcendent realm of values, in God, in Platonism, is nearing its end. At times he sounds like an upbeat Weber, one who welcomes and celebrates this development, because it allows man to recognize as his that which he once attributed to others: "All the beauty and sublimity we have bestowed upon real and imaginary things I will reclaim as the property and product of man; as his fairest apology. Man as poet, as thinker, as God, as love, as power; O, with what regal liberality he has lavished gifts upon things, only to *impoverish* himself and make *himself* feel wretched! His most unselfish act hitherto was to admire and worship and to know how to conceal from himself that it was *he* who created all that he admired."[55] The transcendent values to which men have subordinated themselves have in fact always been their own products; every discovery was in fact an invention, every interpretation a new creation. Nietzsche sees in the advent of nihilism the possibility of a freedom to revalue all values, recognizing them all as human creations, borne of a will to power. But there is an important difference, and it does not simply lie in Nietzsche's tendency to view with gaiety and lightness what Weber announces with foreboding. The *Genealogy of Morals* and other writings provide also a genealogy of the subject, not as a natural being whose essence is to be possessed of consciousness and the capacity to create meaning but as someone created to be able to make promises, feel guilt, subscribe to values, and the like. Thus for Nietzsche – albeit inconsistently so – the subject is not the source and origin of meaning and value but is himself a historical product, forged on the anvil of Christian morality and Roman law. Weber assumes that the value-creating or culture-secreting individual has always existed, but only becomes aware of himself as such in modern times, whereas for Nietzsche this individual is himself a creation or invention. The difference is significant, because if the presumption that humans are the source of all values and meanings is in fact historically and culturally produced, then we may not be entitled to presuppose it where such a subject has not been created.

This, as we saw in the Introduction, is Heidegger's position. Heidegger rejects all talk of Weltanschauung and of different ways of "picturing" the world precisely because it assumes that men have always pictured the world and ascribed value to it. The difference between the medieval and modern worlds is not, however, that modern men and women picture the world differently and have different values. To see the world as picture, to have values and cultures and experiences, is not to have a set of transcendental presuppositions which have finally come into their own, but rather is a consequence of cultural and epistemic shifts, including the rise of a metaphysics of subjectivity that Heidegger labels "anthropology": "That the world becomes picture is one and the same event with the event of man's becoming *subiectum* . . . the more extensively and the more effectively the world stands at man's disposal as conquered, and the more objectively the object appears, all the more subjectively . . . does the *subiectum* rise up, and all the more impetuously, too, do observation and teaching about the world change into a doctrine of man, into anthropology. It is no wonder that humanism first arises where the world becomes picture . . . Humanism, therefore, in the more strict historiographical sense, is nothing but a moral aesthetic anthropology. The name 'anthropology' as used here . . . designates that philosophical interpretation of man which explains and evaluates whatever is, in its entirety, from the standpoint of man and in relation to man."[56]

The contemporary anti-humanists who are the heirs of Nietzsche and Heidegger similarly insist that man, far from always having been a value-creating and meaning-producing being who with modernity finally becomes aware of that fact, is himself a historically produced, and possibly transient, consequence of contingent historical events. One effect of their analyses is that historiography is immediately rendered problematic: if Man is a product of history, he cannot be the constant whose changes and transformations it retells. Indeed, analyses of this sort reverse our normal sequence of cause and effect, suggesting that Man is the subject of anthropology and history not because he is the origin and source of meaning and values, but rather that this presupposition and its correlates, embedded in our culture and our thought, serve to create and secure humanism and anthropology. Historiography is one of the important means by which, and sites upon which, this process is achieved. "Making historical analysis the discourse of the continuous and making human consciousness the original subject of all historical development and all action," according to Michel Foucault, "are two sides of the same system of thought," one characterized by "the sovereignty of the subject and the twin figures of anthropology and humanism."[57] Indeed, history writing has an especially important function to fulfill, for as this humanism and anthropology have come to be assailed in the study of language, myth, sexuality, and kinship, historiography becomes "the last resting-place of anthropological thought,"[58] or in Lévi-Strauss's words, "the last refuge of a transcendental humanism."[59]

Historiography, God, and Tradition

If Weber's transcendental presupposition cannot in fact be presupposed, if it confuses cause with effect, then this constitutes a problem for the code of history whenever it is applied to an object where the anthropological presumptions of the code are absent. Michel de Certeau points out that when historians study religion, they take it as their task to ask what religion tells us about the society from which it sprang. They assume "society," in other words, to be the axis of reference that will render religious phenomena intelligible, whereas for their subjects religion was (often) what made society intelligible: "The religious history of the seventeenth century . . . implicates a difference between two systems of representation, one 'social' (so to speak) and the other 'religious'; that is, between two periods of consciousness, or between two historical types of intelligibility, our and theirs. Thus, we have to wonder what may be the meaning of an enterprise that consists of 'understanding' a time organized as a function of a standard of comprehension other than ours." For "In this [our] perspective, 'comprehending' religious phenomena is tantamount to repeatedly asking something else of them than what they meant to say . . . taking as a *representation* of the society what, from *their* point of view, *founded* that society."[60]

The study of a past that is significantly "other" is here characterized by a reversal which Certeau renders through a metaphor drawn from chess: "Between their time and ours, the signifier and the signified have castled. We postulate a coding which inverts that of the time we are studying."[61] As a modern, rational practice, historiography cannot accord to God the role of a historical actor, and thus we translate seventeenth-century understandings into our terms. Far from being defined by its avoidance of "anachronism," history writing as discipline and practice is in fact based upon anachronism, continually translating the understandings of historical subjects into our modern, anthropological understanding. But the converse is also true: our historical practice is not an ex nihilo creation but arises out of previous debates: "when they refer to their own practices . . . historians discover constraints originating well before their own present, dating back to former organizations of which their work is a symptom, not a cause."[62] "Our" historical discourse is a product of those debates and processes which, beginning four or more centuries ago, rendered religion into a phenomenon susceptible to being explained in sociological terms, rather than regarding the human world as one to be understood as the product of divine instigation. "Just as the 'model' of religious sociology implies, among other things, the new status of practice or of knowledge in the seventeenth century, so do current methods – erased as events and transformed into codes or problematic areas of research – bear evidence of former structurings and forgotten histories. Thus founded on the rupture between a past that is its object, and a present that is the place of its practice, history endlessly finds the present in its object and the past in its practice."[63]

Earlier in this chapter, I examined Gadamer's argument that all encounters with past texts and text analogues were intrinsically interpretive, and that all interpretation in the human sciences is intrinsically historical. His conclusion that such encounters occur within a tradition and can lead to greater self-consciousness of that tradition was, I suggested, an important and potentially fruitful notion, even though it could not ground historiography as a specific practice. I now wish to return to Gadamer to illustrate how fruitful this understanding can be.

If we translate Certeau's observations into Gadamerian terms – recognizing that to do so is not to stay with Certeau's thought – we could say the following: When we encounter a text from, say, seventeenth-century Europe, one which explains society and its functioning in terms of God, the distance between the text and our historical situation cannot be bridged by canceling one of the terms. Understanding is achieved neither by imposing our current understandings upon the text (for example, by treating God as a "projection" or ideology), nor can we seek, as romantic hermeneutics would, to recreate the context and meaning of that text in order to restore it to its original meaning and intention. An acknowledgment of the historicity of our own understanding means that we cannot accord any privilege to our categories of interpretation; but the same acknowledgment of the historicity of our understanding means that there is no way of encountering the text "in its own right." Because this is something more than an epistemological dilemma, it is capable of "resolution." The text is not just an object of the past belonging purely to the present: it comes to us already interpreted, not as a mere object but as a tissue of interpretations. We must remain open to its "truth," and if we become convinced of this, it forces us to rethink our current understandings, and to redescribe the tradition through which it arrives to us. However if we find ourselves, as is more likely, unable to reach an agreement with the text – if there can be no fusion of horizons – we are then entitled to try situating it in terms of its context. But even so, the end-point is not the same as it would be had we dismissed the truth of the text from the beginning, since we have re-encountered, and arrived at a better understanding of, how we relate to a tradition in which God once bestrode the world and made it in his image, but which later gave way to a "secular" view in which God had his historical agency withdrawn from him. The "former structurings and forgotten histories" which have brought us to our present historical situation are no longer "forgotten"; they have been disinterred and reexamined, and we have arrived at a better understanding of the tradition through which we speak, as a result of this encounter. History "finds the present in its object and the past in its practice" self-consciously as result of such a dialogic encounter, even where, as in this instance, we cannot acknowledge the truth of the text nor achieve a fusion of horizons.

Recently, Constantine Fasolt has given us another example of something very much like this in his *The Limits of History*. In this book Fasolt provides a close reading of the *Discoursus novus de imperatore Romano Germanico* (New Discourse of the Roman-German Emperor; 1642) by Hermann Conring (1608–81),[64] in which Conring sought to refute claims that the Roman Empire still existed in any recognizable or significant form; that the king of Germany was the Roman emperor; and that he derived his title from the church and ultimately from God. One of those whom he singled out as upholding these unjustifiable claims was Bartolus of Sassoferrato (1313/14–57), the great medieval jurist. In fact Bartolus was well aware that even by his time the emperor did not in fact rule the world. He explicitly recognized that France, for instance, was ruled by the king of France, and even acknowledged that his *dominium* over France was legitimate. But this did not affect his claim on behalf of the Roman Emperor and church. Why not? Because in his argument, to be ruler of the world does not mean that those whom the emperor rules obey him; it is a question of jurisdiction, not obedience. The emperor has jurisdiction, not the capacity to command obedience; his right is universal, but that is not the same as total; his dominium is distinct from ownership and control – just as a shepherd may have dominium over a flock of sheep without having dominium over even a single one of the sheep in the flock. Conring's refutation, by contrast, is achieved through historical argument. He sets out to show that even at the height of the Roman Empire, the emperor's power was not coextensive with the world; that the Romans never had the right (*ius*) to rule the world; and (this constitutes the bulk of the *New Discourse*) he provides a historical narrative from antiquity to his present, showing that whatever authority the Roman Empire and emperor once possessed had been steadily diminishing. What the detailed arguments so summarily rendered here indicate, according to Fasolt, is that Conring and Bartolus were arguing at cross-purposes: "Bartolus focused on law; Conring focused on politics . . . Bartolus looked to eternity; Conring looked to history. For Bartolus the universe was integrated into one hierarchy; for Conring it was divided into an infinity of separate self-subsisting parts. Bartolus maintained that politics and law were fundamentally the same, Conring that they were essentially distinct. Bartolus thought the nature of things consisted of relationships; Conring, that it consisted of an invariant essence. And so on."[65]

The central difference, the one that renders their arguments incommensurable, is that for Bartolus the source of all overlordship and of the unity of the world is God, the "efficient cause" of the empire and the church; while Conring's argument is historical in a way that Bartolus's is not and could not be. "Could not be" because this mode of understanding was new; the Renaissance humanists had invented it, and Conring was drawing upon and developing their legacy, of which we too are heirs. That is why in reading this debate we cannot but find ourselves in sympathy with Conring. More importantly, it is why even when we exercise historical charity and seek to place Bartolus "in his own context," this historicizing maneuver only aligns us all the more securely on the side of Conring and history: "To seek a historical understanding of the relationship between Bartolus and Conring is . . . an oxymoron: either the understanding will be historical, and then it will confirm the wall of historical consciousness that Conring built to separate himself from Bartolus. Or it will break that wall: but then it cannot be historical."[66]

Fasolt thus makes an argument similar to the one I am seeking to advance: that history writing is informed by certain presumptions that are not themselves "true" (or for that matter false), but rather represent a particular way of construing the world, "one particular and limited form of understanding that is itself party to the proceedings it describes."[67] But he also – and here less self-consciously and thus not explicitly – illustrates the potential value of a hermeneutical approach to the past. Fasolt insists that the intellectual worlds of Conring and Bartolus are incommensurable.[68] But Conring's debate with Bartolus, and more generally his refutation of "medieval universalism," is only possible because both thinkers and bodies of thought are addressing questions of Roman law and the nature of the commonwealth, and both are using a common, inherited language of *ius*, *lex*, *dominium*, and so on to do so. As Fasolt acknowledges, "they are similar in many ways" and "there are connections, echoes, overtones, traditions connecting them."[69] Thus even as he argues that history is an invention of the Renaissance humanists, and seeks to specify the limits of this form of understanding, Fasolt also illuminates the process by which this mode of understanding arose, engaged with, and replaced preceding forms of understanding. Precisely in the process of arguing that history as a code is anachronistic when applied to the medieval world,

Fasolt also sheds light on how the struggle to refute and replace earlier ways of understanding shaped the mode of understanding to which we are now heirs. In Gadamerian terms, one could say that such an exercise shows the impossibility of a "fusion of horizons" with the texts of Bartolus of Sassofer-rato – to engage with Conring and Bartolus historically is already, as Fasolt says, to put ourselves on Conring's side and into Conring's world – but writing such a history in full consciousness of its limits as a mode of understanding also illuminates the continuities and breaks in a tradition where, to put it too simply, once God explained the world, and later history came to do so.

I AM ASKING what it means, using the code of history, to write about those who do not live by that code or recognize themselves in it. I have argued that this question arises with reference not only to the nonwestern world but also to premodern Europe. To explain the world of men and women of medieval times historically is to translate their understandings into our terms or, to repeat Certeau's words, to "postulate a coding which inverts that of the time we are studying." However, this exercise, while anachronistic, is nonetheless productive; even where we cannot accept the "truth" of texts from the past, we gain better self-understanding, that is, understanding of the tradition out of which we reason.

The same is not true when we apply the code of history to Indian pasts, for the simple reason that the object of enquiry does not belong to the same tradition as the enquiring subject.[70] To write a history of India from within western knowledge is to confront the fact that the "now" from which we write is not itself linked in a thousand ways to the "then" of those of whom we write, because a profound caesura has occurred: the tradition from which we write is not the same as that of which we write. The threads connecting the subject and the object have snapped; western education, and the rational-ist historiography which it produced and which it sanctions, do not bear the same relation to India as the knowledge(s) disseminated and the tradition(s) once cultivated in the *madrassa* and the *tol*. Thus what might validate the anachronism which is an inescapable feature of historiography even when it encounters European pasts does not apply here, because here history "finds the present in its object," *but it does not* find an *Indian* "past in its practice."

The knowledge from which we write a history of India – in this case, a his-tory of western education in India – is not continuous with the knowledges of India. These intellectual traditions had not died of inanition when the British first came to India; as we shall see in chapter 6, around the period that

Conring was writing there was an explosion of scholarly writing in Sanskrit, testifying to the vitality of an extraordinarily long and continuous intellectual tradition. Some of the *navya* or new scholars of the seventeenth century self-consciously saw themselves as effecting innovations; but they were still heirs to a tradition going back two millennia, which they actively engaged, disputed with, and developed. The same is not true of historiography, for neither the Sanskrit tradition nor any other indigenous tradition found an echo in the code of history which we now use to write of Indian pasts. This code was an imposition, an act of "epistemic violence," to borrow a phrase from Gayatri Spivak. It did not engage with Indian traditions, did not refute them and thereby displace them. Its victory was won cheaply – through a colonial administrative fiat. As a result, the code of history cannot even fulfill the hermeneutic function that it fills elsewhere, that of being one of the modes by which men and women of the West can, through the self-consciously anachronistic exercise of translating the lives and worlds of their dead forebears into their own terms, illuminate both what connects and what separates them from this past and these forebears. In India that role continued to be performed by the genealogist, the balladeer, and the storyteller, who interpreted and refurbished the tradition to which they belonged, by retelling the past.[71] The historian, however, was closer to the position of colonial officials (many of whom, like James Mill and Macaulay, were also historians); she was discontinuous with, and in a position of pure externality to, the pasts of which she wrote.

Which Past? Whose History?

I have suggested that anthropology-humanism has fostered an illusion, mistaking effect for cause. "Man" does not give rise to the sciences of man; it is these sciences that encode and thus serve to produce and secure humanism. In characterizing modern thought as anthropological, Nietzsche, Heidegger, Foucault, and other writers I have drawn upon to develop my argument also offer a critique of this anthropological presumption. For instance, they argue that the subject is neither sovereign nor transparent to himself; that just as he is an effect of certain events, he may one day disappear; and so on. I am sympathetic to these arguments, but here I have invoked them for their characterization, rather than for their critique. The assumption that Man is a creator of meanings and values, I suggest, is not a "transcendental presupposition" we are entitled and even obliged to make, but rather a form of "transcendental narcissism,"[72] one of the means by which the modern West creates and secures the anthropological-humanist theme that Man is the source and origin of meaning and value – and hence the subject of history. Nonetheless, inasmuch as this humanism *is* in fact secured, inasmuch as the West *is* dominated by a metaphysics of subjectivity, inasmuch as the presupposition that Man is source and origin of meaning, value, and purpose is found in a wide range of practices and institutions and intellectual activities, then a historiography founded upon similar premises is an appropriate way for western societies to conceive of their past and represent it to themselves.[73]

Whether such premises are also valid for writing the history of western education in colonial India – the question with which we are concerned – will depend upon whether the presuppositions found a home in colonial India. That is, it will depend upon whether the "transcendental narcissism" of the West succeeded in also becoming a narcissism in the East; whether this "white mythology," as Derrida terms it,[74] also became part of the mythos of India.

My earlier enquiries help us to answer this question. Western education, as we saw in chapter 1, did not simply stuff new ideas into existing heads. It posited a form of subjectivity, with a specific kind of a relation to knowledge. To gain knowledge was not to come into harmony with an existing order of meanings, which was now seen as a failure of knowledge (as passive rather than active learning, as "mere" memory rather than genuine understanding), but was rather to distinguish oneself as active subject from a realm of objects to be known, with the "knowing" firmly vested on the side of the subject. We also saw that the discourse of cram and instrumentalism registered and on occasion thematized the anxiety that this subject neither existed nor had been produced. In chapter 2 we saw that educated Indians conceived the world they inhabited as one that came to them already organized into a meaningful order. This did not render them passive and supine, for it is a conceit of humanism-anthropology that to fail to be a subject is tantamount to being an object. They debated and interpreted, exercised agency and choice, and sought to live ethical lives – but all the while inhabiting a world that came ordered in ways which the categories of human thought had not created but of which they had to take cognizance, and all the while without conceiving their gods as something they "believed" in. As a result, even when what they learned at school and in university was not consonant with their ways of inhabiting their world and making sense of it, many did not suffer the sense of intellectual and moral crisis that was ascribed to them in the discourse of moral decline. Western knowledge was often assimilated by being treated as a set of competences necessary for the domain of *artha*, rather than as something that clashed with and undermined their ways of inhabiting the world. Their "traditional" Weltanschauung was not challenged and undermined by a new one, either because they assimilated their new learning to their existing intellectual landscape (rather as some Hindus made Christ yet another god in the Hindu pantheon), or because change, where it was effected, was not from one Weltanschauung or world-picture to another but from not seeing the world-as-picture to coming to do so.

I have also argued, drawing upon Gadamer and others, that history writing can serve a hermeneutic function – indeed, that this is its principal function. There is no such thing as the object "history," which historiography rescues and retells well, while myths, epics, and Puranic "histories" tell it badly; there are only human pasts that are constructed as objects by the modes through which they are re-told and re-presented. The code of history is but one way of representing the past, and a recent one. It is eminently useful even where anachronistic, because when written in a hermeneutic mode, it can be a way of engaging, better understanding, and developing and refurbishing the intellectual tradition(s) to which we belong, and out of which we reason. But this is only true where the code of history is applied to the pasts out of which this code itself developed; applied to other pasts, neither is it the "right" way of recounting these pasts nor does it illuminate the traditions of the peoples whose pasts these are.

Traditions are not hermetically sealed, of course. The civilization of medieval and early modern India was itself a palimpsest, born of the meeting of the culture, knowledges, and institutions to which the subcontinent had been home, and those that the Turk and Afghan and Persian invaders brought with them. If we are willing to allow for the existence of a "western tradition" stretching back to a time long before there was any conception of "Europe" or the West, this was a tradition that includes the collapse of Rome and the fusion of Roman law with barbarian institutions, the later revival of Greek learning, and the synthesis of Aristotelianism and Christianity effected by St. Thomas. Moreover, this tradition and those of India never developed in complete isolation from each other; and for some four hundred years now the ways of the western barbarians have been finding a home in India. A fusion of traditions may yet occur, and out of this a new tradition may yet be founded. However, historiography today cannot assume that this has already occurred. For now, to write history in a western mode with even a modicum of self-consciousness is not only to be continually reminded that one is writing from a historical now which is very different from that of the object of study: it is also to be reminded that this difference is not the space of a dialogue where we simultaneously refurbish and reconsider the tradition within which we are located but that it marks a profound break, the full implications of which historiography has yet to register, let alone begin to seriously consider.

From all this it does not follow that a history of western education in colonial India in the mode of modern, rationalist historiography is illegitimate. What does follow is that the presuppositions encoded by such a historiography are not in fact transcendental ones, a meta-code equally adequate to all times and places; rather, these presumptions are parochial ones, themselves borne of the social and epistemic shifts that gave rise to and characterize the modern West. Rationalist historiography cannot, in other words, accord to itself any epistemic privilege. If a history of western knowledge and education from within that knowledge is not to be caught in a "vicious" circle, it must remain alert to the possibility of its inadequacy to its object. In writing such a history, one does not assume the existence of subjects who endow the world with meanings, the objectified forms of which (texts, artworks, coins, monuments) allow us to recreate their world-picture. Instead one charts how various processes, including the dissemination of western knowledge, served to constitute these subjects and the world-as-picture, and sometimes failed to do so. This is what the first part of this book has sought to do.

PART II

Modern Knowledge, Modern Nation

CHAPTER FOUR

Governmentality and Identity
Constituting the "Backward but Proud Muslim"

The beginning of the nineteenth century in Europe witnessed a growing volume of official statistics on agriculture, trade, education, births, and deaths, as well as the institutionalization of regular national censuses. Ian Hacking argues that this "avalanche of numbers" did more than just count: "counting is no mere report of developments. It elaborately, often philanthropically, creates new ways for people to be."[1] Hacking labels this understanding of the relation between counting and that which is counted "dynamic nominalism," and writes, "The claim of dynamic nominalism is not that there was a kind of person who came increasingly to be recognized by bureaucrats or students of human nature but rather that a kind of person came into being at the same time that the kind itself was being invented. In some cases, that is, our classifications and our classes conspire to emerge hand in hand, each egging the other on."[2]

The idea that the enumerative practices have sometimes helped to constitute what they purport to merely count has proved especially fertile in studies of the nonwestern world. Referring to the censuses which began to be conducted in southeast Asia in the nineteenth century under the aegis of colonialism, Benedict Anderson writes that "the new demographic topography put down deep social and institutional roots as the colonial state multiplied its size and functions. Guided by its imagined map it organized new educational, juridical, public-health, police and immigration bureaucracies . . . which in time gave real social life to the state's earlier fantasies."[3] In an earlier and seminal essay Bernard Cohn argued that the operation of the census in colonial India served to "objectify" India's social structure, thus making it possible and sometimes necessary for Indians to "think" and relate to their culture in new ways.[4] Since then a growing number of works have elaborated, amended, and sometimes contested the proposition that colonial sociology

109

and the enumerative practices of the colonial state have been constitutive of group identities in India.[5]

In his contribution to this debate, Arjun Appadurai rightly observes that the extent to which colonial imaginings actually shaped the self-perceptions of those enumerated and classified varied greatly, according to their proximity to the colonial state, their gender, class, and so on. In the same cautionary vein he observes that "while certain components of the colonial state were active propagators of the discourses of group identity, others, such as those involved with education, law and moral reform, were implicated in the creation of what might be called a colonial bourgeois subject, conceived as an 'individual.'"[6] The relation between those knowledges and state practices that presumed and posited the individual subject, and those presuming and positing group identities, Appadurai goes on, is "an important issue that any interpretation of enumerated communities will eventually have to engage."[7]

In this chapter, I engage this question, but I do so by first suggesting that we need to pose it in a different manner. It is not, as Appadurai suggests, that education was a site for the creation of individuals, while other institutional locales and practices were where group identities or enumerated communities were produced. Education was not only where individual subjects were posited and sometimes produced (the subject of part I of this book) but was also an important site where projects for the founding of collective identities were played out (the subject of part II). Indeed, if part I has shown that western education frequently did not succeed in producing the modern subjects presupposed and posited by it, part II will show that this education, and the debates and desires to which it gave rise, played an important role in producing group identities, and in creating new ways for conceiving of existing collective identities.

Below I argue that a statistically driven debate on education, intimately connected with the practices characteristic of a "colonial governmentality," became a key site for the discursive construction of the figure of the "backward but proud Muslim." This figure was one whose "Muslim-ness" was imagined such that it presented a new way of thinking, and the possibility of a new way of being, Muslim.

The "Backward but Proud Muslim"

From about the middle of the nineteenth century the concern began to be voiced in some quarters that Muslims were not being reached by the

government-sponsored western education introduced in 1835, and were consequently falling behind "in the race for life," especially as this was measured
by their representation in government employment. In 1852 the annual report on the progress of education in Bengal noted with concern that Muslims
were not participating in higher education to the same degree as Hindus;[8]
and in 1868, observing that very few of those graduating from Calcutta University were Muslims, the university's British vice-chancellor warned the
Muslim community that while they had every reason to be proud of having
once been the rulers of India, "in these days of competition, those who would
not rise must fall; those who do not keep forward will, perhaps, be left behind
altogether in the race."[9]

But it was in the 1870s that these observations gained sudden momentum.
In 1871 W. W. Hunter's *The Indian Musalmans* was published, which stapled
together three issues: alleged Muslim disaffection with British rule, a decline in the number of Muslims in government employment, and the failure of Muslims to partake of the government-sponsored system of western
education. According to Hunter, Muslims were the least contented of Her
Majesty's subjects. Whereas once they had been the rulers of the land, and
even after being supplanted by the British had continued to staff the courts
and fill the ranks of the colonial administration, more recently "the educated
Muhammadan . . . sees himself practically excluded from the share of power
and of the emoluments of Government which he hitherto had almost mo-
nopolized, and sees all the other advantages of life passed into the hands
of the hated Hindu."[10] Government employ had been delinked from those
skills which Muslims had cultivated as part of their religion and their role as
rulers of India, such as knowledge of Persian. Persian had been supplanted
by the vernaculars and English as the language of the courts in 1837, and after
1844 western education had increasingly become a requirement for securing government employment.[11] However, the secular education imparted in
government and many government-aided schools and colleges through the
medium of English or Indian vernaculars (unknown or despised by Muslims
and transmitted principally by Hindu teachers) was an education which according to Hunter was "opposed to the traditions, unsuited to the requirements, and hateful to the religion, of the Musalmans."[12] Not surprisingly,
Muslims had not taken to it readily or in great numbers, whereas the "pliant
Hindu," who "knew no scruples"[13] and was unperturbed by the nonreligious
character of the education imparted in western schools, took to western education with gusto. The result was that Muslims ceased to supply much of the

personnel for revenue collection, courts, and police, as they had once done: instead, "the staff of Clerks attached to the various offices, the responsible posts in the Courts, and even the higher offices in the Police, are recruited from the pushing Hindu youth of the Government School."[14]

The government immediately gave official endorsement to the idea that Muslims were falling behind in education.[15] Lord Mayo observed in a vice-regal note, "There is no doubt that as regards the Muhammadan population, our present system of education is, to a great extent, a failure."[16] This conclusion underpinned a resolution of the Government of India of August 1871, which noted that in most provinces Muslims were not availing themselves of educational opportunities in proportion to other communities, and called upon provincial administrations to suggest ways and means of redressing this imbalance. A decade later the Indian Education Commission, led by Hunter, endorsed the "fact that, at all events in many parts of the country, the Musalmans have fallen behind the rest of the population,"[17] and made seventeen recommendations designed to redress the problem of Muslim reluctance to participate in western education.

The idea of the backward Muslim was one that was embraced and articulated, in tandem with the government, by a section of the Muslim élites. Thus Sayyid Ahmad Khan, who dedicated much of his life's labors to improving the status of the Muslim community of India (in addition to serving some forty years in the British-Indian judicial system, at a time when a western education was not a requirement for government preferment), responded to Hunter's book by denying the idea that Muslims were a perpetually disaffected and potentially disloyal section of the population; but he endorsed the proposition that Muslims had fallen behind in education and hence in the "race of life."[18] Indeed, this was to be the central premise underlying his involvement as the moving force behind the Muhammadan Educational Conference (founded in 1886, originally as the Muhammadan Educational Congress) and the Muhammadan Anglo-Oriental College, both of which aimed at rectifying the situation through the voluntary efforts of the Muslim community. It was this premise that underlay the Committee for the Better Diffusion and Advancement of Learning Among the Muhammadans of India, which Sir Sayyid, as he later became, helped to found in 1870, just before the publication of Hunter's book; and an essay prize competition which the committee sponsored in the following year set as its topic the reasons for the disproportionately small number of Muslim boys receiving a liberal English education, compared to Hindus, and the possible remedies. The concern with Muslim backwardness was echoed by other Muslim organizations. In 1882 the National Muhammadan Association, in Bengal, presented a memorial to Viceroy Ripon, in which it complained that "while every community has thrived and flourished under British rule, the Muhammadans alone have declined and decayed"; the replacement of Persian learning by English education had meant that the advantage formerly enjoyed by élite Muslims was immediately lost: "English-educated Hindu youths trained for the most part in missionary institutions, from which the Mussalmans naturally stand aloof, now poured into every Government office and completely shut out the Muhammadans."[19] Over thirty years later M. Azizul Huque began his history of Muslim education in Bengal with the lament that things had got worse rather than better: "shut off from all legitimate and noble vocations of life by force of circumstances and stress of competition, we find ourselves hopelessly lost in the battle of life," all because of "want of proper training and education."[20]

If Muslims were "backward" (the main measure of this being their low numbers in government employ), and if this was because they were backward in western education in particular, why had Muslims been tardy in embracing western education? Many explanations were offered, in most of which great stress was placed on language and the secular nature of governmental education (themes already sounded by Hunter in *The Indian Musalmans*). Azizul Huque, quoted above, traced the decline of Muslim fortunes to the introduction of a system of education in which Persian and Arabic no longer had a privileged place: "Mahomedans, fresh with the memory of the past, could not reconcile themselves to the system of liberal education"; and once having fallen behind, "continued to be steeped in ignorance," so that, "poor in education, backward in general advancement and culture, [they] found themselves hopelessly lost in the battle for life."[21] A "Memorial of the Central National Muhammadan Association" dated the decline with precision. It began in 1837, when a colonial government edict replaced Persian with English and the vernaculars as the language of law – "The English-educated Hindus . . . poured forth into every office, and completely edged the Musalmans out year by year . . . Before they had quite awakened to the necessity of learning English, they were shut out from Government employment. Thenceforth their political influence dwindled."[22] It was also sometimes claimed that vernacular education disadvantaged Muslims, for whom Urdu was their mother tongue, though the claim that Urdu was the vernacular of all Muslims was hotly disputed.[23]

That the colonial government's policy of "religious neutrality," which disallowed religious instruction in government schools and colleges, was a cause of Muslim antipathy to western education was a claim very widely advanced. Most of the essayists and almost all the judges in the essay competition sponsored by the Select Committee, for instance, agreed that the disassociation of learning from religion in the government-sponsored system was a major reason why Muslims stayed away from western education.[24] The report of the Hornell Committee, appointed by the Bengal government to investigate Muslim educational backwardness in 1914, similarly concluded that one reason why Muslims "failed to take their proper share in the public life of Bengal" was that "they were at one time afraid that education given through the medium of English and the Vernaculars would sap the principles of Islam and for a long time they refused to take any part in the educational system of Government, thereby failing to profit by the opportunities of which the Hindus took full advantage."[25] The judgment of the committee was soon endorsed by the Government of Bengal, which found that "the primary cause of [Muslim] educational backwardness has been the suspicion with which a conservative people, anxious to preserve their distinctive beliefs and customs, have hitherto regarded the general secular schools."[26] Almost twenty years later the quinquennial report on education for 1927-32 was still attributing Muslim educational backwardness to "loyalty to their traditional learning and religion."[27]

The *Indian Education [Hunter] Commission Report* of 1883 discussed Muslim educational backwardness at some length, summarized the explanations that had been advanced for it, and drew upon them to present its own, comprehensive explanation:

> some held that the absence of instruction in the tenets of their faith, and still more the injurious effects of English education in creating a disbelief in religion, were the main obstacles . . . Some contended that the system of education prevailing in Government Schools and Colleges corrupted the morals and manners of the pupils, and that for this reason the better classes would not subject their sons to dangerous contact. The small proportion of Muhammadan teachers in Government institutions; the unwillingness of Government educational officers to accept the counsel and co-operation of Muhammadans; numerous minor faults in the Departmental system, the comparatively small progress in real learning . . . the absence of friendly intercourse between Muhammadans and Englishmen; the unwillingness felt by the better

born to associate with those lower in the social scale; the poverty nearly general among Muhammadans; the coldness of Government towards the race. . . . these and a variety of other causes have been put forward at different times by members of the Muhammadan community to account for the scant appreciation which an English education has received at their hands . . . but a candid Muhammadan would probably admit that *the most powerful factors are to be found in pride of race, a memory of bygone superiority, religious fears, and a not unnatural attachment to the learning of Islam.*[28] (emphasis added)

The claim that Muslims were "falling behind," and that this was because they were underrepresented in the education system, was not universally accepted. When the Government of India, after the submission of the Memorial of the National Muhammadan Association, solicited the opinions and suggestions of provincial governments on how to remedy the problem, it found that the premise of Muslim backwardness was contested. Some provincial governments declared that the problem, if it existed at all, was confined to Bengal.[29] However, the Bengal government initially responded to the Memorial of the National Muhammadan Association with a point-by-point refutation of its claims, and concluded by declaring that "as Government service as well as positions of unofficial emolument and influence are open to public competition, it is worse than useless for Muhammadans now to plead that Government should show any favour to a particular class or section of the community."[30] The Chief Commissioner for the Central Provinces was even more blunt: "The Muhammadans have had the same chances which others have had . . . He ventures to think that some false sentiment has been expended for some time past on the Muhammadans, their decadence and their grievance. It is a pity because it hinders them from exerting themselves, which is the only way by which they can succeed."[31]

However, such denials and qualifications were usually ignored. When a minority of those who had submitted essays to the Select Committee disputed that Muslims were in fact underrepresented in education, the Select Committee flatly declared their view to be erroneous.[32] Whenever there was a suggestion that the gap was exaggerated, or alternatively that it was being closed, this was denied with some vehemence. For example, Syed Mahmood's detailed *A History of English Education in India*, published in 1895, was partly written to "expose the great fallacy" of the view that Muslims had made satisfactory progress, and that there was "no further room for anxiety, or need of any exceptional effort or special encouragement."[33] And at the highest levels of government the "fact" of Muslim educational backwardness was accepted. Subsequent to the Hunter Commission the Government of India from time to time reiterated its concern about Muslim backwardness;[34] at the provincial level, special enquiries were established to investigate Muslim educational backwardness; and a series of measures were adopted at different times and in different provinces to address the problem.[35]

"Muslim backwardness" was thus to retain its status as a problem needing remedy from the 1870s to Independence. And the Hunter Committee's explanation of the reasons for Muslim educational backwardness, with all its imagery of a ruling race fallen upon hard times, nostalgic for the past, and reluctant to adapt to the new realities – the idea that "Muslims were now laggards, all sulking in their tents, dreaming of lost empires and reciting decadent poetry"[36] – was to have a long life. It was to be approvingly cited and paraphrased in subsequent government enquiries and official writings,[37] as well as in other works. For example, in his India: A Bird's-Eye View (1924), Lord Ronaldshay paraphrased the explanation of the Hunter Commission of forty years earlier; his paraphrase was then quoted in J. M. Sen's History of Elementary Education in India (1933).[38] In this way the idea of Muslim backwardness gained a currency far beyond the in-house documents of the bureaucracy, as the image of the "backward but proud Muslim" was repeatedly reproduced, paraphrased, and elaborated, taking on a life of its own.

"Seeing" Backwardness

Why did the issue of Muslim backwardness come to be foregrounded? The common answer, first given by nationalists, is that the British policy of "divide and rule" was behind the colonial government's sudden solicitude for its Muslim subjects. For a section of the Muslim élites this newfound concern was useful, because the emphasis on religious differences within South Asia allowed them to pose as leaders of "their" community, and gave them an importance and influence to which they could not otherwise lay claim. Our concern is not with the substance of this argument, however, but rather with a prior, epistemological question: What made it possible for "backwardness" to emerge as an object of knowledge? What were the enabling "epistemic conditions" that made it possible to pose the question of Muslim backwardness, let alone posit it as a pressing problem in need of solution?

The importance of statistics stands out, since the discourse of the "backward Muslim" was made possible by numbers, conducted through numbers,

and indeed obsessed with numbers. The issue of Muslim educational backwardness first became a public concern around the time of the first all-Indian
census. This concern was in part reflected in how figures were collected,[39] and
of course the census made it possible to pursue, and seek to prove or disprove,
the fact of Muslim backwardness. Religion appeared as a fundamental category in the census, one that was cross-tabulated against a number of others –
sex, marital status, occupation (after 1881), and education. Numbers on Muslim backwardness proliferated, as concern occasioned by it soon generated
further figures. The Indian Education (Hunter) Commission, confirming the
fact of Muslim backwardness, had recommended that to keep track of this
backwardness, and of the efficaciousness of measures adopted to remedy it,
the annual reports on progress in education should have a section specially
devoted to Muslims. A resolution by the Government of India in July 1885
mandated this, specifying that educational reports must provide information on "the position and advancement of the Muhammadan community,
not merely as a whole, but with reference to local variations, in order that the
Government of India may be kept fully informed as to the state and progress
of this important section of the community."[40] It is perhaps more than a co-
incidence that W. W. Hunter, who was so frequent and important a contributor to the discourse of Muslim backwardness, was also, as director general of
statistics, the compiler of many of the statistics that he mobilized. It was soon
after completing his labors of compiling the *Imperial Gazetteer* that Hunter
took on the role of chairman of the Indian Education Commission.

The importance of information, and of figures in particular, was not a fact
recognized only by government. The "Aims and Objectives" of the Muhammadan Educational Congress, drafted by Sir Sayyid in 1886, observed that
"people in one district ... know little about the state of education of Mahomedans in other districts; they do not know whether their co-religionists outside
their own local circle are going forward or backward, and what are the causes
of the same." It was to enable Muslims from various parts of India to gain an
overall picture of the state of Muslim education, and to allow them to "meet
together to converse on the subject of national education, and think over the
means by which it may be advanced," that an annual meeting was necessary.
Delegates from districts, Sir Sayyid went on to suggest, should "read before
the meeting a statistical report of the condition of Musalmans in their districts," which among other topics would cover the number of Muslims in the
district, their residence (urban or rural), their general condition, the number
and types of schools and colleges, the kind of education imparted in them,

and the number of Muslims being educated in them.[41] At one point there was even an attempt at a nongovernmental census. In 1893 Theodore Beck, principal of the Muhammadan Anglo-Oriental College, launched a "Mahomedan Educational Census," seeking to mobilize "public spirited Mahomedans" to go door to door to collect information from their co-religionists of a type and at a level of detail not covered by the census. The information collected was to be used to urge and cajole those Muslims who had not been educating their sons to begin doing so if they had the means. This was only to be the first step: "The work of this Census must take at least ten years' steady effort. Money, clerks, statistics, books, pamphlets – the apparatus of this Census will become in itself a great organization."[42]

Beck's grandiose vision was never realized, but the annual sessions of the Muhammadan Educational Conference did function, among other things, as an occasion to hear reports on the educational status of Muslims, sometimes in mind-numbing detail. The original text of what later became an ample-sized book on the history of western education in India, and especially on the education of Muslims, was delivered as a lecture in two parts by Syed Mahmood at the eighth and ninth annual sessions at Aligarh, in 1893 and 1894; each lecture lasted five hours.

Statistics were thus critical to posing the problem of Muslim backwardness. However, it is not that statistics allowed the state to finally "see" and measure what was always there. Historians and philosophers of science have been at the forefront of cautioning against the variety of epistemological naïveté that assumes the objects of new knowledges to have always already been there, only awaiting the rise of the knowledge that would unveil them and bring them into view. In fact the discoveries made in the laboratory, for instance, are products of specific technologies; it is usually impossible to distinguish whether they are "discovered" or "produced."[43] Georges Canguilhem points out that sickness, as experienced and understood by the sick person, is different from disease, which comes to be known as a statistical deviation from socially normative, "average" states.[44] The latter understanding is not one naturally and immediately available to ordinary consciousness; it is one of "various kinds of cognition that are the historical accomplishments of specific intellectual technologies," and the cognitions are not available in the absence of the technologies.[45] With regard to Muslim backwardness, statistics were the "intellectual technology" that enabled the cognition of backwardness.

To say that backwardness is a phenomenon produced by rather than simply measured by statistics is still, however, not a complete characterization of the epistemic conditions which made it possible to "see" the "fact" of Muslim backwardness. We can further pursue this question by means of a contrast with indigenous education. Many Muslims, we know, received "instruction" of different types and in different settings: *maktabs, madrassas, patshalas,* mosques where they learned to recite *quranic* verses from a learned man, and so on. These forms of instruction were a feature of Indian society up to and after the introduction of modern, western education. It was often, though not always, an explicit object of this instruction to pass on and reproduce the values and norms of communities characterized, among other things, by their adherence to Islam.[46] Indeed, if "Muslim" and "education" are to be juxtaposed, they were more meaningfully juxtaposed here than in the nonreligious education system authorized by the British.

However, the problem of "Muslim backwardness" could not be posed from within this system of instruction. Why not? Because although the madrassa and the maktab did indeed contain a conception of "Muslim" as transcending the limits of class and region, it did not easily imagine this as a subset of a wider social field. As we had occasion to observe earlier, "education" in colonial India was not predicated upon a conception of society as a horizontal field, as a population, but rather as a series of segmented and hierarchically organized domains with correspondingly different needs and practices. Consequently, "education" was not conceived of as the transmission of a unitary body of knowledge but rather as different knowledges and different forms of instruction for different social groups — *tols* and maktabs and madrassas, *maulvis* teaching recitation of Quranic verses in the mosque, village patshalas providing some very basic skills, specialized patshalas providing instruction for certain professions and castes, and so on. Within this learning, the unified social field which makes judgments about backwardness and forwardness possible was lacking. This social field became thinkable only with the emergence of an educational "system" which presupposed the object, "population."

The intellectual field in which comparisons could be made and backwardness discovered — including educational backwardness — was thus provided by the idea of population. Population in turn becomes available as an object for cognition, measurement, and regulation from a particular perspective (it too is not an object for practical consciousness), and the perspective is that of the state, a state concerned with the health, productivity, and numbers of the population it governs. "Backwardness," statistics, and population thus imply each other, and they all imply the presence of a state with a particular kind of relation to its subjects.

Colonial Governmentality

That state is the "governmentalized" state discussed by Michel Foucault. In his later published works and in his lectures at the Collège de France, Foucault traced a shift from a power coded in the form of sovereignty, operating through juridical means and having as its ultimate exercise the taking of life, to a new power that "gave itself the function of administering life," "a power whose highest function was perhaps no longer to kill, but to invest life through and through."[47] This new power was one that sought to safeguard and promote the health, productivity, and happiness of the population, as a way of maximizing the wealth and power of the state. The "transition which takes place in the eighteenth century ... from a regime dominated by structures of sovereignty to one ruled by techniques of government," Foucault writes, "turns on the theme of population."[48] Foucault names this new form of power "governmentality," a neologism suggesting a particular rationality which came to underpin the exercise of government. However, this new rationality of government was distinguished from sovereignty not only by its solicitude toward the health and productivity and even happiness of its population (hence the importance of statistics, to produce knowledge of the population – their numbers, longevity, health and ill health, rates of mortality), but also in that it recognized that it was not possible for the state to completely regulate the population. If the health of the state depended upon the well-being of its population, this was best secured by governmental regulation *and* by paying scrupulous attention to the development of individual capacities for *self*-regulation. This new power worked upon people as aggregates, as "population," but also as individuals; through the regulation of populations, but also through freedom. Foucault neither denounces this liberty as an ideological delusion nor accepts the liberal naturalization of it, but rather seeks to analyze, in the words of one of his interpreters, "the conditions under which the practice of freedom is possible,"[49] conditions which are shown to be intimately linked with (rather than at odds with) the modern state.

Part of the explanatory power of the Foucauldian account of governmentality lies precisely in its affording the possibility of understanding a defining and yet seemingly paradoxical feature of the modern world, namely that an immense increase in the reach and intervention of the state has often been accompanied by the creation of a certain field of individual liberty. The paradox dissolves in Foucault's account, because the two go hand in hand in the form of a governmental rationality that governs through freedom. Analysis need not be locked in a sterile antithesis where it constantly counterpoises individual liberty to governmental regulation, presuming that the advance of the one must mean the diminution of the other. Liberal and radical analyses of the development of modern education, Ian Hunter points out, are usually organized around a similar antithesis, "organised around an opposition between a pedagogy 'imposed' by social utility or political necessity and one developed 'for its own sake' as part of the self-realisation of 'man' or the 'universal class.' "[50] Depending upon one's understanding of the social system of which education is a part, one can then either conclude that at some point education was finally freed of its subordination to social utility and allowed to fulfill its proper function of individual self-development, or that this is still a task to be completed. Once thought is liberated from this opposition, Hunter argues, we can recognize that the development of popular education in nineteenth-century England did not oscillate between this "exemplary opposition between the self-realising and the utilitarian, the self-expressive and the normative";[51] nineteenth-century educational reformers like David Stow and Kay-Shuttleworth explicitly proposed a model of popular education in which "moral norms would be realised *through* self-expressive techniques . . . [and] forms of self-discovery organised around the individual would *permit* the realisation of new social norms at the level of population."[52] Indeed, the importance attached to education derived from precisely its status as a site where administering the population and inculcating habits and techniques of freedom and self-regulation, by which individual members of the population would administer themselves, could be combined. The educational system that emerged in England was a "distinctive governmental apparatus formed . . . in an unprecedented investigative and administrative network which made the 'moral and physical' condition of the population into an object of government. It was in this network that the old techniques of pastoral surveillance aimed at the individual soul, and new forms of social discipline aimed at whole populations, could combine to form the technology of moral training."[53]

As has often been noted, there are parallels between the processes described by Foucault and developments in colonial India from about the latter third of the nineteenth century, when the forms and scope of colonial power were extensively reorganized. In this period the censuses were begun, the law codified, bureaucracy reorganized and rationalized, and "a whole apparatus of specialized technical services was instituted in order to scientifically survey, classify, and enumerate the geographical, geological, botanical, zoological, and meteorological properties of the natural environment and the archaeo-logical, historical, anthropological, linguistic, economic, demographic and epidemiological characteristics of the people."[54] However, those who have noted and drawn attention to these parallels have also insisted that there are important differences between governmentality in the metropolis and its operations in the colonies. The "colonial" in "colonial governmentality" needs to be understood as an adjective designating the ways in which the specificities of colonial rule qualified the functioning and character of gov-ernmentality.[55] How did it do so?

While it is premised upon a technology which seeks to govern through freedom, liberal governmentality, as Barry Hindess reminds us, has always also included a large number of people who are governed illiberally: "If we were to do a head count of those subjected to liberal rule, we would have to say that before the middle of the twentieth century, the vast majority consisted of those who [it was thought] would benefit from being subjected to authori-tarian rule: the subject peoples of western imperial rule and, throughout the nineteenth and early twentieth centuries, substantial groups in western soci-eties themselves."[56] The central justification for this view was the presump-tion "that the capacities required for autonomous conduct and the social con-ditions that foster and sustain them can be developed in a population only through compulsion, through the imposition of more or less extended peri-ods of discipline."[57] This was of course the prime justification for colonialism in its heyday – the idea that colonial rule was necessary to foster "moral and material improvement," and that an extended period of tutelage was neces-sary in order that one day natives might be capable of autonomous conduct and self-rule. We could dismiss these justifications of colonial rule as hypoc-risy and bad faith, which indeed they were; but at the same time we need to recognize that they had real effects in shaping the character and function-ing of colonial rule. Colonial governmentality functioned to at once posit the possibility and desirability of governance through liberty, but always within a frame where that possibility was deferred, and where autonomous conduct was not possible – yet.

Education occupied an especially privileged place in this constellation. We have seen that the knowledge diffused through western education, and the practices associated with this diffusion, did posit a subject capable of making knowledge his own; and that the concern with "moral development," with the capacity to make judgments and decisions by reference to clear and rationally derived criteria, was also very much present. The notions of order and orderliness which accompany this conception of the self-regulating subject were also present, as became apparent whenever modern education was contrasted with "indigenous education." The latter was denounced for being autocratic, but at the same time seen as highly disorderly. Lieutenant T. B. Jervis of the Statistical Survey complained that at the indigenous schools he had observed in the Bombay Presidency, pupils "sit without order, or distinction into classes and leave their work when called for to assist their young companions, thereby occasioning much confusion and hindrance to others."[58] The secretary to the Bengal Council of Education described his visit to an indigenous school, where the students "were squatting upon the clay floor, without order or regularity," and contrasted it to a government-established vernacular school across the way, which held its classes "in a neat, open, small puckah [permanent] building," and where the activities of the students displayed "order, regularity and earnestness."[59] In the modern, government-funded or government-inspected schools, discipline and order were thought to go hand in hand with self-regulation, for the discipline in question was self-discipline; in indigenous schools harsh authoritarianism and disorder went hand in hand, for an external and coercively imposed authority could only operate intermittently and harshly, and therefore ineffectively.

Colonial governmentality, we might say, functioned to posit the possibility of self-governance and incite the desire for it, while simultaneously declaring it unachievable – for now. At the same time, and with perhaps greater success, it facilitated the emergence of new collective identities.

Being Muslim

Anticolonial nationalism is South Asia succeeded in producing not one but two nations. Why this should have been so, and how and why the bloodbath of Partition occurred, have been among the central questions in the historiography of modern South Asia. Education has sometimes been held responsible for having widened the divide between Hindu and Muslim, and there is a certain plausibility about attributing Hindu-Muslim divisions to educational and occupational disparities, because these accord neatly with the emergence and organizational expression of new interests and voices. One of the first Muslim organizations of the new and modern (voluntary and associational) type to be established, the Muhammadan Educational Conference, was founded, as we saw, to further the cause of Muslim education; but it soon came to present itself as the Muslim counterpart and competitor to the Indian National Congress, founded the year before. The Muslim League, formed in 1906, was the child of the Muhammadan Educational Conference, to which it functioned as an adjunct for the first few years of its existence. Given all this, it is tempting to explain communal separatism as partly arising out of educational inequality between the two communities, an inequality which translated into unequal access to the new sources of status and advancement, and the attempts to redress which (through organizational forms such as Muslim associations, and government policies treating Muslims as a distinct group) only exacerbated the communal divide.

Here I have not joined the historical debate over whether Indian Muslims were "in fact" backward or not,[60] nor have I speculated on whether and how their alleged backwardness contributed to divisions along communal lines. I have instead sought to explore the epistemic conditions that made it possible and necessary to cross-tabulate "Muslim" and "education," and produce the figure of the backward Muslim. The production of statistics was clearly a necessary condition, but statistics did not simply enable one to see the fact of backwardness, and measure it, but embodied a particular perspective from which this fact could both be brought into being as a fact and seen as such. The perspective was that of the governmentalized state, which governs a population.

But as should be apparent, the "perspective" that made backwardness visible only did so inasmuch as it also entailed conceiving of "Muslim" in a new way. The peoples of South Asia, belonging to castes, religious communities, village communities, and so on, were reconceived once these came to be seen as subsets of the more inclusive category, "population." David Lelyveld writes that

> there were many ways to construe group identity among the people of India. Labels existed on many levels of generality and cut across each other in complicated ways. Those based on birth might involve a wide range of identities, from household to property holding group, to lineage, to endogamous group to a far-flung cultural category supposedly indicating shared status. A person might also be labeled by locality – a

section of a village, a village, a cluster of villages, an old administrative unit, a large geographic region. Language identification was similarly ambiguous, because most Indians had command of a whole continuum of linguistic styles and dialects. Religious designations were often unclear; below the surface of the well-known scriptural religions one might detect an immense variety of ritual practices and objects of worship, some purely local, others amalgamating widely different great traditions. What is more, many of these labels were outsiders' constructs, unfamiliar to the people they purported to describe.[61]

Sudipta Kaviraj describes these forms of group belonging as "fuzzy communities," communities without a strong sense of boundaries, and communities which did not ask "how many of them there were in the world."[62] They were also fuzzy because in them identities were relational and varied according to context, whereas colonial categorizations of these identities assumed so many isolated corporate groups which then entered into relations with one another. The Muslim was at once member of an *ummah*, a worldwide community of the faithful, and someone who belonged to a particular locale, to a subcommunity, spoke one or more of several possible languages, and (in some regions of the subcontinent) was a member of the high-status *ashraf* class or the plebian *ajlaf*. Life was lived as a network of dense and complicated hierarchical relations that usually made one's identity relationally determined, and changing according to context, rather than fixed in the manner presupposed by enumeration. This was a fact registered, for instance, in the names of Muslim *ashraf*, which apart from a personal name also had prefixes and suffixes indicating (in lieu of a surname) their "title," their lineage or local connections, and sometimes other information, such as the place with which their family was connected. Biographies and autobiographies are a good guide to this, for they give the texture of such a complex and shifting range of identity-positions in a fashion that the social sciences, products of the modern that seek to grasp the modern, seldom can.[63]

The discourse of the "backward Muslim" not only brought into being a backwardness that was not thinkable and seeable in precolonial society, but in so doing it also and equally abstracted from the differences of region, class, and culture that characterized the Muslims of South Asia. Thus in reconstituting the category Muslim the discourse of the backward Muslim – enabled by statistics, and representing the perspective of the governmental state – also made it available to practical consciousness, and in doing so made it possible for others to think and be Muslim in a different way. As a result education figured not only as the site where a "colonial bourgeois subject" was posited but also as a site where new forms of collective identity were enabled. Education proved to be transformative, but not, as modernization theory would have it, because the modern knowledge disseminated through it replaced pre-modern superstition with modern Reason, thereby transforming the "traditional" Muslim into the modern Muslim. Education proved important rather because modern, western education, unlike the maktab and the madrassa, was tied up with the governmental practices of the colonial state, and thus was a site for elaborating new ways of understanding and governing the "population." Through the material changes they effected, these ways of understanding then became available to sections of that population. It is not that Muslims were "transformed" or remade into modern subjects (though no doubt some were), but rather that new ways of being Muslim became possible. To what extent these possibilities were grasped, and by whom, varied. In this explanation, unlike in modernization theory, there is no inevitability about these processes. The caution issued by Appadurai, with which we began – that whether the self-perceptions of those enumerated and classified in these ways changed, and how much so, depended upon a range of circumstances – is very much to the point. For many it is no doubt true, as Ayesha Jalal concludes in her study of Muslim conceptions of selfhood in South Asia, that the meaning given to Muslim identity through colonial schemes of enumeration "remained more of an abstract legal category" than a living social entity.[64] Perhaps the greatest proof of this is that Muslim reformers like Sir Sayyid spent much of their time berating their fellow Muslims for continuing to be mired in petty minutiae and disputes – that is, for failing to discard, and rise above, the local allegiances and conflicts that gave shape and texture to their lives as Muslims.

But at the same time, this new way of being Muslim shaped others' projects for their own and their community's future. The idea of the backward Muslim, which presumed and made possible a new way of thinking "Muslim," also made it possible to conceive of, and conceive the desire for, the "forward" or modern Muslim. This conception and desire was to animate a number of diverse projects. Sayyid Ahmad Khan desired a "new generation of Muslims who would have the knowledge, skills and values necessary to qualify them for public leadership,"[65] and hoped that the Muhammadan Anglo-Oriental College would be the crucible in which this new generation could be forged. Maulana Abul Kalam Azad, as Congress nationalist and then as education minister of independent India, sought a Muslim identity which would be securely anchored both in Islam and in Indianness, the two combined in part by being "modern." Muhammad Ali Jinnah, Qaid-e- Azam or father of Pakistan, had his own visions of what the Muslim who was not backward, but master of his own fortunes, needed to be like. Indeed, the heterogeneity of these desires, and the variety of projects to which they gave rise, ensured that the figure of the "backward Muslim," whether he "in fact" existed or not, would have real and lasting historical consequences.

CHAPTER FIVE

Gender and the Nation

Debating Female Education

The debates to which western education gave rise, and the intensity with which these were debated, bore little relation to the actual numbers of Indians receiving such education. If this was so of education in general, it was especially so of female education. In 1882 there were, in all of British India, six girls in college, just over two thousand in secondary schools, and 124,000 in primary or "mixed" schools, the vast majority of these in the provinces of Bombay, Madras, and Bengal, leaving a minuscule number of girls receiving any formal education in the rest of British India.[1] Well under 1 percent of girls of school-going age (narrowly defined) were enrolled in any educational institution at any level,[2] and for every thousand boys enrolled, there were only forty-six girls.[3] By early in the new century there were 160 females in arts colleges, but of these 124 were European, Eurasian, Indian Christian, or Parsi, leaving thirty-six Hindu and Muslim girls attending college. Similarly, of the thirty thousand girls enrolled in the higher echelons of secondary education and receiving instruction in English, two-thirds were European or Eurasian.[4] Where female education was discussed, the director general of education in India observed in his quinquennial report for 1902–7, "In the main . . . it connotes primary education, that is to say, the teaching of little girls to read and write in the vernacular, to do easy sums and a little needlework."[5] Very often it did not even mean that: many girls attended coeducational schools, which usually meant boys' schools with all-male staff that had been encouraged to enroll girls but where, it was widely observed, girls received little education and indeed little attention.[6] A government statement in 1913 acknowledged, "The education of girls remains to be organised."[7]

Nonetheless, female education was the subject of constant discussion in colonial India, in staggering disproportion to the number of girls affected. Why was this so? The obvious answer might be that the depth and intensity of the discourse bore witness to its controversial and contested character; that those who urged female education were confronted with those who denied the need for it, or argued against it. In fact, however, the discourse on female education was very one-sided: by the latter nineteenth century most of the many voices heard on the subject accepted its desirability, and urged its importance. Far from being an answer to our question (Why was there so much said and written about female education despite the small number of girls receiving it?) this observation only yields a second question: Why so much discourse, if there was agreement? In other words, why such belaboring of a point on which a public consensus had seemingly been reached? And given that the volume of discourse on this subject was not matched by dramatic increases in the numbers of girls receiving education, yet another question: What did this discourse on the desirability of educating women signify, if it did not signal a newfound willingness to educate girls and women?

The discourse on women's education was tied up with controversies over "the woman question" in colonial India, controversies which, it has often been noted, had less to do with women than with what women were seen to signify, or could be made to signify. That is, debates on the woman question were connected to differing characterizations and assessments of Indian (or Hindu) society and tradition, which often emerged and took shape in the course of polemical exchanges between the colonial ruler and nationalists. To investigate why female education was so extensively discussed (despite the lack of opposition), and what the debates signified (if they were not translated into results), we need to begin with these exchanges and recreate the discursive contexts in which they took place.

Representation and Backwardness

When confronted by demands from a section of the Indian élites for a greater degree of self-rule for India, and later by demands for full independence, the British rulers of India would seek to refute the viability of the claims on which the demands were based. There were voices within officialdom declaring that the British had conquered India by the sword and had to rule by the sword, but for the most part the British response mixed repression with argument. One of the arguments was that India was not a nation but rather a congeries of castes, religions, and "races," none of which could legitimately represent the others. The British would claim that demands for "home rule" or "independence" articulated the sectional and selfish interests of an edu-

cated and urban élite, which was in no way placed to speak for the vast majority of India's population; that they purported to speak for them was a cloak
for their own ambitions. Claims for self-rule or independence, if yielded to,
would result in the domination of the untouchable by the Brahmin, of the
Muslim by the Hindu (or else in a fratricidal war between the two), or of
the sturdy, yeoman peasantry (sometimes rendered as the "martial races") by
the effete but cunning Bengali babu. This denial of nationalist claims to speak
for other Indians, on the grounds that there was no "India" but only sectional and competing interests, simultaneously functioned to validate British
claims to rule; the very alienness of India's foreign rulers was a virtue, because
it meant that they stood above the fray. Not party to any interest of its own,
the colonial government claimed to dispassionately and impartially preside
over India, wisely adjudicating between the contending interests and claims
of the Indian subcontinent's peoples.

Another argument, and one of the principal justifications of colonial rule,
was that India was too economically and socially backward to join the rank of
self-governing nations. The British claimed to rule India for her own benefit,
in a fashion designed to slowly but steadily result in a "moral and material
improvement." This claim was usually understood and articulated in historicist and evolutionary terms. Not only was India economically poor and
technologically inferior, but this poverty and inferiority meant that India
belonged to the past, that it was "medieval" rather than modern. Having
proved incapable of progressing to the next rung of the historical, evolutionary ladder on its own, India required an extended period of foreign rule to be
transformed or, as it was often put, "regenerated."

To these claims nationalists developed a number of replies. The charge
that there was a gulf separating the western-educated élites from the Indian
peasant was one which nationalism in its earlier, moderate, and constitu-
tional phase would partially concede, but would then turn to its own account by arguing that this élite "mediated" between its colonial rulers and
the vast mass of the Indian people, and therefore needed to be given more
say in governing the country.[8] A later nationalism denied the charge, and
sought to offer a practical and political refutation of it by bridging the divides
of caste, class, religion, and region through mass nationalist mobilizations,
and through efforts to attend to the distinct needs of some sections of the
Indian population, of which the Non-Cooperation-Khilafat movement and
the Poona Pact (or Gandhi-Ambedkar Pact) were instances. At an ideological
level the alleged disunity of India was answered by varied attempts to prove

that underlying all the diversity of India was a historical and cultural unity, attempts ranging from sophisticated discursive elaborations such as Nehru's *The Discovery of India* to the metaphorically charged imagery and iconography of a Mother India crying out to her sons for liberation from alien tutelage.[9] Independent nationhood, nationalists came to argue, would consolidate this unity and give full and free expression to it.

As for the colonizer's claim that India was backward, and hence ill equipped to exercise democratic freedoms and self-rule, nationalists would sometimes concede the sorry state of contemporary India but seek to rescue national honor by constructing a picture of a once-golden Indian (usually Hindu) past. India had fallen from greatness, rather than having failed to advance beyond a "rude" state of development. Later nationalists came to argue that much of India's economic and material backwardness was in any case a consequence of colonial rule and the exploitative economic relations which characterized it. In the latter nineteenth century Dadabhai Naoroji and others publicized the idea that British rule brought about a "drain of wealth" from India to England;[10] and in the twentieth century Nehru and others drew upon Marxist ideas to indict British rule for having retarded India's economic growth and propped up "feudal" social structures, rather than aiding modernization.[11] It became a central nationalist plank that Indian poverty and economic backwardness, far from constituting a justification for continued colonial rule, could only be adequately addressed and remedied in an independent India governed by Indians.

The Iconic Woman

The status and condition of India's women loomed large in these conflicts, and many of the arguments briefly sketched above were also played out with specific reference to women. In his immensely influential *The History of British India* – "the hegemonic textbook of Indian history" in the nineteenth century[12] – James Mill drew upon the writings of Scottish Enlightenment historians to claim that the condition of women reflected the degree of civilization that a people had attained: "among rude people, the women are generally degraded; among civilized people they are exalted." By this test India ranked low on the civilizational scale, for "A state of dependence more strict and humiliating than that which is ordained for the weaker sex among the Hindus cannot easily be conceived."[13] The degraded condition of women, exemplified in customs like sati, prohibitions against the remarriage of widows, purdah, child marriage, and so on testified to the "rude" status of Hindu society. For Mill – as for numerous other colonial officials and missionaries, as well as many "maternal imperialists" who willingly shouldered the "white woman's burden"[14] – this was unshakeable proof that India required the benign and improving rule of a civilized European country.[15] At the same time, the "sensitivity" of this question, which touched upon religious observance and the delicate matter of relations between the sexes, provided the colonial government with a reason for doing very little to ameliorate the lot of degraded Indian womanhood, even while drawing attention to it as one of the prime instances of the social backwardness of Indian society.

Many Indians concurred that the status of women in India was low, and that this reflected badly upon their society. An eminent Indian convert to Christianity, the Reverend K. M. Banerjea, wrote in 1841 that Bengali women "drag on lives of the utmost wretchedness and degradation, and are regarded only as servants of the household, and ministers of carnal gratification to their husbands."[16] Indian students were often required to reflect upon this aspect of Indian society: the status of women was a popular essay and exam question, particularly in the first half of the nineteenth century. While a student in Hindu College, Michael Madhusudan Dutt, later to become one of Bengal's greatest poets, wrote in answer to one of these, "In India, I may say in all Oriental countries, women are looked upon as created merely to contribute to the gratification of the animal appetites of men . . . The people of this country do not know the pleasures of domestic life, and indeed they cannot know, until civilization shows them the way to attain it."[17]

Others expressed resentment at the wholesale and harsh condemnations of Indian or Hindu customs. When K. M. Banerjea repeated his comments on the "wretchedness and degradation" of Hindu women in a talk to that remarkable body, the Society for the Acquisition of General Knowledge, Peary Chand Mitra replied with a rebuke: "There are some persons," Mitra observed, "who are ready at all times to find fault with everything relating to the Hindu," and to pass "sweeping condemnations on our institutions respecting females."[18] Mitra went on to observe that the condition of women in Europe had not always been, nor was it currently, an exalted one; and to suggest that while the lot of women in contemporary India was indeed a poor one in many respects, it had not always been so – in the past women in Hindu India had exercised much greater liberty, had been possessed of civil rights, and had often been educated. That this rebuke was delivered at the Society for the Acquisition of General Knowledge made it all the more significant, since neither Mitra nor his listeners belonged to the ranks of those "ortho-dox" who denied that women's condition was in need of reform, and who a decade earlier had opposed legislation outlawing sati. On the contrary, this was a body of the radicals and iconoclasts of the 1830s and 1840s which histo-riography has often described as the most advanced and rationalist vanguard of the "Bengal Renaissance."

Mitra's claim regarding the position of women in earlier times antici-pated what from the mid-nineteenth century came to assume something of the status of an orthodoxy, namely that in ancient India women's condition had been altogether different, and very much more exalted, than it was in the present. From pamphlet and in press, in English and in the vernacu-lars, in prose and poetry, people with otherwise differing views on issues to do with women regularly cited historical and mythical figures from the an-cient past such as Maitreyi, Gargi, Damyanti, and others as examples of how once women in India had been "learned, free and highly cultured."[19] In an eponymous poem on Savitri by Toru Dutt (1856–77), the mythical, ideal wife of Hindu tradition appears as the opposite of the ignorant and superstitious woman confined in the *antahpur*:

> In those far-off primeval days
> Fair India's daughters were not pent
> In closed zenanas. On her ways
> Savitri at her pleasure went
> Whither she chose, – and hour by hour
> With young companions of her age,
> She roamed the woods for fruit or flower,
> Or loitered in some hermitage,
> For to the Munis gray and old
> Her presence was as sunshine glad,
> They taught her wonders manifold
> And gave her of the best they had.[20]

If reform of the condition of Indian women was required, it could now be cast as a consequence not of India being insufficiently civilized (with "Europe" standing for civilization), but rather of her lapse from her own tra-ditions and customs. It was not the "Hindu religion" or "native customs" which were the source and cause of woman's plight, but their decline: as Annie Besant put it in the course of urging reform of the practice of child mar-riage, "I am pleading . . . for a restoration to women in India of the place that was theirs when India was greatest."[21] With history reconstructed thus, it followed that improving the lot of women required recapturing some essential Hinduness or Indianness, rather than remaking Indian women in the image of their western counterparts. Numerous speakers and writers waxed lyrical on the special qualities of the Indian (or Hindu) woman, whose "clean innocence . . . simple faith . . . sweetness and geniality of temper . . . [and] natural courtesy . . . are unsurpassed."[22] Rather than being an object of pity, Indian womanhood now assumed a privileged status in nationalist discourse. Tanika Sarkar describes how woman was discursively produced as a potent signifier in the course of elaborating this discourse: "An icon was constructed of the patriotic subject, the good Hindu woman with her simple dress, her ritually pure conchshell bangles and red vermilion mark, her happy surrender and self immersion in the sansar [domesticity], and her endless bounty and nurture expressed by cooking and feeding. She was charged with an immense aesthetic, cultural and religious load in nationalist writings."[23]

In part this was an aspect of a more general reassertion of the value of indigenous culture and tradition, a reassertion which became especially marked in the 1870s and 1880s. It was also more than this, however. Partha Chatterjee has illuminatingly argued that anticolonial nationalism in India divided the world of social institutions and practices into two domains, the "spiritual" and the "material," which corresponded to a distinction between that which was integral to national identity and that which was extrinsic to it. In Chatterjee's summary of the position that Indian nationalism had arrived at in the second half of the nineteenth century, "The material is the domain of the 'outside,' of the economy and of statecraft, of science and technology, a domain where the West had proved its superiority and the East had succumbed. In this domain, then, Western superiority had to be acknowledged and its accomplishments carefully studied and replicated. The spiritual, on the other hand, is an 'inner' domain bearing the 'essential' marks of cultural identity. The greater one's success in imitating Western skills in the material domain, therefore, the greater the need to preserve the distinctness of one's spiritual culture."[24]

From the second half of the nineteenth century, Indian womanhood and the home which she was seen to embody came to be seen as one of the most important sites where the "essential marks of cultural identity" were located and reproduced. The middle-class Indian male had perforce to engage with the colonial civil sphere to make a living, and the nationalist had to engage with it to acquire the scientific and technological skills needed if India were to liberate herself from foreign rule. In the process cultural compromises were necessitated. All the more necessary, then, that the Indian woman, through her religious devotion and her "traditional" dress and demeanor, function as an emblem and repository of an identity which was pure and unsullied. She signified an Indianness that had to be retained and preserved, even as the nation-to-be sought to acquire the material and technological resources necessary to prepare to fight for national Independence, and to build a modern nation thereafter.

Not only did the Indian woman signify Indianness, but as wife and mistress of the home she provided the anchor that kept her western-educated husband, immersed in the "material" world of colonial society, from losing all touch with his national essence. Annie Besant wrote, "Hinduism needs the support of educated Hindu women, reproducing in modern days the Brahma Vadinis of old, and saving English-educated men from the scepticism which they imbibe from their secular or missionary education. The future of Hinduism depends largely on women."[25] A highly idealized conception of women's role, no doubt, but occasionally there were men who testified that this was the role their wives had played. G. S. Dutt, one of few Indians who gained entry into an Indian civil service dominated by the British, described how as a result of his western education and a period spent in England he became almost wholly Anglicized, so much so that he insisted on having his wife speak to him in English, and take lessons in ballroom dancing. As a traditional wife she complied with his wishes, but over time it was her deeply rooted Indian identity and Hindu religiosity which remade him, such that "she succeeded in making" him "a Bengali again."[26]

At the same time, the need for change was not rejected. On the contrary, strengthening the nation and preparing for the struggles ahead required that middle-class Indian women also had to change, had to become "modern" and yet remain quintessentially Indian. As Chatterjee goes on to suggest, nationalism did not reject the West or modernity: "the nationalist paradigm in fact supplied an ideological principle of selection ... not a dismissal of modernity but an attempt to make modernity consistent with the nationalist project."[27] What did follow, if remaking women and domesticity required recapturing and preserving some essential Hinduness or Indianness rather than using western counterparts as models, was that this project of preservation-cum-transformation could only be undertaken by Indians, not by the colonial state. There thus begins in the nineteenth century what one historian has termed a project of "ideological-aesthetic meddlesomeness,"[28] with a segment of the Indian middle class striving to refashion its women. Female education was a defining aspect of this project.

Female Education: Virtuous Wives and Modern Mothers

When it was decided in 1813 that the colonial government was to undertake some responsibility for educating its Indian subjects, and again in 1835 when it was decided that this education was to be education in western knowledge, the authorities had only their male subjects in mind. The education of women was not high on the agenda in Britain at the time, and the small resources to be devoted to educating England's Indian subjects were not to be wasted on the lower classes or on women. Thus the earliest efforts at providing formal education for girls came from private agency – from the private initiatives of colonial officials, and most notably from missionaries.[29] It was not until 1850 that the Indian government declared government support for female education (though not yet any financial commitment), and then on the grounds that through their influence as mothers and wives, educated women would have a disproportionate and beneficial impact on the general spread of European knowledge.[30] Here, as through much of the colonial period, the colonial state urged female education not because of its value to girls but rather because it was thought conducive to the more effective education of boys; and conversely, because it was felt that uneducated wives and mothers "stand for ideals and modes of thought which are often sharply in conflict with those which their men have learned to entertain," leading to a "dualism" in the life of the educated Indian,[31] and contributing to the "moral crisis" discussed in chapter 2.

The very circumstance which made it desirable to educate girls – that the home they represented was different from, even at odds with, the world of colonial, modern civil society – was also, however, cited as an obstacle to the spread of girls' education. The peculiarities which characterized relations between the sexes and domestic arrangements in Indian society, including the custom of purdah (the seclusion of women), child marriage, the prejudice that a woman who learned to read and write would end up as a widow or become immoral – were widely seen as impediments to female education. Citing some of these "peculiar difficulties," the *Report of the Indian Education [Hunter] Commission* of 1883 stated, "For many years to come, the respectable native community will desire to shelter their daughters from public observation, and to seclude them from contact with males not belonging to the

family. The problem is how to reconcile school-life with these popular feel-
ings."[32] The solution to this problem, it concluded, would depend less on government initiatives than on the "growth of public opinion among the natives
themselves."[33]

There were indeed many prejudices against female literacy and education
in most parts of India, including the ones mentioned by the Hunter Commission. Often the most vigorous opposition came from the older women of
the joint family.[34] However, by the mid-nineteenth century the idea of female
education was also finding some support among sections of the new middle
class, especially the "reformed" sections of Hindu society such as the Brahmo
Samaj.[35] The education envisaged in this early period was mostly at home,
either in the form of husbands educating their wives,[36] or *zenana* education,
in which "missionary ladies" or young members of the Brahmo Samaj would
visit middle-class women in their homes to provide some instruction, usually
more to do with the graces required of the wife of a middle-class gentleman
in government service than with reading or writing.[37]

By the latter half of the nineteenth century there were growing voices
in favor of female education, including formal schooling,[38] mostly from the
new middle classes who occupied a subordinate position in the colonial public sphere of offices and law courts. These voices made themselves heard
through a raft of journals and magazines directed at women, which both
presumed literacy among their readers and urged the need for women's education;[39] through public debates in newspapers, magazines, and pamphlets,
which urged upon western-educated men the importance of educating their
womenfolk; through didactic pamphlets directed at women and seeking to
persuade them of the merits of education;[40] and through native efforts to
establish girls' schools.

IN *VANITABODHINI* (1898), a dialogue in Hindi between two women – the
dialogue was a favored form in didactic works – Vidavthi seeks to answer
the doubts and objections of her friend Sarala concerning women's education. It is not true, she explains, that the Shastras forbid women's education; pandits who are genuinely learned tell us that on the contrary, they
enjoin it. The custom of educating women was lost, like many other good
Hindu customs, during the oppressive Muslim rule. To Sarala's fear that educated women will become widows, Vidavthi replies that this could not possibly be true, else all memsahibs would be widows. The fear that education
leads women to romantic intrigues and immorality is similarly refuted. Con-
ceding that her fears and objections may be groundless, Sarala nonetheless

asks what, if anything, is gained by education. Vidhavthi answers that currently men dismiss women's views as "women's talk," and even little boys, having read one or two books, come to regard their mother's words as nonsense.[41] Education will therefore lead women to be taken more seriously and to be better mothers, able to instruct their children. They will also be able to read the Shastras and thus better understand their dharma; and be less likely to quarrel (hence men will be more likely to linger at home) and break up the joint family, since a great deal of female quarrelsomeness derives from ignorance.[42]

The two themes which were to dominate the numerous pamphlets, dialogues, and newspaper and magazine articles in which the discourse of female education proliferated are present here. First, for women to receive education is not contrary to Hindu traditions, but is rather to return to them (here, as in many but not all writings, the "Muslim invasions" and "Muslim rule" are the scapegoat for the decline of good customs and the introduction of oppressive ones). This was a theme endlessly elaborated, in humble pamphlets such as this one and in more elevated settings. Addressing the Indian Social Conference in 1906, the poet and nationalist Sarojini Naidu began by observing that it was "a paradox, at once touched with humour and tragedy," to have to urge female education in India: India of all places, "which, at the beginning of the first century was already ripe with civilization and . . . examples of women of the highest genius and widest culture." She urged her (mostly male) audience: "restore to your women their ancient rights."[43]

The second theme is that female education will modernize and improve existing domestic arrangements, rather than fundamentally reorder and transform them. Specifically, it was urged on behalf of female education that it would make women better wives, especially given the changing public worlds that their husbands inhabited; make them better mothers; and give more substance to their piety by making them more moral and virtuous.

The claim that educated women would make better wives was made on a number of grounds, which are worth distinguishing even if collectively they all amounted to a call for a reformed and modernized domesticity. One was the Victorian notion that household management was a serious, even scientific affair, requiring the sort of knowledge which could not be provided by the older women of a joint family, who themselves were usually illiterate. One of the early *bhadramahila* (genteel, middle-class) contributors to this discourse, Kundamala Debi, wrote in 1870 that "an educated woman can do housework thoughtfully and systematically in a way unknown to an ignorant, uneducated woman."[44] Another educated Bengali woman, Bamasundari, similarly wrote: "How to do housework, deal with family members and domestic servants as well as educate them – these are areas in which women . . . are singularly ignorant."[45] Another ground was that female education was required as an adaptation to the changing nature of middle-class occupational roles, and the increasing importance of western education for a small but socially significant group of men. The gap between the worlds of women and men had always been significant, and was metaphorically and physically rendered in some parts of India through the distinction between the *antahpur*, or "inside," and the outside world. What was new, and required adaptation on women's part, was that this gap was no longer even cut of the same cultural cloth. As a result, a distance which was once unexceptionable now loomed for some as one which undermined domestic harmony. An advocate of female education in the *Brahmo Public Opinion* wrote, "an educated Bengali, when he returns home, fagged and wearied by the day's over-work, wishes very much to be refreshed either with music, or with pleasant conversation on topics familiar to him, and feels very much disappointed when his hopes are frustrated . . . he very much feels the want of a help-mate."[46] We can see in this statement and others like it the emergence also of a new desire. Although the English model of domesticity was in general thought one to be avoided – not least because the practical and emotional economy of the joint family placed inherent limitations upon the idea of the "companionate marriage" – the idea of a wife who could share her husband's interests and understand the cares of his work was one which found appeal in some quarters.[47] Traveling in England in 1870, the Brahmo leader Keshub Chunder Sen was much impressed by the "sweet English home";[48] and Amrita Krishna Basu urged his listeners at a meeting of the Simla Literary Society to educate their wives and daughters, because they would "enjoy better domestic pleasures in the company of educated and enlightened wives and daughters."[49] Others saw a danger in the gulf between the nationalist man's public life, necessarily immersed in voluntary associations and all the other institutions and paraphernalia of modern life, and his pre-modern home: "It is dangerous that from a vivid public life, full of interest, full of keen and strenuous struggle, a man should go back into the women's quarters of the house, and find himself carried back over centuries."[50]

It was also widely argued that educated women would make better mothers. A student essay at the Elphinstone institution favored female education on the grounds that "philosophers like Bacon, and linguists like [William] Jones, who afterwards became so famous for their learning, were indebted in their early lives to their learned and intelligent mothers, under whose care their youthful minds were formed."[51] A regular theme in the discourse of female education was that the educated mother – capable of instructing her children, running an orderly house, maintaining hygiene, providing a "scientifically" sanctioned diet, and tempering affection with discipline – was superior to her uneducated counterpart. As an essayist in the *Calcutta Review* wrote, "Intelligently educated mothers, and sisters, and wives [are] essential to the training of a race of intelligent and high-spirited sons, and brothers, and husbands."[52] As this and numerous similar statements testify, motherhood – in its newly defined, enlightened, and "modern" variety – was ennobled such that it was not only a domestic duty but also a national obligation. "By the turn of the century," Meredith Borthwick writes in her study of the changing role of Bengali women, "motherhood had been invested with a new meaning . . . raised from a natural function to an exalted duty . . . a vocation so complex that only a well-educated woman could manage it."[53]

The education of women, it was also claimed, would lead to greater virtue and morality. From the mid-nineteenth century many came to see the confined world of women, represented by the *antahpur* and *zenana*, as breeding grounds for intrigue, quarrelsomeness, and a piety which, while admirable in the abstract, in the concrete was full of idle superstitions and empty rituals.[54] The educated woman would continue to be religious, but in an enlightened rather than superstitious fashion; she would be at least as moral and chaste as her uneducated predecessor, and far more virtuous than her female attendants and entertainers from the lower classes, from whom she was to be sharply distinguished and separated as never before.[55]

By the late nineteenth century few voices were heard in public arguing against women's education – divisions between "advanced" and "orthodox" opinion, which did occur around other issues concerning the status of women, were largely absent from public discussions of female education, with "conservatives" and "reformers" agreeing that female education was a desired goal. My examples have principally been drawn from those who explicitly referred to Hindu women, or who equated "Hindu women" with "Indian women." But there were parallel and sometimes overlapping debates among Muslim reformers. Gail Minault writes, "discussions of women's education and construction of plans to effect it had become an obsession among many north Indian Muslim men in the late nineteenth century." These men argued that with education "women would become better companions to their husbands, better mothers to their children, and better homemakers," as well as "better Muslims . . . observant of sanctioned, as opposed to "useless," rituals."[56] And while in both cases there were some debates around the type and extent of education appropriate for women, and the debates sometimes generated heat,[57] for the most part even these were rather muted, and the curriculum for girls in government schools was not substantially different from that for boys.

A great deal of this debate paralleled those in Britain, where the proponents of women's education similarly argued that it was necessary to produce a well-regulated domesticity. The Victorian themes of discipline, order, efficiency, organization, regularity, and economy figured large in Indian discussions. The Indian discourse on female education was even marked by a similar anxiety – those who advocate education for women went to great pains to make clear what the educated woman should *not* become, namely disaffected and unfit for domesticity, or competitive and "mannish." The words of a speaker championing female education at the Beharee Student's Conference of 1907 could have been delivered at any gathering in Britain: "we do not want a lady graduate, whose knowledge is replete with calculus, Astronomy and Metaphysics but who is at the same time quite innocent of the arts of cookery and domestic hygiene."[58]

Desexed and Denationalized

There was, however, a very important difference.[59] The anxiety being articulated was not only that the educated woman might be "desexed," but that she might be "denationalized." Indeed, to become desexed *was* simultaneously to be denationalized. To the very degree that woman had become an icon, the symbol and guardian of all that was Indian, for her to lose her feminine attributes (recall Sarkar's description of "her simple dress, her ritually pure conchshell bangles and red vermilion mark, her happy surrender and self immersion in the sansar") would mean that she would no longer signify and embody Indianness. The middle-class and nationalist project was to educate women so that they would become modern and yet able to represent Indianness; the anxiety that was the underside of this project was the fear that Indianness might be effaced by the pursuit of modernity. Some warned that this was happening, or had happened. The headmaster of a high school wrote, "The effect of this indiscriminate imparting of high western education to our girls has had the unfortunate result of unsexing our educated women and of denationalising them – a result bad enough in the case of boys, but infinitely worse in the case of future mothers."[60] Annie Besant, who urged female education as a patriotic necessity, also warned that it must not denationalize: "it is bad enough to denationalize your men. It would be a thousand times worse to denationalize your girls."[61] Why was it "infinitely" or a "thousand times" worse to denationalize women than men? Because then they could no longer perform the function which had been assigned to them, as icons and guardians of national identity – as Besant immediately went on to say, the denationalizing of girls "would be the death-knell of India."[62] Or as the author of *Bharatlakshmi* (1931) bluntly put it, "If, like the so-called enlightened, westernized Indian man, the Indian woman also takes its western education and changes her own nature and religion then our subjection would be extended from the outside to our innermost core."[63]

Thus what was also part of the discourse urging female education – often as part and parcel of writings urging it, at other times from those who warned of its dangers yet without opposing it – was the figure of the Indian woman who had become "westernized" by her education, rather than become an icon of modern Indian femininity. Throughout the nineteenth century the educated woman who had become Anglicized was a figure of rebuke, dread, and satire – in discursive and polemical writings, on the stage, and in novels. Numerous Bengali farces, with titles like *Miss Bino Bibi B.A.*, delighted their audiences with depictions of westernized women whom audiences could join in condemning and ridiculing.[64] Similar anxiety and condemnation continued into the twentieth century, and was by no means confined to the more conservative sections of society.[65] Munshi Premchand, earliest and one of the greatest of modern Hindi prose writers, wrote stories which sympathetically portrayed the lives of peasants, the poor, and of women, and he became a member of the left-wing Progressive Writers Association. But his stories also provide portraits of the "westernized" woman which are anything but affirming. In *Shanti* (1920), a western-educated husband encourages his wife to become modern and western, with disastrous results for the happiness of the husband and the well-being of the joint family. The husband eventually declares, "I want to again see you as a woman who is shy, walks with her head down, reads Ramayan, does household work, spins charkha, is scared of god and is completely devoted to her husband."[66] The wife complies, and order and happiness are restored to the household.

A lecturer at Calcutta University told the Calcutta University Commission, "we do not want that women in India should continue to labour under the darkness of ignorance and superstition . . . But we do not want at the same time that women in India should be steadily anglicised, importing into our peaceful homes the evils of suffragetism or the spirit of revolutionary and rationalistic iconoclasm."[67] Just as modest dress, the *sindhur* and the *bindi*, and other such markers signified Indian femininity, so images of European ways regularly stood in for the loss of a distinctively Indian feminine identity and the decline of domestic virtues. A pamphleteer advocating female education nonetheless also wrote, "Your educated wife knows only how to talk and dress, how to attend visitors in the drawing room . . . She knows also how to read novels lounging in[sic] the sofa . . . She cannot stand the sight of the kitchen . . . they disregard their parents, defy their husbands and hate their children."[68] Balkrishna Bhatt, no admirer of the uneducated and "ignorant" Indian woman, contrasted the traditional Indian wife, frugal and self-sacrificing, with the profligate, nagging, and dominating Englishwoman and her Indian imitator.[69] In 1937 the mayor of Calcutta told the All-India Educational Conference of "ominous signs which spell the ruin of our homes": "Our sisters and daughters have begun bobbing their hair, smoking cigarettes, and enjoying themselves in company with their men friends and seem to be averse to undertaking the duties of a home."[70]

We have seen that a public consensus had emerged around the desirability of female education. This appears to have been reached first in Madras and Bombay, and by the latter nineteenth century in Bengal; by the beginning of the twentieth century, even in what were thought to be the "socially backward" Hindi-speaking regions, a nationalist like Purushottam Das Tandon could assert that the debate over whether women should be educated had been won, and had given way to discussions of what sort of education they should receive.[71] The consensus was such that it could even be described, as I have done, as a "project"; provided we recognize that an anxiety surrounded the project, or better yet, was built into it as one of its elements. What dogged this project—as a critique, but usually produced as part of the same discourse and thus as an auto-critique, as the alterity which defined and delimited the identity of this project—was the figure of the Indian woman who had lost her Indianness and become a brown memsahib. It is this, I suggest, that explains the heatedness and density of the discourse of female education; it is not that female education became the site of competing positions, but rather that the discourse in favor of it was underlain by an anxiety, which it found necessary to harp on endlessly, as if constantly referring to and warning against the danger would ward it away.

Who Signifies?

I began this chapter by observing that debates on the woman question in colonial India were overdetermined by conflicts between nationalists and India's British rulers. The British claimed to be improving an India that was economically but also socially "backward," as the condition of her peasants, untouchables, and women indicated. The spokesmen of Indian national-ism, most of them western-educated, assumed that they were exempt from this charge and argued that their uniquely privileged position – as mediators between their rulers, whose modern world they participated in, and their countrymen, whom they were in the best position to understand – required that they be given a greater role and say in the governance of India. Later they came to argue that the British were not an agent of modernity at all but rather an impediment to achieving it, and that with Independence a mod-ernizing élite, with the consent and participation of the backward, could lead India into the modern world.

The character of these debates changed in response to political and other changes. The isomorphism posited between woman, the untouchable, and the peasant – all exemplars of backwardness – was challenged by national-ism as it came to assert that while transforming the peasantry and reform-ing or uprooting the caste system might have to await the gaining of state power,[72] the remaking of Indian women and of the Indian home was within its power – and moreover, was its exclusive domain. There thus began the project of "ideological-aesthetic meddlesomeness," discussed in the preced-ing pages, to remake the middle-class Indian woman. She and the home that she was seen to preside over were to be rendered more modern, but at the same time were to retain, and were charged with the function of signifying and preserving, all that was distinctively "Indian" in a project that might otherwise become nothing more than an attempt to make India resemble England. Female education was an important part of the project to produce this woman and this home, but the absence of any serious public opposition to the project obscured the deep anxiety which was part of it, manifested in repeated injunctions against letting the educated woman resemble the west-ern woman.

As with other debates concerning the "woman question" in colonial India, debates on female education were not about women but rather about what they signified, or could be made to signify. But also at issue was *who* was to make her signify; who could claim to be legitimately authorized to modernize Indian women. The Indian élites sought to convince others, and perhaps themselves, that they recognized the need to remake Indian women, and that they were capable of formulating an agenda mapping out the character of this transformation. They endlessly elaborated to others, and to each other, what the iconic woman was to signify, and agonized over the lurking dangers inherent in this project. Actually effecting this transformation mattered less, since that was not what this elaborate discourse was about. Hence the curious impression of two parallel discussions going on. One was about the desirability of women's education, and those taking part in and observing this discussion were struck by the unanimity which had been reached on the issue. The other discussion was among educational officials and others directly involved in providing education, and those taking part in this discussion were struck by the wretchedly slow progress being made: in the number of students enrolled, in the level to which they progressed, and in the knowledge and skills gained. Thus at the very time when, according to Purushottam Das Tandon, the debate over whether to educate girls had been won even in the Hindi-speaking regions, the director general for education was observing – as we saw at the beginning of this chapter – that there was very little of the education in question actually happening, and what there was occurred mostly at the lower levels of primary education. There is a curious air of unreality surrounding the discourse on female education – so many discursive moves and declarations, so much argument produced to justify the necessity and urge the importance of it, and yet so little happening "on the ground."[73]

This, I suggest, was because the discourse of female education was less about effecting change than about staking out a claim: that only Indians were authorized to act in this domain, and to map out what changes were required. This claim was made on the grounds that the ability of the middle-class Indian to speak for and represent his women and his home was not contestable, in the way that his ability to speak for the peasant was.

However, the very circumstance that made nationalists choose woman as a signifier and as a site of contestation – that male nationalists could, given patriarchal assumptions shared by ruler and ruled, plausibly claim the right to speak for and intervene in the lives of women – also constituted a potential weakness. To the very degree that "his" home was construed as his sovereign domain and as constitutive of his identity, the middle-class, western-educated Indian was marked by it, in a way that he was not marked by the continued backwardness of the Indian peasant. The backwardness of the peasant signified the backwardness of India; but the backwardness of the middle-class Indian woman could be seen to testify also to the backwardness *of the middle-class Indian.* This much was to become especially clear during the curious affair of Katherine Mayo's *Mother India;* and the ensuing controversy was also to prove a catalyst for a new urgency in nationalist ranks, which sought to match discourse to results.

Mother India

In 1925–26 Mayo, an American journalist and author, made a three-month trip to India with the intention of collecting information for a book. In 1927 *Mother India* was published in New York and then in London. The idea of India as a mother had been a common and potent signifier in nationalist iconography since the nineteenth century, and Mayo later explained that she had chosen her title precisely to make "inescapable the contrast between, on the one hand, florid talk of devotion and 'sacrifice' poured out before an abstract figure, and, on the other hand, the consideration actually accorded to the living woman, mother of the race."[74]

Her book was thus an "exposé" of the true condition of India, especially of Indian women, and through this also a critique of nationalist demands for greater self-rule. Mayo purported to show that Indian society and custom – for the most part Hindu society and custom – condemned women (and also the untouchable castes and others) to lives of ignorance, slavery, and extreme degradation; that it had always been thus; and that all talk of a "Golden Age" of India, when a greater measure of equality and dignity prevailed, was therefore myth. Whatever improvement there had been in the condition of women was due to the efforts of India's British rulers, who had not been assisted and had very often been impeded by their Indian subjects, especially nationalist politicians and speechmakers. Indians blamed England for woes that were deeply rooted in their own culture, a fact they were unwilling to even acknowledge, let alone address. The only prospects for improvement lay in the hope that the educated classes in India might concede that the chains that bound them were of their own making, and earnestly help the British to improve India, rather than engage in nationalist mythmaking and speechifying. Mayo's book was presented as the effort of a well-wisher – it was dedicated to "the peoples of India" – undertaking the onerous and potentially thankless task of holding up a mirror to Indian reality so that Indians could more clearly see themselves, the necessary prelude to their improving themselves.

The meat of the book lay in its graphic descriptions of child brides psychologically and physically damaged by premature intercourse, often with middle-aged husbands; of child mothers giving birth under the most unhygienic and primitive conditions, their reproductive organs irreparably damaged if they survived at all; of the despair of these same mothers at giving birth to daughters, who if not killed to relieve the family of future financial burden were condemned to a future like that of their mothers; and of the lives of women who lived in the utmost ignorance, imprisoned in purdah, slaves to husbands whom they were taught from early childhood to regard as their god. All these practices were rooted in Indian custom and Hindu tradition, which the mass of the people regarded as immutable, a view in which their leaders concurred or which they lacked the courage and will to seek to reform. *Mother India* documented other horrors as well, including the oppression of low castes by Brahmins, but it was the depictions of Indian women in unbearable conditions, and the linking of these conditions to an alleged Hindu obsession with sex (manifested in practices such as early marriage, worship of the Siva lingam, and temple prostitution), which excited the most comment.

And excite comment the book did – more accurately, it provoked a furor. In England many hailed it as "independent" confirmation of what the British authorities had been saying all along – the liberal *New Statesman*, which had been relatively sympathetic to Indian nationalist claims, carried an unsigned review by its editor which both captured and endorsed the tone of the book: "All who know anything of India are aware, of course, of the prime evils of Hinduism, of the horrors of the child marriage system, of the universality of sexual vice in its most extravagant forms, of the monstrously absurd brutalities of the caste system, of the filthy personal habits of even the most educated classes – which, like the degradation of Hindu women, are unequalled even amongst the most primitive African or Australian savages – of the universal cruelty to animals, and of the equally universal prevalence of laziness, untruthfulness, cowardice and personal corruption." Mayo, the review concluded, "makes the claim for Swaraj seem nonsense and the will to grant it almost a crime."[75] Some British feminists joined in the condemnations of India on behalf of their oppressed Indian "sisters." In America *Mother India* sold in huge numbers and shaped public perceptions of India for a long time to come.[76]

The biggest reaction was in India, and it was almost unanimously hostile. Within one year of its publication nine books appeared in reply, including one by the nationalist Lala Lajpat Rai and another by the indefatiguable social reformer K. Natarajan; more appeared over the next few years.[77] Some Indian respondents saw Mayo's condemnation of the alleged Indian obsession with sex as evidence that she was herself "sex-mad."[78] Most Indian respondents read *Mother India* as a politically inspired attack upon nationalist aspirations.[79] And almost all condemned the book as an attack upon Indian women. Thus in Calcutta *Foreward* characterized the book as a "Libel against Indian Womanhood" and a headline in *Amrita Bazaar Patrika* read, "Gratuitous Insult, Indian Women Blasphemed"; and a large protest at the Calcutta Town Hall was advertised as being held "to repudiate the scurrilous attacks and malicious allegations made against the Indian womanhood by Miss Mayo."[80] This was in addition to a host of responses in the press, including ones by Indian women and by Gandhi and Tagore. Numerous public meetings were held to denounce the book, and proposals to proscribe it were raised by Indian members of the Central Legislative Assembly.

The content of *Mother India*, as noted by contemporaries, Mayo herself, and many others since, was not new.[81] As we have seen, the backward and barbaric character of Indian or Hindu society, exemplified above all in its treatment of women, had been a theme of some British writings since the late eighteenth century, receiving formulaic expression with Mill in the early nineteenth, and becoming an orthodoxy thereafter. Numerous Indian social reformers had drawn attention to the social ills which beset India and had sometimes described them in vivid terms, urging sweeping reforms of Indian social practices. Yet the book became an event, the subject of a controversy which, it has been observed, is perhaps only rivaled in recent times by that surrounding Salman Rushdie's *The Satanic Verses*.

Why was this so? If there was little new in the book, why such a fury of denunciation? Mayo, who in 1931 published a sequel entitled simply *Volume Two*, suggested that the response, most of which came from the politically minded western-educated intelligentsia, was "simply and solely because the book was being read in America";[82] seeking independence from Britain, Indian nationalists were cultivating sympathy in America, and *Mother India* was a serious setback in that effort. Malicious and self-serving, this explanation was nonetheless not without some truth. Indian nationalists had been publicizing their cause in America and elsewhere, and after the publication of the book Sarojini Naidu, with the blessing of the Indian National Congress, went on a speaking tour of the United States to publicize the nationalist cause and to undo the damage that Mayo's book had done. However, this was hardly an adequate explanation for the extent of the response in India, nor for the indignation that the book aroused.

According to Mrinalini Sinha, whose introduction to a recent reprint of Mayo's book is the best study of the controversy, the key to the extraordinary affair of *Mother India* lay in its timing rather than its content. The book appeared just as a Conservative government in Britain was preparing to appoint the Indian Statutory (Simon) Commission to examine the workings of the Government of India Act of 1919. This act had conceded the principle of self-governing institutions by creating elected assemblies in the provinces, with control over some governmental functions. The concessions were limited – the elected provincial governments had control over only local matters, the British governors of the provinces continued to exercise supervisory control and veto powers, and the franchise upon which provincial governments were elected was a very narrow one – but the act had nevertheless been vehemently opposed by many in Britain and by large sections of colonial officialdom in India. It was hoped by die-hard imperialists (and feared by nationalists) that the all-white Simon Commission was designed to check any further concessions. Since the passage of the Government of India Act Indian nationalism had also been transformed, for the first time becoming genuinely India-wide during the Non-cooperation Movement of 1921–22, during which the gap between middle-class nationalism and the peasantry had seemingly been bridged. The years since the mass upsurge was called off had been a period of relative quietude, but the transformation of the Indian National Congress into a mass organization signaled the coming to maturity of the nationalist cause, reflected in part in the declaration by Congress some months after the appearance of *Mother India* that independence was its goal, a radicalization which was affirmed at the 1929 Congress. A second wave of India-wide mass protests followed during the Civil Disobedience campaign of 1930–34. Thus it was "the changing imperatives of British imperialism and Indian nationalism in the 1920s that helped make a book, which was hardly original in its subject or exceptional in its argument, the centre of an unprecedented international controversy."[83]

Sinha's explanation of the *Mother India* controversy thus hinges upon the context in which the book appeared, and dismisses its content as "hardly original or exceptional." The most that could be said about the book's content is that it provided one of "the most systematic elaborations" of the "old imperialist theme" of India's backwardness being manifested in the treatment of Indian women.[84] I find this explanation persuasive in part, but incomplete.

What I offer below, through a close reading of *Mother India*, is a supplementary reading, one which draws attention to its content and the "artistry" with which it was presented, and which focuses on a theme in the book which, while not exactly original, gave it a polemical edge that helps explain why it fueled so much debate, as well as what was at stake in that debate.

Reading *Mother India*

The first chapter of *Mother India* is titled "The Argument" and lays out Mayo's reasons for undertaking her trip to India, and what she discovered and concluded after her investigations. The chapter is preceded by an introduction which functions to set the scene for what is to come, not by outlining what the book is about – chapter 1 performs that task – but by providing what is part camera-eye description and part first-person eyewitness account and travelogue.[85] It is the best-written part of a book that is in parts exceedingly well written – as Gandhi for one conceded.[86]

This introduction begins with images of Calcutta: "Calcutta, big, western modern, with public buildings, monuments, parks, gardens, hospitals, museums, University, courts of law, hotels, offices, shops, all of which might belong to a prosperous American city"; "Decorous, sophisticated Calcutta, where decorous and sophisticated people of all creeds, all colors and all costumes go to Government House Garden Parties, pleasantly to make their bows to Their Excellencies, and pleasantly to talk good English while they take their tea and ices and listen to the regimental band." Just outside the Government House Gardens, obscured by their walls, is a busy street filled with limousines, cars, taxis, and "rolling among them now and again, a sort of Fifth Avenue bus, bearing the big-lettered label, 'Kali Ghat.'" The cinematic descriptions continue, now through a tracking shot – we follow the bus as it proceeds past further signs of the modern and the western – "past the Empire Theater, the various clubs, St. Paul's Cathedral, past the Bishop's House, the General Hospital, the London Missionary Society's Institution" – till it finally reaches its destination.

Kali Ghat or "the place of Kali," Mayo explains, is the root-word from which Calcutta gets its name, and the Hindu goddess Kali is the wife of Siva, the god of destruction and blood and death sacrifice. The description now shifts from the impersonal eye of the camera to the first person. One of the Brahmins who owns Kali Ghat, accompanied by a Brahmin friend named Mr. Haldar ("Mr Haldar might have been taken for a well-groomed northern

Italian gentleman. His English was polished and his manner entirely agree-
able"), leads Mayo around it. Cleaving their way through the masses of devotees and the booths where sweets, amulets, and the like are sold, Mayo and
her party arrive inside the shrine of the temple. As they survey the figure
of the goddess ("Black of face . . . with a monstrous lolling tongue, drip-
ping blood") there is a shrill bleating, and the party turns the corner to see
two priests sacrificing a young goat: "A crash of sound, as before the goddess
drums thunder . . . with a single blow of his cutlass [the priest] decapitates
the little creature. The blood gushes forth on the pavement, the drums and
the gongs before the goddess burst out wildly. 'Kali! Kali! Kali!' shout all the
priests and the suppliants together . . . Meantime, and instantly, a woman
who waited behind the killers of the goat has rushed forward and fallen on
all fours to lap up the blood with her tongue – in the hope of having a child."
Mr Haldar tells her, "with some pride," that 150–200 kids are killed in this
manner each day.

The members of the party resume their tour, now passing the minor
deities – the little red goddess of smallpox, the five-headed black cobra, the
monkey-god "to which rich merchants and students of the University pray,
before confronting examinations or risking new ventures in trade," and the
phallic symbol of Siva. They proceed down a lane, where scores of holy men
and mendicants sit, "mostly fat and hairy" (this is one of the few places in
the Introduction where Mayo allows herself to comment, rather than let descriptions and images stand in for the authorial voice). They pass a young
man who is tied by a scarf to the "tiny wrist" of a little girl – a husband and
his new wife, Mr. Haldar informs her, come to the temple to pray for the
birth of a son. There follows a description of the cremation of a "beautiful
young Indian woman," whose forehead, hands, and feet are painted red, to
indicate that she is blessed and fortunate to have died before her husband,
rather than being left a widow. Some further scenes, before Mayo and the
party find their waiting car and depart, once again past the General Hospital
and the Bishop's House.

Many of the themes that will figure in the book – child marriage, primitive religious customs, the horror of widowhood which renders death auspi-
cious for a married woman, and so on – are presented here. But they do not
figure as "themes," for there is no elaboration and condemnation – that will
come later in the book. They are instead introduced as tableaux, a series of
images, discrete and yet related (Kali Ghat, and the Hinduism that it stands
for, provide the context which relates these diverse tableaux and makes them

part of one larger scene). The Introduction does not outline themes that will be the subject of subsequent repetition, but rather presents a picture of, and a context for, what is to come. Or rather, two pictures. For what this introduction artfully does is present a vivid contrast between modern Calcutta and the Calcutta that cannot be seen through the walls of the Government House Gardens, the Calcutta of Kali Ghat.

When James Mill penned his famous assessment and criticism of Indian civilization, it was at a time when the significant distinctions usually made between various aspects of a complex society were those between religious communities, between regions, and between urban and rural India. But there was no need to differentiate between a modern and a nonmodern India, since there was very little of modern Calcutta or modern India. More than a hundred years later, the "old imperialist theme" must also account for the markers of modernity, the hospitals and universities and law courts, and more especially the men "of all colours and creeds" who are apparently at ease in these settings, who speak good English and take their ices and listen to the regimental band. Some of these men now claim that India has begun the process of becoming a modern country, and that Indians like themselves are capable of governing India. The Introduction to *Mother India* draws attention to modern Calcutta, dwelling on the modern buildings, all the better to show that this is not the only India – that just outside the walls enclosing the artificial world within is another India, more numerous, more typical, more "real."

But it is not just that on the one hand there is a modern India and on the other a Hindu India of ancient superstitions and barbaric practices, which is the more representative of the real India. It is also that the two Indias are connected – the bus that functions as a device to shift scenes from one to the other also, and more literally, connects them, in that there is a constant trafficking between the two. These are not hermetically sealed worlds but rather overlapping ones; Kali Ghat is populated not just by ignorant peasants from the "old" India but also by the urbane Mr. Haldar, and the "rich merchants and University students" who pray to their monkey-god. And Mayo does not end her introduction with the image of the party which has toured Kali Ghat motoring back to the India of hospitals and law courts. It ends instead with a conversation, in which the events and images of the preceding pages are summed up – again, not by Mayo but by two interpreters: "Why did you go to Kali Ghat? That is not India. Only the lowest and most ignorant of Indians are Kali worshipers," said an English Theosophist, sadly, next day." Mayo repeats the words to "one of the most learned and distinguished of Bengali Brahmans," whose response she reports, and with which the Introduction concludes: "Your English friend is wrong. It is true that in the lower castes the percentage of worshipers of Kali is larger . . . But hundreds of thousands of Brahmans, everywhere, worship Kali, and the devotees at Kali Ghat will include Hindus of all castes and conditions, among whom are found some of the most highly educated and important personages of this town and of India." An English Theosophist – the foreignness of this enthusiast for Hinduism is mentioned twice – is contradicted by "one of the most learned and distinguished of Bengali Brahmans," who testifies that the traffic from the India of modern buildings and the university includes some of the most highly educated and distinguished of Indians.

THIS THEME – that whatever the differences, modern, western-educated India is as much steeped in barbaric practices and superstitious ways as traditional India – then runs through the book, accompanying its most important descriptions. Among the more graphic is one of a child bride (married to a fifty-year-old "Hindu gentleman") who goes mad from premature sex and arrives at a hospital "fouled," her internal wounds "alive with maggots," and whose husband is suing to recover his marital rights; she is, we are told, "of well-to-do, educated, city-dwelling stock," but her case "differed in no essential" from the next one that Mayo recounts, that of a simple village girl (54–55). In another chapter a "high-caste orthodox Brahman scholar easily at home in his European dress" tells Mayo that he will marry off his daughter at the age of five or seven, but in no case later than nine (68). This same chapter, "The Earthly God," details how Indian girls, once married, become servants in their new household, unable to rebel because the Hindu code enjoins absolute subservience to their in-laws, and teaches them to regard their husband as their god. She quotes in extenso from an account of life in the zenana, where a woman's job is to serve her mother-in-law and please her husband, and the only source of respect and status is the act of giving birth to a son, and adds, "this general characterization of the wife in the *zenana* of educated, well-to-do, and prominent Hindus finds its faithful echo . . . in humbler fields. For the orthodox Hindu woman, *whoever she be*, will obey the law of her ancestors and her gods with a pride and integrity *unaffected by her social condition*" (78, emphasis added). The eponymous chapter on Mother India, with famous descriptions of the dirty and barbarous practices of childbirth, cites doctors who declare that the practices are by no means confined

to the lower classes but also common among men with university degrees –
some of them college lecturers. Mayo adds her own voice to those of her informants, "Evidence is in hand of educated, traveled and well-born Indians,
themselves holders of European university degrees, who permit their wives
to undergo this same inheritance of darkness" (101). The chapter on the slow
pace of female education cites testimony presented to the Calcutta University Commission to show that even western-educated Indians are extremely
ambivalent about educating their daughters and wives, and that even where
they loudly proclaim their commitment to reform of women's condition,
they seldom translate their words into deeds.[87]

Here and elsewhere, and at almost every point in her indictment of Indian
customs and practices, Mayo is at pains to demonstrate – always by quoting
expert authorities and witnesses, Indian and British, and sometimes by also
interposing her own voice – that her catalogue of horrors is not confined to
the "old" India but is very much a part of the India that includes Government House Gardens and the "western educated, well-to-do Indians" who
inhabit this domain. Her claim is not merely that this latter India is only
the tip and that the India of superstition and degraded women is the ice-
berg, but also that they are, as this metaphor suggests, of one piece – that
western-educated Indians are as much part of backward India as their poor
and uneducated countrymen are. Modern Indians clamor for self-rule and
constantly denounce the British, but their claim, and nationalism's claim, to
be the agency for the modernization of India is negated not only by their
ignorance of the India of poverty and of the villages and their lack of interest in finding out about it, but also and equally, as Mayo endeavors to show,
by their being part of the same religious and mental world: "Britain, by her
educational effort, has gradually raised up an element before unknown in
India – a middle class. But this middle class – these lawyers and professional
men – are in the main as much dominated today as were their ancestors five
hundred years ago by the law of caste and transmigration – completest denial
of democracy. They talk of 'the people' simply because the word bulks large in
the vocabulary of that western-born representative government which they
now essay" (295–96).

The Agency of Modernity

Mother India did not simply draw attention, as others had done, to the allegedly "backward" practices of the Indian home, and document the bar-

barities inflicted upon women. It additionally used this backwardness and these barbarities to suggest that not only was India something less than modern, but that those who claimed to be in a position to lead her to modernity were themselves not modern; incapable of transforming their homes, how could they transform the nation they wished to lead? The very claims that nationalism made for sovereignty over the Indian home, and thus for exclusive authority over the project of modernizing it, also rendered the project vulnerable; and it was this that Mother India adroitly tapped into, and why it aroused such a furor of denunciation.

This is seen not only in the controversy generated by Mother India but especially in the specific character of the response to it. Among the range of reactions which Mother India provoked in India, from a purely defensive denial of all its charges to counter-accusations that the West was obsessed with sex and that its family structures were riddled with oppression and breakdown,[88] one was to denounce the book but urge that the best response to it was to proceed with a reform of women's condition. Gandhi, in a response titled "Drain Inspector's Report," denounced Mayo's book but also wrote, "it is a book that every Indian can read with profit . . . Overdrawn her picture of our insanitation, child-marriages etc undoubtedly are. But let them serve as a spur to much greater effort than we have hitherto put forth in order to rid society of all causes of reproach . . . Our indignation which we are bound to express against the slanderous book must not blind us to our obvious limitations."[89] This was the response adopted by the women's organizations which had begun to emerge in India in the early twentieth century. At a large protest meeting called by these organizations in Triplicane in Madras, Jayalakshmi Kumar declared, "we want political freedom so that we may compel social improvement . . . Let us endeavour to change the really bad social customs [in India] and let that be our protest against all such books"; a resolution passed at this meeting denounced the book while urging the need for legislation against child marriage and enforced widowhood.[90] One of the results of this furor was the passage of the Child Marriage Restraint Bill; those who had been pressing for it long before Mayo's book appeared now received strong support from nationalist ranks, and were able to pass it in 1929, over the timidity of the colonial authorities.[91] Mayo's book proved the catalyst – though not of course the cause – for a newfound commitment in nationalist ranks to matching words with deeds.

In the area of female education, similarly, things begin to change in the late 1920s and 1930s. From this time we see a narrowing of the gap between the discourse of female education and educational statistics on the numbers of girls enrolled. The gap remained – the quinquennial survey of education for 1932–37 found that only 14 percent of girls who enrolled in school proceeded to even reach the fourth grade, completion of which was conventionally defined as the minimal requirement for attaining literacy,[92] and on the eve of Independence there were only 232,000 girls in high schools, compared to almost two million boys[93] – but whereas in an earlier period official reports lamented native resistance to the education of girls, now they began to note that demand for girls' education was outstripping supply,[94] and that for the first time the increase in the number of girls enrolled was greater than the increase in boys.[95] That the small amounts of government spending on education were principally spent on boys now began to be widely lamented,[96] and for the first time it was noted that the private initiative of Indians in setting up girls' schools was meeting part of this gap,[97] as had happened decades earlier for boys' education. By the 1930s, Francesca Orsini points out, college girls and even educated working women began to appear in Hindi writings without any opprobrium being attached to their status, even as the usual injunctions against "westernization" continued.[98]

Mother India was not the "cause" of any of this, but it was a catalyst for nationalists seeking to reform the condition of women with greater vigor than before. Mrinalini Sinha characterizes the consequences of the debate as follows: "The debate on the woman question during the *Mother India* controversy would become a vehicle for Indian nationalism to stake its claim as the only truly modernising force in colonial Indian society, wresting that claim away from the colonial government."[99] I think that is exactly right, but would add that the controversy over *Mother India* led nationalists to seek to translate into action a claim which they had begun to make much earlier. As we have seen, by the latter nineteenth century an emergent nationalism had divided the world into an "outer," material domain, where western superiority was conceded and was to be emulated, and an "inner," spiritual domain, seen as the repository of essential Indian values. The spiritual domain included India's women, over whom nationalism claimed exclusive authority, including exclusive authority to "modernize" middle-class women and to modernize Indian domesticity, so that it would keep pace with the changing needs of a modern nation-to-be while continuing to signify and embody an essential Indianness. Female education was a part of this project, and the many voices urging it seemed to indicate that the nationalist élites were both cognizant of and capable of undertaking the necessary task of modernizing India's women and Indian homes. But the discourse on women's education was also marked by an anxiety that modernizing India's women might in fact undermine woman's role as the embodiment and guardian of Indianness. Indeed, the sheer voluminousness of this discourse made it function as a substitute for, rather than a prelude to, concerted action.

In claiming to show that the very area over which nationalism claimed exclusive sway was one where "backwardness" and "medievalism" continued to reign, and thus that those who claimed to lead and remake the nation had not the will to even remake their women and their homes, *Mother India* ignited a debate. The peculiar place and function of the woman question in nationalist discourse had prepared the grounds for that debate. It was here that nationalism had staked a special claim to sovereignty, but where it was, consequently, most vulnerable to the charge that its claims to being the agency of modernization were belied by a mismatch between rhetoric and results. *Mother India* and the controversy that it generated thus proved the catalyst for a claim staked out much earlier, the claim that nationalism was the only agency with the authority and ability to modernize Indian women and Indian homes.

CHAPTER SIX

Vernacular Modernity
The Nationalist Imagination

The British claim that colonial rule was a pedagogic enterprise for the improvement of India, and that western education was one of the means toward this end, was largely accepted by the new élites emerging under British rule. The members and leaders of the nationalist organizations founded in the latter part of the nineteenth century – most of them western-educated[1] – often singled out western education as one of the most important and valuable instruments through which the British were transforming India. The annual sessions of the Indian National Congress were frequently the occasion for such effusions: Sankaran Nair told the 1897 Congress session, "British rule . . . furnished us with the one element, English education, which was necessary to rouse us from the torpor of ages"; at the 1902 Congress Surendranath Banerjea declared, "The three great boons which we have received from the British Government are High Education, the gift of a free Press and local Self-Government . . . but High Education is the most prized, the most deeply cherished of them all"; and B. N. Dhar told the 1911 session of the Congress that "the educational system which has immortalised the names of Bentinck and Macaulay is perhaps [Britain's] greatest gift to the people of India."[2] If nationalists and educated Indian public opinion more generally had a misgiving, it was that the colonial government did not provide enough of this much-valued western education. By the latter nineteenth century the complaint that the colonial authorities were not doing enough to promote education had become ubiquitous; at the same time that notables in Congress were lauding British rule for having provided India with western education, the annual sessions of the Congress that they addressed were passing resolutions urging the British Indian government to provide more of it.[3]

At the beginning of the new century educational reforms undertaken by the viceroy, Lord Curzon, were interpreted by educated Indians as an effort to

diminish Indian access to western education and to assert dictatorial government control over the educational sector, and were vigorously condemned.
Officialdom and Indian opinion were from this time polarized on the subject
of education, often bitterly so. The British characterized the Indian position as
a selfish one – so eager were the Indian middle classes to obtain the precious
certification regarded as a passport to employment that they cared nothing
about the poor quality of this education, and resisted all attempts to improve
it. "Multiply senators, multiply colleges, multiply university centres, courses
and faculties – and all will be well," was how one critic of the Indian position characterized it.[4] Indians conversely saw in every government initiative
a hidden agenda directed at whittling back and controlling the education
sector. Sir Narayan Chandarvarkar, judge in the High Court of Bombay and
one-time vice-chancellor of Bombay University, explained that the educated
classes were not unconcerned about efficiency and quality, but expressed the
fear "that in the name of 'efficiency' of University education the interests of
its diffusion are likely to be sacrificed in India";[5] and Curzon himself referred
with frustration to the "suspicion that [the government] encounters among
the educated classes that we really desire to restrict their opportunities and
in some way or other to keep them down."[6]

The demand for "more" education did not abate. However, from the last
decade of the nineteenth century demands for more education were joined by
a growing volume of criticism directed not simply at the insufficiency of education but at the inadequacies of the existing system.[7] By the early decades
of the twentieth century the criticism had become a torrent, commented on
by all observers of the educational scene. Government statements on education policy regularly noted the many criticisms of the system of education,[8]
and at convocation ceremonies it was observed that university education was
being criticized from all quarters, for all manner of sins. In 1938 the Indian
vice-chancellor of Dacca University complained that "the blame for every evil
from which the country is suffering is laid at the door of the University. The
unemployment problem, the acute economic distress, the physical weakness
of girls and boys, backwardness in trade and industry, absence of a proper
national spirit, lack of reverence for one's own society and country, the way-
ward conduct of youth, and the irreligious outlook of the present generation
are all supposed to be due to the defective system of University education."[9]
An inspector of schools attempted to sum up the indictment: "The Indian intelligentsia has attempted to diagnose the defects of the educational system

variously: it has made men mercenary and does not build character; its aims have been secular and leave no room for godliness; it has neglected physical, moral and religious training; it has made men unpractical and has neglected vocational education . . . ; it imparts instruction through a foreign tongue and has made sound education impossible; it has estranged the masses from the educated classes . . . and lastly, it has utterly ignored India's past culture, traditions, philosophy, arts, learning and history and has bred in the youth no love for their country."[10]

This plethora of criticisms fell into two broad categories. The first was that western education was failing to produce the effects which it had been expected would follow from its provision. Education was meant to be producing young men who could think for themselves and were prepared for a variety of tasks and challenges, but for the most part was producing men who regurgitated information they had crammed in examinations and were fit for nothing but clerkdom in the government service; was meant to instill a modern outlook on the world but had instilled intellectual and moral confusion instead; was meant to reshape lives, but was so far removed from the Indian's home life that life at school and life at home never connected.[11] In short, education was to be the instrument for modernity, and in this it was failing. This was more than the complaint that there was not enough western education for it to perform its modernizing role; it was rather the complaint that it was failing in this role because the vehicle of transformation was itself counterfeit. Indeed, there was a widespread perception that western education in India was the name of the thing, rather than the thing itself. We encountered evidence of this in previous chapters: a pamphleteer in Cuttack lamenting, "There are hardly any such things as students in the proper sense of the term in our country";[12] an eminent Indian convert to Christianity complaining of the mechanical way in which students studied ("A copying machine could do the same");[13] the editor of an important newspaper describing Indian universities as "bad imitations" of the (already imperfect) English originals,[14] and Indian colleges as "coaching agencies mis-named colleges."[15] These and other witnesses decried, time and again, that India had only the shadow of students, not the substance; colleges which were really mere coaching agencies; learning processes which could be performed by copying machines; schools and universities which had neither real students nor provided real learning, and which were themselves only the name-of-a-university. The debate on western education in India, one could say, came to be haunted by the specter of nominalism: the fear that the agency of modernity was not the real thing but merely something bearing the name of the thing, not the genuine article but a simulacrum.

The second category into which we can group criticisms of education were laments about the effects that western education was having, rather than what education was failing to do. Rooted in an alien culture, under the control of a foreign ruler, not having been adapted to the character of those subject to it, western education was alienating its products from their own traditions. Lajpat Rai described the existing system of western education as "emasculating and enervating . . . denationalising and degrading."[16] Har Dayal referred to "the utter wreck of national self-respect which has followed the establishment of the British schools and colleges in India."[17] The art historian A. K. Coomaraswamy described the educational system as one "that has ignored or despised almost every ideal informing the national culture," the products of which were "stranger[s] in their own land."[18] The latter observation – that in becoming alienated from their culture the western-educated had also become cut off and estranged from their compatriots – was very commonly made. When first introduced, western education had been widely expected to produce a class who would function as intermediaries between their rulers and the masses of their countrymen. This had been one of the justifications for government patronage of education, and had become part of the self-understanding of educated Indians. Now it was said, "Neither trusted by their masters nor by the masses they form a class by themselves."[19] Rabindranath Tagore described the gulf between the western-educated and other Indians as "the worst caste system that prevails at present in the country,"[20] and Bipan Chandra Pal similarly adjudged this chasm to be even greater than that between high castes and untouchables.[21]

These two broad criticisms – that western education was failing as a vehicle of modernity, and that it was "denationalizing" its products – were not, on the face of it, logically related. The first criticism was voiced not only by Indians and Indian nationalists but also often by the colonial authorities themselves. Below I focus on the second criticism, which was more explicitly nationalist, and on the various efforts to devise an education that would reinforce rather than undermine national identity. It will turn out, however, that in the nationalist imagination the two criticisms were seen to be closely connected, and this being so, the various schemes for a "national" education sought a single solution to both problems.

National(ist) Education

The criticisms of the new, western education system led to various attempts at providing alternatives, which would compensate for the perceived short-comings of the official system. The Arya Samaj, a reformist Hindu move-ment with its base in Punjab, founded the Dayanand Anglo-Vedic (DAV) High School in 1886 and the DAV College, Lahore, in 1889. The DAV "movement" – the high school and college were soon joined by many schools all over Pun-jab – sought to provide an education which would combine "modern" and therefore western knowledge with knowledge of Sanskrit and training in the "true," Vedic origins of Hinduism, before these were corrupted by evil social practices and idolatry. The management of the school, and its curriculum, reflected these goals.[22]

On a smaller scale, but very much in the public eye, were the educational experiments of India's Nobel laureate Rabindranath Tagore. Tagore founded his school at Santiniketan in 1901, the Viswa-Bharati university in 1919,[23] and Sriniketan, his school for "rural reconstruction," in 1921. All were outside the official system, which Tagore characterized as mechanical and productive of imitation rather than originality. "We had to sit," Tagore wrote, referring to his own unhappy encounters with schooling as a young boy – "inert, like dead specimens of some museum, whilst lessons were pelted at us from on high, like hailstones on flowers."[24] The contrasts that Tagore continually drew in his writings and speeches – between discipline and freedom, nature and the natural versus the artificial and mechanical, passive versus active – provided the background to his own pedagogic mission. At Santiniketan it was recog-nized that the "restless wings given them [children] by nature" are absolutely necessary for discovery and growth, and that seeking to discipline this rest-less enquiry usually killed learning.[25] "In proper schools boys ... must never be boisterous, they must not laugh too loud. But boys are born savages and must pass through the stage of savagedom. I let them run and climb and swing and when the rain fell, go out and get thoroughly drenched in the open air."[26] As in the ancient *tapavana*, or forest school, after which Tagore's school was modeled, teachers and pupils lived as a community, freedom con-quered discipline, play was preferred to work, classes were conducted outside in the open air, and the aim was to allow the child to develop rather than force him into a mold. Tagore's educational endeavors were an always implicit and often explicit critique – as much on Rousseauan and Pestalozzian grounds as nationalist ones – of the existing educational system.[27]

The Muhammadan Anglo-Oriental College (from 1920 the Aligarh Muslim University) and the Benares Hindu University (1915) were both self-conscious attempts to provide to religious communities an education that would equip them with the modern knowledge necessary to face the (colonial) world, as well as instruction in their cultural and religious tradition.[28] Knowledge of and pride in their ancestral (religious) traditions was to be a hallmark of the education provided at AMU and BHU. The Muhammadan Anglo-Indian College played an important role in the development of a new Muslim identity,[29] and BHU played an important role in the development of syllabi and textbooks in Hindi, produced a great many Hindi writers and critics, and trained teachers who would go on to teach in Hindi.[30]

These various efforts were all nationalist inasmuch as part of what they stressed and sought to offer to students was some quality of "Indianness" (or Hinduness or Muslimness) felt to be lacking in the official government system, if not directly undermined by it. Tagore's schools and university additionally sought to provide a more creative education than the officially mandated one. But one of the persistent problems to plague such alternatives was that the instrumental advantages of education – recognized certification, prestige (especially that associated with knowledge of English), and the like – all belonged to the official system. Any alternative, "national" or otherwise, usually sought to retain some of the attractions of the official system, for fear of losing students;[31] and in most cases (with the partial exception of Tagore's institutions) they sought to achieve recognition as bona fide institutions from state authorities, and to add to or amend the authorized curriculum rather than altogether replace it. The result, as the editor of the *Dawn* put it in 1908, was that institutions established and controlled by Indians tended to become "replicas of the Government model, without a separate mission or nobler reason for existence."[32] Thus it was in one sense a measure of the DAV High School's achievement that its students sat for the matriculation exam for entrance to university with great success, and that the school and college came to be commended by the government; but in the eyes of some supporters this also came to be seen as a failing, with some Arya Samajis complaining that the school "began to turn out not Gautamas and Kanads, but babus."[33] Disagreements over the direction which education was taking was one of the reasons behind a split in the Arya Samaj in the early years of the twentieth century, with the departing members seeking to establish schools which provided an education fundamentally different from that provided within the official educational system.[34] Tagore's school ignored the official curriculum, and its students took the matriculation exam for entry to Calcutta University as "private students" rather than as pupils of Santiniketan, but late in his life Tagore was to complain that even his college and school "are every day becoming more and more like so many schools and colleges elsewhere in this country: borrowed cages that treat the students' minds as captive birds, whose sole human value is judged according to the mechanical repetition of lessons, prescribed by an educational dispensation foreign to the soil."[35]

There were also more overtly nationalist challenges to the dominant education system. The slogan of "national education" was raised during the Swadeshi agitation in Bengal (1905–8), which followed upon the announcement of the colonial government's decision to partition the province of Bengal. As part of the general protest the call was raised for students to withdraw from government schools and colleges. Frantic efforts were then made to establish alternative educational institutions. The National Council of Education (NCE), established in 1906 to found a "national" education system, sought to establish a network of schools under Indian control, unfettered by government inspections and direction; the aim was to provide an education drawing upon and emphasizing the richness of Indian traditions, delivered in Indian languages, with English taught as a second language.[36] For a period the NCE met with an enthusiastic response, and it succeeded in raising money and establishing a network of schools, as well as its flagship, the Bengal National College and School, in Calcutta. However, the usual problems soon began to appear, including inadequate funds and the low esteem in which the certification offered by the alternative schools was held in the marketplace; and as the Swadeshi agitation itself began to wane, so too did enthusiasm for the NCE system. The historian of the Swadeshi movement, Sumit Sarkar, sums up the results thus: "One or two model institutions, at Santiniketan or Calcutta, surviving as examples of non-political constructive swadeshi; a number of national schools in East Bengal serving as seminaries and recruiting grounds for revolutionary terrorism – such were the remnants of national education in Bengal in the decade succeeding 1910."[37]

The call for a "national" education to replace the existing educational system was, however, now on the agenda. In 1911 and again in 1916 the annual session of the Congress passed a resolution declaring that "the time had arrived for people all over the country to earnestly take up the question of national education ... and organize a system of education ... suited to the requirements of the country, on national lines and under national control"[38] – a significant departure from earlier years, when Congress resolutions had simply called upon the colonial government to provide more education. The call to boycott the officially sanctioned education system was raised again during the Non-cooperation movement of 1920–22, this time nationwide. The premise behind the mass campaign of "non-cooperation" was that British rule survived principally because Indians were complicit in it, and conversely, that it would be morally and politically undermined if they refused to co-operate. Thus the call for non-cooperation or boycott included education, and no one raised the clarion call as loudly, nor as emphatically, as Gandhi. Again, efforts were made to establish an alternative system. *Vidyapiths* and other national schools and colleges were established to offer an alternative to "cooperating" with institutions that maintained the legitimacy of British rule, institutions which, in Gandhi's words, made of Indians what they "were intended to become – clerks and interpreters."[39]

"The aim of national education," Gandhi wrote in *Young India*, "is just the opposite. It is to turn out . . . men determined to end the alien rule."[40] At times it seemed that national schools were not principally about schooling at all: "We did not start the Vidyapith and other institutions connected with it merely for the sake of education," Gandhi told the students of the Guja-rat Vidyapith, with which he was closely associated: "We started the Vidya-pith as a part of the campaign for non-cooperation . . . [. It is] an associa-tion for Swaraj."[41] Accordingly, what was important was not simply whether these institutions remained independent of the government-mandated sys-tem of grants and inspections, or which textbooks they used or how they taught history.[42] What was most important was whether they furthered the aims of self-purification which were an essential and defining element of swaraj, namely spinning, fighting the practice of untouchability, and pro-moting amity among India's religious communities. Gandhi told the stu-dents of the Gujarat Mahavidyalaya that they were not there principally to learn good English, or even good Sanskrit: "You are here to learn and acquire things which you will not get elsewhere and which are far superior to those enumerated above. These are: the Charkha, removal of untouchability . . . and the unity of Hindus and Muslims and Parsis . . . It is of no account if you pass in all other things except these."[43] National schools were less schools than (as Gandhi told the annual session of the Indian National Congress at Belgaum in 1924) "factories where the first instruments of our freedom are forged."[44] At other times, however, Gandhi would emphasize pedagogic and not simply political differences. He would declare: "[There is] a world of differ-ence between our method of teaching and theirs."[45] And indeed, in national schools all teaching was done in the mother tongue of the region; history and economics were taught from an Indian, patriotic point of view; even in the teaching of math, the examples used sought to relate to Indian life; and manual training, a favourite theme of Gandhi's, received great emphasis.[46]

Gandhi, Tagore, the Arya Samaj, and various other proponents of national education all adjudged the existing education system to be disastrously flawed. It disseminated knowledge alien to the history and traditions of India, through institutions and practices which were foreign imports. It was thus necessary to substitute an education that was "national." But what, precisely, was "national" about national education? The nationalist, educationalist, and Arya Samaj leader Lajpat Rai put the question with his customary directness: "What do we mean by national education? Is it the language which is the medium of instruction, which makes it national, or the agency through which it is imparted, or the agency which controls and regulates it, or the books which are taught or the standards or ideals which underlie it?"[47]

As we have seen, the answers varied, from the Arya Samaji stress on Sanskrit and reformist Hinduism, to Tagore's mix of Pestalozzian pedagogy and Bengali romanticism, to Gandhi's ferocious championing of the self-reform of Hindu society. The variety of answers is testimony to the richness of the nationalist imagination. However, no one seriously proposed what might seem the most obvious answer of all: that national education purvey the traditional or indigenous knowledges of India.

Tradition and Indigeneity

In October 1931, while in London to attend the "Round Table" conference occasioned by the civil disobedience movement against British rule, M. K. Gandhi gave a lengthy speech at the Royal Institute of International Affairs, in the course of which he declared that the British had come to India with little understanding or respect for Indian institutions, and with an arrogant conviction of their superiority. Everywhere, "instead of taking hold of things as they were, [they] began to root them out," replacing the tried and true with elaborate schemes and programs. In the field of education, "ancient schools have gone by the board, because there was no recognition for these schools, and the schools [newly] established after the European pattern were too expensive for the people." "I say without fear of my figures being challenged successfully," Gandhi continued, that as a result "today India is more illiterate than it was fifty or a hundred years ago."[48]

Gandhi's figures were in fact challenged at the meeting and subsequently by Sir Philip Hartog, who had played an important role in educational affairs in Britain and India.[49] Pressed by Hartog, Gandhi declared that if he were shown to have erred in reasoning or facts, he would publicly acknowledge as much. With all the tenacity of the proverbial British bulldog, Hartog hounded Gandhi over the next eight years with census data and other figures which he claimed proved Gandhi wrong, and pressed Gandhi to either refute the figures or else keep his promise and publicly retract. Gandhi offered what statistical evidence he could and stuck to his guns, though with characteristic courtesy he did not discontinue the correspondence, even after the British Indian government had placed him in Yeravda Central jail.[50]

Gandhi's was not the only voice at this time to raise the specter of a once-flourishing system of indigenous education and its sad decline. A spate of articles and books attested to the existence of an extensive system of instruction throughout pre-British India, and indeed stretching back to ancient times. The first scholarly book of this kind was by a European, F. E. Keay's *Ancient Indian Education* (1918), and it noted that the subject matter was "unexplored"; in the next decade it was extensively explored, such that by 1930 a contributor to the growing literature on ancient Indian education could refer to it as a "branch of Indology."[51] Scholarly books were supplemented by numerous articles and essays in the press which sought to show that Indians were not barbarians, but rather had valued and cultivated learning for centuries before the advent of the British – enough that Edward Thompson and his co-author G. T. Garrat remarked in irritation, "The state of education in India before the British occupation is, unfortunately, a favourite subject for political dissertations."[52]

The idea that India had had a rich tradition of learning was useful for promoting national pride. The charge sometimes made, as by Gandhi – that the British had destroyed a well-functioning indigenous system of education, and had thereby made Indians illiterate – was a useful stick with which to beat the British. But for all this, very few nationalists suggested a return to the "nonscientific" learning of the *tol* or the *madrassa*; few disputed that the day of nonmodern knowledges was long gone. There were some exceptions. According to Har Dayal, British political conquest had been supplemented and reinforced by the "social conquest" of the Hindus, and western education had been the prime instrument for effecting it. The knowledges of which the Brahmin had been custodian had been replaced by the western knowledge dispensed by the Englishman, with the result that "the respect and influence which he used to command . . . is resigned by the Brahman and occupied by the Briton."[53] The implication, though not clearly spelled out, seemed to be that Indians needed to turn their back on western learning and western institutions, since these functioned to place the colonizer in the position of teacher, with the Indian as pupil. Benoy Kumar Sarkar, one of the teachers at the Bengal National College, argued that the traditional "pedagogy of the Hindu" needed to be revived not only for the sake of Hindu but to guide a West that had lost its way.[54] Pramatha Nath Bose, one of the first Indians to obtain a B.Sc. from England, in his old age declared himself an opponent of "progress" and modern civilization, and expressed skepticism toward the various attempts to leaven western knowledge with doses of Indian identity; instead he advocated a return to the "traditional" or indigenous system of learning that had served India well through many centuries.[55]

But even such voices were not always consistent,[56] and in any case they were very much in the minority. Nationalists typically sought to harness and synthesize western knowledge with some quality of Indianness, to forge a "national education" that would equip the nation with science and modern knowledge while making the recipients of this knowledge more, rather than less, conscious of and proud of their Indian identity. Thus Lajpat Rai declared that while there were things to admire in the indigenous system, "any widespread revival of the ancient or medieval systems of education is unthinkable,"[57] because that would mark national regress rather than progress. Of those few who did advocate a return to the older systems, the outspoken Lajpat Rai wrote, "I do not know whether they are idiots or traitors."[58]

When proposals were made for a revival of Oriental learning, they were usually rejected by those for whom they were intended. In the 1870s, after the establishment of Punjab University College, the Anjuman-i-Punjab and its European president, Dr. G. W. Leitner (principal of Lahore Government College) campaigned for a full-fledged university run along "Oriental" lines. This was met with a shower of criticism, and the *Tribune*, an Indian-owned newspaper in Punjab, led a determined campaign against it.[59] A growing band of critics pointed out that the proposal was an official creation, dressed up to look like a "spontaneous" demand from élite Indian opinion. The Indian members of the Anjuman, it was pointed out, were dignitaries dependent upon official goodwill for their prestige – the *Tribune* wryly observed, "if to-day the Government is to decide that education is to be imparted through the Hebrew language, to-morrow our big wigs will come forward with their money to help their new scheme."[60] Critics claimed that the proposal to establish a university in Punjab different from those earlier established in Madras, Bombay, and Calcutta was driven by political and not pedagogical imperatives. The real agenda of government, these critics alleged, was to protect Punjab from the criticism and "sedition" which colonial officialdom thought was a consequence of creating a class of English-educated babus in Bengal. But this attitude of colonial officials, critics argued, overlooked precisely one of the main virtues of a western education in English, which was valuable not only for the knowledge it imparted but because it was "producing a great revolution in the character of the people of this country ... greater courage, greater resolution, and greater firmness are being installed into the minds of young India by English education."[61]

A return to indigenous knowledges was thus never part of the nationalist agenda, which sought instead the wider diffusion of western education, albeit with a strong leavening of "national" content. Indigenous knowledges were not cast aside. They continued to be studied and cultivated, sometimes with encouragement and support from government. However, in these cases the knowledges themselves underwent a transformation and ceased to be the repositories of a living intellectual tradition. The fate of Sanskrit learning is a good example, worth considering at some length.

From Living Tradition to "Critical Knowledge"

Even before the British made provision for government funding of indigenous instruction in 1813, individual Englishmen had established, or induced the colonial government to establish and patronize, institutions devoted to cultivating and teaching Oriental knowledges. Governor General Warren Hastings established the Calcutta Madrassa in 1780, initially out of his own pocket. In 1791 Jonathon Duncan, British resident in Benares, established Benares Sanskrit College and sought government support for his move, on the grounds that patronage of traditional Hindu learning would endear the British government to the Hindus, and also because the college would produce natives qualified to assist European judges in administering Hindu law.[62] Self-interested calculations played a role in colonial patronage of Oriental knowledge, but so too did the enthusiasm aroused by the first translations of Sanskrit works, and by William Jones's discovery of the common linguistic roots of Sanskrit, Latin, and Greek. By the late eighteenth century and into the early decades of the nineteenth, there was an enthusiasm throughout Europe for the language and literatures of Sanskrit, an enthusiasm that has even been characterized as an "Oriental renaissance."[63] Thus when the colonial authorities began to provide money for education, it was indigenous education that they funded; the founding of Benares Sanskrit College was followed in the 1820s by the founding of similar colleges in Calcutta and Pune.

Benares Sanskrit College, for instance, employed Indian *pandits* and *vaids* as teachers, and initially they were free to determine the curriculum. However, classes occurred in an institutional setting, and the relation between *guru* and *shishya* [pupil] was replaced by a system in which teachers were paid by the government – as indeed were their students, who were in receipt of government stipends. In the 1820s examinations, prizes, and public debates were introduced, marking a significant mutation of "indigenous learning." For as we observed in chapter 1, in Indian traditions of learning the form in which knowledge was transmitted was inextricable from the content of the learning; the relationship between guru and shishya, for instance, was not an incidental form for transmitting a knowledge which existed and could be conceived independently of the modes of its transmission. If, as shown in chapter 1, "old" methods of learning "infected" the "new" learning, leading to rote learning of the new curriculum, then in this case it was the new form in which traditional learning was disseminated that effected a mutation in its content. Bernard Cohn sums up the results as follows: "The British conceived of education taking place in institutions . . . There were to be fixed positions of professors, teachers and assistants, who taught regular classes in subjects. The students' progress had to be regularly examined to measure their acquisition of fixed bodies of knowledge. The end of the process was marked by prizes and certification . . . Even with the undoubted good will and best intentions . . . a British metalogic of regularity, uniformity, and . . . fiscal responsibility could not help but participate in the erosion and transformation of what the British wanted to preserve, that is, Hindu and Muslim learning."[64]

Soon even the "goodwill" began to evaporate. The orientalists and colonial officials who entertained some admiration for Indian knowledges and traditions were soon vigorously challenged by evangelicals and utilitarians, who saw in Indian knowledges only the sources of religious errors and economic and social backwardness. Colonial rule increasingly came to be premised on the idea that the British were in India to educate and improve their subjects, and had nothing to learn from them. The victory in 1835 of the "Anglicist" party, which advocated spending government funds upon western learning rather than the cultivation of indigenous knowledge, was at once a mark of this mode of conceiving colonialism as a form of pedagogy and a milestone in its advance.

The institutions of indigenous learning earlier established by the British were continued, but in most cases also "reformed." Poona Sanskrit College, established in 1821, soon had an English school added to it, and in 1851 the English School and the Sanskrit College were combined to form an institution now renamed Poona College. The Bombay Board of Education explained the reasoning behind its decision: "By this amalgamation, the undue encouragement which . . . is at present given by the existence of a Sanskrit College, to the almost exclusive cultivation of a dead language and very ancient literature, would cease; while, at the same time, sufficient support would exist for the acquirement of sufficient Sanskrit for all philological purposes."[65] The Sanskrit College in Calcutta was reformed along similar lines, and much later the Indian Education (Hunter) Commission observed with satisfaction that the institution began to perform a useful function after the reforms, when "abandoning the idea of employing Sanskrit as a medium of instruction . . . it confined its study of that language to points literary and philological."[66] Similarly, in Benares Sanskrit College an English department was introduced, so that the college no longer exclusively taught nonwestern knowledges. In 1843 John Muir, a civil servant with the East India Company, was appointed to conduct an enquiry into the college. Muir was an accomplished Orientalist and a devout Christian who had engaged in polemics seeking to discredit Hinduism and prove the superiority of Christianity. Indeed, his two passions had come together only a few years earlier, in 1839, when he published *Matapariksa* (An Examination of Religions), a Christian polemic against Hinduism, in Sanskrit. Not surprisingly, Muir's report into the college recommended that the Hindu schools of philosophy or *darsanas*, "notoriously characterised by grave errors,"[67] be downgraded in the curriculum, a recommendation that he proceeded to implement when he was appointed in the following year to reorganize the college. His successor as principal of the college, J. R. Ballantyne, was similarly critical of aspects of "traditional" learning, and continued the process of downgrading indigenous knowledges.

The introduction of western education did not, however, have the effect of simply effacing knowledge of Sanskrit. There were institutional and curricular reasons why this was not so. Under the educational system introduced by the British, Sanskrit was offered as a subject in high school – compulsory in some regions, optional in others. The universities of Calcutta and Bombay, though they did not require study of a modern Indian language, required a second language for the entrance or intermediate exam, and for most students this was Sanskrit.[68] Perhaps more important, knowledge of India's ancient literature in Sanskrit did not disappear during the colonial period—on the contrary, it is sometimes said that the researches of European orientalists are what "gave back to India its forgotten past."[69] Far from seeing Sanskrit disappear, the years of British rule were a time when Orientalism and the discipline of Indology were established and flourished, just when Sanskrit and many of the knowledges connected with it were ceasing to be a living tradition. The paradox is captured in the frequent lamentations of Indologists at the decline of a particular kind of Sanskrit learning, such as Franz Kielhorn's comment in 1874 that "It is sad to see the number of sastris, distinguished no less for their humility and modesty than for their learning and intelligence, diminish year after year, and to feel that with them there is dying away more and more of that traditional learning which we can so ill dispense with in the interpretation of the enigmatic works of Hindu antiquity."[70] Kielhorn was a professor of Sanskrit at Deccan College; his contributions, as of others like him, were made possible by and presupposed the new colonial dispensation, and the new methods of scholarship. But the colonial order and the new forms of scholarship that it brought into being also foreshadowed the decline of another mode of engaging with Sanskrit. This was one in which ancient texts and authors were not simply objects of study but also interlocutors, living disputants. This mode or tradition had by no means exhausted its vitality at the advent of colonialism. The two centuries immediately before the consolidation of colonialism around 1750, Sheldon Pollock tells us, "witnessed an explosion of scholarly production unprecedented for its quality and quantity,"[71] constituting "one of the most innovative epochs of Sanskrit systematic thought (in language analysis, logic, hermeneutics [and] moral-legal philosophy)."[72] Many of the contributors to this intellectual efflorescence identified themselves as *navya*, or "new" scholars; they were not blindly repeating and transmitting an ossified tradition but producing new and innovative scholarship. Yet at the same time they were also heirs to a tradition going back two millennia, and the long-dead members of this tradition remained their "partners in argument."[73]

Colonial rule did not bring the study of Sanskrit to an end, but it fundamentally changed the manner in which, and the purposes for which, Sanskrit was studied. The character of this change can be discerned from an exchange in 1884, when the director of public instruction solicited views on how best to develop the study of Sanskrit at Benares Sanskrit College. In his response George Thibault, the principal of the college, advocated

> gradually improving the methods on which the study of Sanskrit is at present carried on in the Benares Sanskrit College and of converting Pandits of the old school into accomplished Sanskrit scholars, in the European sense of the word. I do not by any means wish to under-rate the Sanskrit learning possessed by the [Indian] Professors and many of the students of our Sanskrit College. Their deep and extensive reading, their most accurate knowledge of the technicalities of the Sanskrit Sha-stras, and their command of the Sanskrit language may well raise the envy of European scholars. On the other hand, not even the best of our Pandits can be said to possess a critical knowledge of the Sanskrit literature and language. They know nothing of the history of their lan-guage and the place it occupies among cognate languages. They have no idea of the gradual growth of their literature and the fact that it mirrors different phases of national and religious life. They are quite unable to discuss intelligently historical and chronological questions. They proceed most uncritically in editing texts etc etc. . . . in institu-tions maintained by a European Government some efforts should be made to render the study of Sanskrit more critical and – viewing the matter from a European point of view – more fertile than hitherto.[74]

The other respondent was Babu Pramadadas Mitra, a member of a well-to-do Bengali family steeped in the "old" knowledge but also versed in the new western learning, who had previously been a member of the faculty in the Sanskrit department. In his response to Thibault's suggestions Mitra did not dispute that "Pandits of the old school" lacked a historical and critical sense. What he contested was that a living tradition of enquiry should be regarded as only so many "materials" for critical editions and historical reconstruc-tion: "the great authors of India have not laboured only to furnish materials for a conjectural history of the rise and growth of a national and religious life." There were, he averred, "higher objects to be aimed for by a Sanskrit scholar"; the poetry and ethics and philosophy and theology of ancient India, the works of Valmiki and Vyasa and Sankara and Abhinavagupta, could also be studied "for intellectual delight and moral elevation, the culture and wis-dom that they afford." The "old" learning of the pandits was not redundant as long as that which they studied was an ongoing tradition, rather than so many sources for the re-creation of a lost and dead past. In the name of "that learning which has from remote antiquity had its most celebrated seat in this city [Benares]," Mitra protested against any scheme that "may eventually lead the Pandits to turn their backs upon the old ways and lines of study . . . ways and lines of study which I may say have produced the very literature that has engaged and still engages the earnest and admiring attention of many a liberal-minded European scholar."[75] Such an outcome was to be avoided at all cost, lest it bring about "that day of universal lamentation for India when her glorious past shall be divorced, irrevocably torn off from the present."[76]

In fact, the study of Sanskrit in the ensuing decades did increasingly become "critical" and "historical" and "comparative" and "philological"; the study of Sanskrit did not decline, but the type of study undertaken by the pandit was devalued, and decayed. A government statement on educational policy in 1913 declared that the Government of India attached great importance to Oriental studies, but "through the medium of western methods of research and in relation to modern ideas."; and it approvingly paraphrased the observation of a conference of Orientalists held at Simla two years earlier that "the world of scholarship . . . would suffer irreparable loss if the old type of *pandit* and *maulvi* were to die out before their profound knowledge of their subjects had been made available to the world."[77] The bearers of "traditional" learning should not die out – at least not until their lore had been extracted, put through the sieve of western "critical" methods, and processed into knowledge. Just as the intellectual traditions once embodied in Sanskrit were now so many source materials, so the pandit had become the handmaiden of the Indologist.

Soon Indian Indologists emerged, fully trained in the new methods, sometimes displaying a similar mix of admiration and condescension toward the learning of the pandit. Ramakrishna Gopal Bhandarkar (1837–1925), one of many of Kielhorn's students to achieve eminence as a Sanskritist,[78] was the first "modern" Indian professor of Sanskrit, one who did not come from a background as a pandit but rather learned Sanskrit in western educational institutions. In his presidential address to the All-India Oriental Conference, he distinguished between those scholars who employed the "historical, comparative and the critical method" and "the pandits of the old school who have spent long years in studying, in the traditional way, the authoritative Sanskrit learning such as Vyakarana and Nyaya," whose studies, while "no doubt, deep and sound . . . are lacking in historical, comparative and critical outlook."[79]

IN THE COURSE of his polemics against government patronage of indigenous knowledges in the 1830s, Macaulay had protested that to teach in Sanskrit and Arabic would be to use state revenues to encourage men "to waste their youth in learning how they are to purify themselves after touching an Ass, or what texts of the Vedas they are to repeat to expiate the crime of killing a goat."[80] But even as Macaulay wrote, and certainly in the decades after, what was for him a "problem" ceased to exist, as the languages which had once been the bearers of intellectual traditions increasingly became disassociated from these traditions. To quote Pollock once again, "In the face of European modernity, Indian systems of thought, or rather Sanskrit systems, simply vanished as a significant force in Indian history."[81] It was not that the Sanskrit language was no longer studied, or even that "Indian systems of thought" were consigned to the dust heap, but rather that one could now study the Vedas, or Bhatrihari or Panini, less for obtaining guidance on how to live or continuing a conversation of considerable antiquity than for producing critical editions, or engaging in historical reconstructions and philological investigations. It became possible to study Sanskrit and Arabic "critically" – that is, without reference to the traditions of knowledge with which they were imbricated. The paradox was that Indology advanced in direct proportion to the slow demise of once-living Sanskrit intellectual traditions.

These knowledges, and the practices associated with them, never entirely died out. But they did not occupy a place of importance in nationalist thought. By no means were all nationalists ignorant of these traditions – some were learned in them, and bore titles indicating their learning, like *acharya* or *pandit* or *maulana*, including the nationalist leader who went on to become independent India's first minister for education, Maulana Abul Kalam Azad. But while nationalism took pride in such learning as evidence of the "glorious traditions" of ancient India, it did not ascribe to these indigenous knowledges an important role in the *future* of the independent nation-to-be. Why was this so?

Vernacular Modernity

In India as elsewhere, anticolonial nationalism embodied the desire to be "modern but different" – to acquire the characteristics that made the colonial power strong, but to do so in the name of an irreducible difference that was conceived in national terms, and for which nationalism purported to speak. As Lajpat Rai put it, "We do not want to be English or German or American or Japanese . . . we want to be Indians, but modern, up-to-date, progressive Indians."[82] It was not enough to imitate the colonizer: if the project was simply to become a mirror image of the original, there could be no ratio-

nale for the nationalist project. Chakrabarty writes that "the colonial experience of becoming modern is haunted by the fear of looking unoriginal . . .
Nationalist writings therefore subsume the question of difference within a
search for essences, origins, authenticities, which, however, have to be amenable to global-European constructions of modernity so that the quintessentially nationalist claim of being 'different but modern' can be validated."[83]
Partha Chatterjee, as we saw in chapter 5, argues that one of the means by
which nationalism sought to reconcile the search for national difference with
the pursuit of modernity was by dividing the world of social institutions
and practices into two domains, a "material" domain where "Western superiority had to be acknowledged and its accomplishments carefully studied
and replicated," and a "spiritual" or "inner" domain, where national identity
was located, and which had to be safeguarded and preserved.[84] In Chatterjee's account, education was part of the "inner," spiritual domain rather than
the "outside" of "economy and statecraft, science and technology." Hence
"nationalism sought to bring this area under its jurisdiction" by starting secondary schools and seeking to assert control over the universities.[85]

Here it seems to me that Chatterjee's very fruitful distinction between
"inside" and "outside" threatens to become coterminous with the more conventional distinction between civil society and state, yielding the conclusion
that nationalism engaged in a Gramscian war of position, seeking to exert
control over civil society before the decisive struggle for state power. Such an
account would not be wrong, but it would be less insightful than the original distinction between inside and outside, between that which is modern-
universal and must be imitated and acquired, and that where the "essential
marks" of identity are located, and which therefore must be protected and
secured. Education, I submit, was both important to and problematic for
nationalism, because it *straddled* this distinction. On the one hand, education
was where the knowledges, skills, and techniques of the modern, which the
nation-to-be had to acquire, were disseminated. That is why one could not
reject education, for to do so would be to give up on the aspiration to be modern. Herein lies the answer to the question I posed, namely the question of
why nationalism never sought to revive the study of indigenous knowledges,
such as a long and rich intellectual tradition in Sanskrit, as an alternative
to the dissemination of western knowledge. It did not do so because these
knowledges and traditions were not seen as conducive to modernity; however
plausible they were as assertions of difference, they were not "amenable to
global-European constructions of modernity." But neither was colonial edu-

cation (unlike, say, the railway system) simply a site where the skills of the modern could be acquired, because it was also a site where identities were produced and secured. As a project to be modern, nationalism sought more western education, which was seen as necessary to becoming modern; but as a project to be "modern but different," it also sought an education that would preserve difference, even bring it to self-consciousness, rather than efface it. In the words of Lajpat Rai, quoted earlier, it was necessary to become "modern, up-to-date [and] progressive," but more specifically to become "modern, up-to-date [and] progressive *Indians*" (emphasis added).

Hence the nationalist project to found a "national" education, an education that would be modern without ceasing to be Indian. We saw that the question of what was to count as "national" about national education was one to which there were varied answers, rather than a single one. But—and it is not the same thing as a common answer—across the spectrum of nationalist opinion, and amid the diversity of types of "national" education on offer, there was one element held in common: whatever else made this education national, it had to be in the "vernaculars," that is, in the languages of India.

Gandhi and Tagore, who despite great mutual regard disagreed on many issues (including the desirability of boycotting government schools and colleges during the Non-cooperation Movement), spoke as one on this issue. In an article in *Young India* titled "Evil Wrought by the English Medium," Gandhi wrote, "No country can become a nation by producing a race of imitators."[86] As long as Indians gained knowledge through a language alien to them, learned with great difficulty and only ever imperfectly acquired, they would be condemned to being imitators, a nation "in itself" (a mere country) but not yet a nation *for* itself. A metaphor invoked again and again by Gandhi was that of blotting paper; because Indian education occurred in English, "we have become blind imitators of European civilization—mere blotting papers."[87] The point was not whether Indians should acquire western knowledge. Gandhi would often (though not always) concede that knowledge of western science and literature might be a good thing, but only as long as it was acquired in the vernaculars. On this Gandhi was consistent and emphatic, from his early pronouncements to his later ones. Gandhi's scheme for a Basic National Education, announced in 1937, proposed compulsory and free education for all children from seven to fourteen, with the education in the vernacular tongue of the region where the school was located, a strong focus on handicraft production, and the goal of using the handicrafts and productive work to eventually make these schools economically self-supporting. This plan, intended for an independent India, was a very radical departure from both the colonial education system and indigenous traditions, not least because the centrality it accorded to manual, handicraft labor had no precedent in either.[88] After this plan had been adopted by Congress (with the modification that schools were expected to become only partly self-supporting, and that too over time),[89] Gandhi declared, "the medium of instruction should be altered at once and at any cost, the provincial languages being given their rightful place. I would prefer temporary chaos in higher education to the criminal waste that is daily accumulating."[90]

More than Gandhi, Tagore would emphasize the richness of European culture and acknowledge that India had much to learn from Europe. The idea behind his "East West" university was precisely that the East and West *could* meet, and enrich each other. But all instruction had to be in the vernacular. The importance of the mother tongue was the main subject of Tagore's address to the convocation of Calcutta University in 1937, the first time the convocation had been addressed in Bengali.[91] Where Gandhi employed the metaphor of blotting paper, Tagore favored the image of a parasite: "our modern school and college education . . . has from its inception been parasitic on a foreign tongue . . . Accustomed to live by borrowing, it has come to measure attainment by largeness of debt" (115). There was nothing wrong with borrowing per se – Tagore rejected the criticism of those who decried everything western as foreign, for "What if the seeds came from foreign parts, did they not fall and sprout on our own soil? That which can grow and flourish in the country no longer remains foreign" (119). Thus there was no question of rejecting the West, or the English language, or modernity. The issue was rather one of recognizing that under the official system students had been "brought up to absorb the thoughts of others . . . and their own faculty of thought . . . their creative inspiration, have all been enfeebled" (116). "Those who receive such education," Tagore told his audience, "cannot produce what they consume" (115–16). For Indians to become producers and not simply consumers of modernity, it was necessary for them to assimilate "the subject-matter of education through one's own language, just as, in order to incorporate foodstuffs into the body, they have to be chewed with one's own teeth, saturated with one's own digestive juices" (116).

But this answer also met the other major criticism of these years, namely that the existing education system was simply inefficacious, that it was failing to make Indians modern. Tagore told the Calcutta convocation: "On behalf of writers in Bengali, and for myself, I would claim that we have been

engaged in the work of implanting modern culture in the heart of our country"; indeed, writers in Bengali had been doing so with greater success than
the university had done, because they implanted this modernity in the language of the people, so that it could take root (122). Even Gandhi, sometime
critic of modern civilization, could write, "Under my scheme there will be
more and better libraries, more and better laboratories, more and better research institutes. Under it we should have an army of chemists, engineers
and other experts," with the important difference that "all these experts will
speak, not a foreign language, but the language of the people."[92]

To champion vernacular education was therefore not to choose Indianness over modernity; it was a means of reconciling national difference with a
global modernity, making it possible to be both modern and Indian. Not only
could one be Indian and modern at the same time, but it seemed that the one
presupposed the other. The nationalist resolution of the "problem" of education thus provided two seemingly unconnected problems with one solution:
vernacular education was a critical element in making education "national,"
and also in making it an effective vehicle for modernity. For India, declared
her nationalists, the Indian modern had to come in the form of vernacular
modernity.

Education in the Nationalist Imagination

On the day in question, Gaur Mohan, leaving Ramtanu in the sweetmeat shop,
went to Mr Hare and asked him to take the boy as a free student. The gentleman
was not then in a mood to confer the favour. He had received too many applications
of the kind . . . But the pandit . . . told Ramtanu for a few days continually to run
with the sahib's palanquin, and to repeat in his ears the prayers of being taken in
as a free pupil . . . Two months passed in this way, Ramtanu being the pursuer, and
David Hare the pursued, after which the latter, being convinced that the boy was
really anxious to learn English . . . promised him a free education.[93]

This story of a young Ramtanu Lahiri importuning the Scottish watch-
maker and philanthropist David Hare for admission to the English school
that Hare had helped to establish could almost stand as a metaphor for the
reaction of the urban middle classes in India to the introduction of English
education. After the victory of the Anglicists in 1835, the middle classes in
the presidency towns of Calcutta, Bombay, and Madras began to flock to
the newly established government schools teaching western knowledge in

English. Western education became an important feature defining the lives of the emerging urban middle class in the nineteenth century, and indeed became a new source of status differentiation in colonial India, demarcating a "new" middle class from older ones. Soon, especially in Bengal, privately established schools began to make up for the shortfall between rapidly growing demand and scanty, government-provided supply.

Indian nationalists would sometimes describe western education as a "gift" of British rule, or even as its "greatest gift." Until the latter part of the nineteenth century their chief complaint about education was principally that their rulers did not provide enough of it. By the end of the nineteenth century, as we have seen, education was also becoming the subject of increasing criticism, and not just because of its insufficiency. As a more assertive and "extremist" strand of nationalism began to compete with its "moderate" and constitutionalist predecessor, such nationalists claimed that the existing system, introduced and controlled by the British, had made little attempt to adapt itself to its Indian surrounds. At best, the system remained "foreign" to the sensibilities and culture of many who subjected themselves to it; at worst, it had the effect of "denationalizing" students, of alienating them from their own culture and traditions, and thus from their countrymen. By the early years of the twentieth century the Congress was calling for the educational system that had been introduced and controlled by the colonial power to be replaced by a national system. Nationalists, as well as others, also complained that western education was proving inefficacious as the vehicle for modernity.

Faced with these problems, nationalists advocated a variety of solutions. The alternatives to the existing system that they advanced, and sometimes sought to implement, varied quite considerably – nationalism was not a monolith – but almost all had two elements in common. The knowledge that they proposed to disseminate was modern, western knowledge – a revival of traditional, indigenous knowledge was not seriously contemplated. And teaching in the languages of India was a central element in virtually all the alternative schemes, howsoever else they may have differed. In the nationalist imagination, providing modern knowledge in indigenous languages, through a curriculum rooted in and emphasizing Indian traditions, would solve the two glaring deficiencies of the existing system in one stroke. It would press the imprint of Indianness on the knowledge and at the same time ensure that this knowledge was effectively disseminated, fulfilling its transformative, modernizing potential. Indians could then finally become producers of modernity rather than passive recipients – "blotting paper" or "parasites," in the descriptions of Gandhi and Tagore.

After independence Abul Kalam Azad, independent India's first minister for education, told an audience at Patna University, "Our educational system was not introduced by us. It was founded and controlled by foreigners. Whatever they decided to teach us was right, but their method of imparting education was wrong."[94] What was "wrong" about it – Azad went on to tell his audience in an address delivered in Hindustani rather than English – was that the language of instruction was English rather than the Indian vernaculars, a fault urgently in need of remedy.

In postcolonial India, it is what "foreigners decided to teach us" that has continued to be disseminated, and that too, as far as the higher levels of the educational ladder are concerned, mostly in English. Other knowledges have not disappeared, but they have been for the most part marginalized to the quotidian, where they are frequently the subject of strictures from the modernizing postcolonial state, condemned as markers of an "ignorance" or even "superstition" yet to be overcome. What such admonishments reveal is that in addition to reigning supreme, modern western knowledge is not seen as "western" at all, as a particular mode of knowledge; it is knowledge as such, everywhere and for everyone. Today all "serious" knowledge that is produced in India, whether the site for this production is the academy, the state bureaucracy, or any other, is produced according to the canons and protocols of the knowledge that emerged and was systematized in the West in the early modern period. And this outcome, or "gift," if such it be, is as much the fruit of nationalist strivings as it is of colonial imposition.

Epilogue
Knowing Modernity, Being Modern

I concluded chapter 6 by observing that almost all "serious" knowledge about the nonwestern world, whether produced in the West or in the non-West, shares the presumptions and guiding categories of a conception of knowledge that began to emerge in Europe in the early modern period. A knowledge born in the modern West has thus become global. It is global precisely because, notwithstanding its European origins, it is seen as universal rather than parochial.

This knowledge is seen as "modern" not just in the sense that it is historically recent, but also because it is seen as part and parcel of *modernity*. Scientific, rational knowledge is seen as the knowledge which comes with the transformations that mark entry to the modern; just as the steam engine replaces horsepower, the powerloom the handloom, so another mark and measure of a society's passage into the modern is that premodern ways of knowing come to be replaced by modern, rational knowledge. Conversely, the adoption of such knowledge is seen as necessary in making the transition to the modern; embracing modern ways of thinking and the "modern outlook" are necessary for those who would wish to be modern. Modern knowledge is thus at once a cause, a consequence, and an emblem of modernity.

Those working with this knowledge display a keen awareness of its historicity. Its chroniclers are all agreed that one can locate a time and place where it first made its entry into the world, even if they may disagree on precisely when and where that was. Yet almost miraculously, an acknowledgment of this historicity in no way circumscribes its claims: although it is recognized that this knowledge emerges in the course of the recent history of the West, it is bounded neither by time (its core presumptions can be used to analyze premoderns) nor by place (it can be used to understand all societies). Indeed, an acknowledgment of its historicity seems to enable, rather than diminish, the extravagance of the claims that can be made for it. What makes this miracle possible?

The answer lies in an account or understanding that emerges in the eighteenth and nineteenth centuries, according to which modern knowledge is the self-consciousness of modernity. Just as social and technological changes are the "material" face of modernity, modern knowledge is what underlies these changes. It is seen both as a force in the emergence of the modernity, *and* as that which enables us to understand the changes that brought the modern world into being. Indeed, it is in part *because* modern knowledge is regarded as important in the making of the modern world that the same knowledge is treated as the privileged means by which to know that modern world. At the same time, modernity itself is regarded as a privileged historical moment and a privileged site, one where the facts and processes that have always governed the natural world and human history finally became discernable. In this narrative modern knowledge is doubly privileged: it is the privileged means by which to know the modern, which is itself the privileged vantage point from which all of human history finally becomes explicable.

When in the early nineteenth century Burckhardt wrote that the "veil" which made man "conscious of himself only as a member of a race, people, party, family or corporation" finally lifted in Renaissance Italy, enabling him to recognize himself as a "spiritual individual," he was contributing to this narrative.[1] So too were Marx and Engels when, in characterizing the revolutionary effects of capitalist production, they wrote: "All that is solid melts into air, all that is holy is profaned, and man is *at last* compelled to face with sober senses, his *real* conditions of life"[2] (emphasis added). Marx's work provided a distinctively Marxist version of this account or understanding; according to this account, only when production becomes determinate or clarified, differentiating itself from ritual and gift – as it does in modern, capitalist society, where generalized commodity production is the norm – is it apparent that production is and has always been the basis of *all* human societies. And when Weber wrote that disenchantment was what allowed men to recognize the melancholy fact that the world had never been imbued with purpose and meaning, he too was making the claim that only at a certain point in the history of humankind could certain truths finally be discerned, truths which, however, had retrospective validity.

It is this that makes the claims to universality on behalf of western knowledge so novel and efficacious. This account, far from being yet another set of parochial assumptions claiming universal validity, like a proselytising religion, purports to explain both why we humans were once bound to get things wrong and how it became possible to get them right. The core presumptions of western knowledge are homologous with modernity – it is only in the modern era that they can be recognized or unveiled – but they are not limited to the modern. That we are free individuals; that being determines consciousness, and production determines being; and that values and purposes are human products rather than features of the cosmos – these, according to this understanding, are universal truths, and not just truths for our modern world. Moreover, while this knowledge originated in the modern West, it is not inherently western. That is precisely why nationalists and others could seek to embrace it – this knowledge was universal and could make us modern, without our having to "become" European.

The perceived close connection between modern western knowledge and modernity is no doubt the reason why debates about this knowledge can generate passion. The critiques of Enlightenment Reason that are a feature of contemporary intellectual life generate charges of irrationalism and are sometimes seen as attacks on the project – whether finished or unfinished – of modernity. These debates have been conducted impassionedly in India, with the additional complication that the knowledge in question, and modernity itself, are not home-grown but products of the colonial encounter. Some Indian intellectuals have argued that critiques of the Enlightenment and modernity are reactionary, or at any rate run the risk of unwittingly playing into the hands of reactionary forces. Their opponents sometimes reply that such criticisms only reveal the degree to which their proponents remain intellectually colonized, long after their colonial masters have departed.

I have avoided engaging in such polemics, treating the arrival of western knowledge in India neither as the triumph of Reason over ignorance or unreason nor as an insidious form of intellectual and cultural colonization. I have "bracketed" questions of this nature, instead addressing myself to a study of how modern western knowledge was disseminated through western education, the effects that it had, the debates to which it gave rise, and how we might interpret these effects and these debates. Or rather, I have not so much bracketed the question of the "truth" of western knowledge as I have sought to recast it. I suggested in part I that knowledges, western knowledge included, are not forms of cognizing a world external to them but rather are constitutive of this world. As modern western knowledge "traveled" to India, various agents of change (not least the dissemination of this new form of knowledge) succeeded in reconstituting that locale (not least by transforming the Indian into a subject). But I have also suggested that this knowledge only partly constituted what it purported merely to explain. Chapter 1 showed that Indian students often engaged with western knowledge in instrumental ways, and "acquired" it through rote learning. The knowledge disseminated in the new schools and universities presumed that knowledge resided in a subject, who confronted a world of objects; but this knowledge did not always succeed in producing subjects who conceived of knowledge in these terms. As I showed in chapter 2, the explanation that Indian students were in danger of being plunged into a mental and moral crisis through their encounter with western education was mistaken, because their morality was not, as this explanation presumed, a matter of "beliefs" held in the "mind." Thus to the degree that modern western knowledge did not remake Indians, it never became fully adequate to knowing India. This conclusion, I have been careful to insist, is one that we reach not because we are somehow able to step outside of western knowledge to assess its truth, but rather because it can be seen in the discourses that came to surround its diffusion through western education. Read carefully, these discourses can be seen to register, however dimly, a recognition that what I have called the "core presumptions" and "background assumptions" of this knowledge were in fact absent, or contravened, and that in this specific sense, western knowledge was not adequate to knowing India. This recognition makes writing a history of western education a problematic exercise, as argued in chapter 3. One cannot assume, as modern historiography does, that all human pasts consist of subjects who endow the world with meanings, the objectified forms of which allow us to recreate their world. In writing such a history, one must remain alert to the possibility of its inadequacy to its object.

In the highly polemical context of some current debates, even what I see as the "agnosticism" of this position – neither embracing what we have learned to call Reason, nor denouncing it as merely the colonizer's Reason – will be seen by some as taking sides, and will no doubt lead to charges of irrationalism, nativism, and relativism. But I take the vigor with which these arguments are sometimes advanced as confirming my own, that what is at stake is not principally Truth or Reason, but a will toward a certain way of life, with which this Reason is identified. That way of life is usually glossed as "modernity," and the desire for western knowledge in colonial India, as part II sought to show, was indissolubly connected with the desire and the project for a national-modern. Or rather, it was indissolubly connected with heterogenous desires and projects for the national-modern – for the "advanced" and thus modern Muslim, for the Indian woman who would at once safe-guard and embody an essential Indian identity and yet be the wife and mother of modern men, and for a citizen whose particularity as an Indian could be reconciled with "global-European constructions of modernity," and who had been equipped to participate in building a modern and independent nation through western knowledge acquired, for the most part, in his native tongue.

BUT IF MODERN western knowledge was not "adequate" to India, in the specific sense indicated above, is this because India was, or is, premodern? Is it the implication of the arguments mounted in this book that modern knowledge is a fruitful means for knowing the modern world that it helped to bring into being, but for this very reason, not a useful medium by which to "think" premoderns?

If these were the implications of my arguments, I would then have pro-vided an amended and more complicated version of what is, however, a very familiar narrative. This is one in which the site and image of modernity is Europe, and the recent history of India is read as a history of lack and in-completeness. The phenomena I have discussed, as well as many others that differentiate India from European modernity, would then be interpreted and explained as signs and consequences of a transition to modernity that has begun but not yet been completed. In this narrative (or narratives, because there are different versions of it) the knowledge which allows us to recognize incompleteness is not called into question; the "incompleteness" or "lack" is not of our categories but rather that of the real. What I have offered can thus be seen as an argument which differs in that the knowledge by which we judge absence and incompleteness is itself problematized. The incomplete-ness of our Indian modernity is demonstrated not by the serene assurance of the categories through which we know it but by the difficulties encoun-tered when these categories traveled to India. In the first case, our confidence in the ability of our intellectual categories to understand and identify the modern enables us to recognize that India is premodern, or only partly mod-ern. In the second case, it is the discourses which western education gave rise to, read as indicating that the core assumptions of modern thought could not be assumed in India, that allow us therefore to see that India must be premodern.

If this was indeed where my arguments led, the results would not, I think, be inconsequential. We would be obliged to regard knowledge not as a form of knowing a world external to it but as one of the ways in which worlds are constituted. With a more reflexive understanding of our knowledge, we would have gained a better sense of its possibilities and limits. And with a sense of its limits, we might be less disposed to regard other knowledges as simply "wrong," and more open to recognizing them as different ways of being in the world. However, in closing I will outline why I reject the possible conclusions briefly sketched above, to draw out more fully what I think are the intellectual and ethical possibilities that flow from preceding arguments.

Being Modern

Characterizing some of our contemporaries as premodern, and in this sense as belonging to the past even as they inhabit the present, should now be ethically unsustainable. There is an enormous condescension in such a "denial of coevalness"[3] and the social engineering that often springs from it – the attempts to gift peoples with modernity, by force if necessary – has been disastrous. It is also intellectually unsustainable. The peasants in the Bolivian tin mines who worshiped the god Tio were nonetheless part of a world capitalist market.[4] The aboriginal peoples who have survived dispossession and genocide are not a "survival" of an ancient past but are very much imbricated in the modern-present.[5] Indian peasants who do not display the "modern outlook" participate in the world capitalist market, and since 1947, as citizens, they have been participants in India's parliamentary democracy. And the motley figures encountered in this book – crammers and dowry seekers, vice-chancellors who consulted astrologers, Brahmin clerks and industrialists, "proud Muslims," nationalists, modern housewives and mothers – all engaged with and negotiated modern institutions, ideas, and practices. What could it possibly mean to characterize them as premodern? Or depict them as caught in a no-man's land, stranded between the banks of a premodern that they have left behind, borne along by various currents to the shores of a modernity not yet reached? As one historian (also rejecting this all-too-familiar narrative) plaintively asks, "Why should modernity still await us in India, more than two hundred years after its career was launched in India by European imperialism? How long does it take for an Indian to become modern?"[6]

A similar dissatisfaction with the narrative of an incomplete transition to modernity has led some to suggest that we should cease to privilege the process and the form in which modernity first arrived in Europe, such that all other regions of the world appear to have only an imperfect or incomplete version of this original. It has been proposed that we allow for alternative modernities, or multiple modernities, so that we can think of India, China, and areas elsewhere as also part of the modern, even though their modernity does not look like modernity in the West. But if this is to be more than just a matter of tinkering with definitions, it requires a fundamental rethinking of our understanding of modernity.

Recognizing this, Charles Taylor rejects the narrative which privileges the European experience, and which treats it as what all societies must undergo if they are to be classed as modern. He characterizes this narrative or theory as one in which "modernity is conceived as a set of transformations which any and every culture can go through . . . Modernity in this kind of theory is understood as issuing from a rational or social operation which is culture-neutral . . . a general operation that can take any specific culture as its input."[7] In this theory, the specificities that distinguish "premodern" cultures do not matter, not because they are all seen to be alike but because the culture-neutral processes of modernization run steamroller-like over all such specificities. That is why modernity is always singular, why India and China, when they become modern, will look like Europe, minor differences aside. But modernity is more than just a set of economic and institutional arrangements: it is also the practices, beliefs, and background assumptions that enable these economic and institutional arrangements to function. Why does this account assume that the background assumptions and practices of the modern will not even be inflected in any major way by the traditions they encounter – and replace? Because what is implicit and often explicit in this account is the view that the presumptions connected with modernity, or what Taylor calls the "culture of modernity," are not on a par with other cultures. It is not simply one more way of construing and constructing human identity and its place in the world: "At the heart of this explanation is the view that modernity involves our 'coming to see' certain kernel truths about the human condition,"[8] such as instrumental rationality, and the assumption that the individual is somehow more basic and more real than any collective.[9] What Taylor is referring to is precisely the narrative discussed above, a narrative in which the core presumptions of modern thought are unjustifiably accorded privilege, because they are regarded not as just one possible way of construing the world but as the right way, finally uncovered.

Taylor rightly rejects this account of modernity, and the accompanying narrative telling us that the culture of modernity is the privileged bearer of certain universal and trans-historical truths. He offers instead a way of conceiving modernity in which the cultures of regions that become modern leave a lasting imprint on that modernity: "If the transition to modernity is like the rise of a new culture [then] the starting point will leave its impress on the end product . . . transitions to what we might recognize as modernity, taking place in different civilizations, will produce different results that reflect their divergent starting points . . . new differences will emerge from the old. Thus, instead of speaking of modernity in the singular, we should better speak of 'alternative modernities.' "[10] And just as our usual understanding rests upon the presumption that the culture of modernity becomes universalized because it "unveils" the truth that has been there all along, so too the pluralization of modernities can only proceed by rejecting this idea, *including* with reference to the West: "It is not that we [modern Westerners] sloughed off a whole lot of unjustified beliefs, leaving an implicit self-understanding that had always been there to operate at last untrammelled. Rather, one constellation of implicit understandings of our relation to God, the cosmos, other humans, and time was replaced by another in a multifaceted mutation."[11]

Disputing the account which claims that modern thought uncovers universal truths opens the way to recognizing that societies can be part of the modern without having their peoples become individuals, live in a disenchanted world, or embrace instrumental rationality. This account confuses products with processes—it wrongly assumes that bureaucratic rationality presupposes rational bureaucrats, that the production of universal science requires universalist scientists, and that capitalism requires maximizing individuals.[12] The account might only be adequate to characterizing and understanding western modernity—if that. I say "if that" because Taylor's argument has a double implication. The reason why we have thought of modernity as singular is *not* that we arrogantly generalized from the experience of the West. It is rather that in this understanding, premodern or "traditional" cultures—including those of the West—are assumed to have had representations and enchantments and metaphysics and cosmologies, whereas we moderns have come to grasp (or been forced to see) the bedrock truths that underpinned these various constructions all along. If that is mistaken—if modernity does not mean the replacement of "mere" representations and misunderstandings by truth, but rather the replacement of what Taylor calls one "social imaginary" by another, a fact obscured or even repressed by the knowledge through which we grasp the modern—then there is an important sense in which this explanation is simply mistaken, and not mistaken only inasmuch as it is unjustifiably generalized to account for the nonwestern world. If modernity need not imply disenchantment, individualism, and instrumental reasoning, and yet modern knowledge is often conceived as the fruit of that disenchantment, then that modern knowledge cannot be modernity grasped in thought.

Knowing Modernity

Taylor makes some bold intellectual moves, with radical implications. Rejecting the idea that the presumptions and the knowledge produced by modernity are the unveiling of universal truths, he suggests instead that what marks modernity is the shift from one constellation of background presumptions to another. But there is one move that he is reluctant to make, one element that he explicitly exempts from his argument – science. Although, as we have seen, Taylor rejects the idea that modernity involves our "coming to see" certain truths, and writes that "facets of what we identify as modern, such as the tendency to try to split fact from value or the decline of religious practice, are far from reposing on incontestable truths which have finally been discovered," he also immediately adds that this *is* a claim that can be made for modern physics.[13] "There is some justification," Taylor writes, "for talking of our "coming to see" the truth when we consider the revolution of natural science which began in the seventeenth century."[14] Taylor is here not just saying that science and technology are among the stuff of any modernity, a claim that is unexceptionable if the term modernity is not to be emptied of all meaning. The problem with the conventional account of modernity, he is saying, is its tendency to lump together those truths that we do "come to see" (science) with those presumptions (instrumental reason, individualism, etc.) that are part of the social imaginary accompanying and produced by western modernity, but that are not universal truths finally uncovered. The reason for this exclusion is presumably that to extend the argument to include science might be tantamount to declaring that just as individualism and instrumental rationality are a social imaginary like any other, and cannot lay any claim to being the truth revealed, so too modern science and nonmodern cosmologies are just, and equally, parts of different social imaginaries. This is not a conclusion that Taylor is willing to embrace, and if these are the choices, which is how matters are often presented – one thinks of older debates on whether Azande witchcraft is as good as modern science – there are few willing to embrace it.

But these are not the only choices, and Taylor's exclusion of science from the general thrust of his argument derives from his having insufficiently emancipated himself from the explanation that he criticizes. At the heart of Taylor's exclusion is the idea that while cultures produce the world they then inhabit, there is also a nature, which is outside culture, though different cultures regard and explain it in different ways. Once we accept an ontology that declares the world to be divided thus, it follows naturally that knowledge of the world should also be divided thus. All that remains to be determined is where the line is to be drawn: over which territory the "human sciences" can claim sovereignty, and how far the writ of "natural sciences" runs. The most aggressive champions of Nature have sometimes come close to claiming that even culture can be explained by neurons and evolution. The diviners of culture, by contrast, have for the most part accepted the duality, and with great humility have sought only to point out that causes did not always explain meanings, that the world man created was different from the one he found, and so on – in short, that culture had its own domain. In more recent times, in the wake of aggressively "constructivist" arguments, they have ventured to claim more than that. And so we continually redraw the lines and thereby seek to annex territory, through extravagant claims for nature and science on the one hand and an increasingly solipsistic "culturalism" on the other;[15] or rather, the majority in each camp happily till their own fields, leaving their generals, the theoreticians, to dispute the no-man's land in between.

For a long time we have assumed that this division is real – indeed, we began to do so at the beginnings of the modern age, when Bacon, Descartes, Hobbes, Hume, and many others rejected and sometimes mocked the idea that "natural philosophy" could use concepts of "final causes" and "purpose" in explanation. The conventional way in which we understand this history is to regard these moderns as having "come to see" that Nature did not embody meanings or "have" ends, and thus as reassigning purpose and meaning to Culture. But the modern idea of nature is not the Greek *physis* with "purpose" eliminated from it, and neither was it constituted by simply reshuffling and reassigning the medieval and early modern categories of the supernatural, preternatural, artificial, and unnatural into already available categories of culture or nature. "To reconstruct the meanings and resonances of early modern nature," Lorraine Daston writes, "requires setting aside the modern opposition of nature versus culture," for "the very categories of nature and culture, conceived in yin-yang complementarity, are of relatively recent provenance."[16] Historians of science like Daston, and Shapin and Schaffer,[17] and philosophers like Latour, have in recent times offered the beginnings of an alternative account, one that has us see modernity as that which *invents* the idea or artefact of nature, and does so at the same time as it invents society and culture.

What characterizes modernity, Latour argues, is not its discovery that "Nature" was disenchanted, but its creation of Nature on the one hand and society and culture on the other. Meanings and values belonged by definition to the societal and cultural pole, and thus the very idea of Nature had disenchantment "built into it": in modern self-understandings "becoming" modern "consists in continually exiting from an obscure age that mingled the needs of society with scientific truth, in order to enter into a new age that will finally distinguish clearly what belongs to atemporal nature and what comes from humans, what depends on things and what depends on signs."[18] Latour calls this – the separation of humans from nonhumans, of Nature from culture, of that which has no meaning but can be known from that which is nothing but meanings and values – the "Great Divide." He argues that it explains the other great divide, that between us moderns and the premoderns. As Michael Adas shows, some of the initial ways in which Europeans conceived of their superiority to non-Europeans (such as the notion that they had true religion, while others had false gods) increasingly yielded to explanations emphasizing the superiority of European science and technology, a superiority seen as attesting that "European modes of thought and social organization corresponded much more closely to the underlying realities of the universe than did those of any other people or society, past or present."[19] Or in Latour's words, since the time that we created Nature and Culture as opposites, and organized our knowledge around their opposition, we have with great self-satisfaction regarded ourselves as "the only ones who differentiate absolutely between Nature and Culture, between Science and Society, whereas in our eyes all the others – whether they are Chinese or Amerindian, Azande or Barouya – cannot really separate what is knowledge from what is Society, what is sign from what is thing, what comes from Nature as it is from what their cultures require."[20]

In arguments such as this science is not privileged, as it is for Taylor. That is because the object to which it corresponds – the nonhuman, Nature in opposition to society and culture – is not regarded as the surplus or residue once we have pushed to the limit the argument that knowledge is a way of organizing and being in the world, and not simply a way of knowing it. Weber was wrong to see disenchanted nature as a "discovery," as an unveiling of a truth, but right to see it as a defining feature of how western moderns thought, and how they constituted their world. It is what, in the view of western moderns, most clearly distinguishes them from all the premoderns – but that view needs to be reconsidered. The rethinking need not take the form of concluding that moderns also project their cultural categories onto nature, while pretending otherwise – it need not lead us to declare that nature too is part of culture, and that nuclear physics is as constructed as water divining (and no more true). It can more fruitfully lead to questioning and problematizing the distinction between nature and culture. Daston does so through a historical enquiry which demonstrates the contingency of our organizing categories. Latour's way of doing so is to argue that we moderns, and others, are all "nature-cultures." [21] According to Latour, as this becomes increasingly apparent (for a variety of reasons), we can recognize that the way we thought and constituted ourselves as modern is deeply misleading. Historically, drawing a distinction between Nature and Culture was constitutive of modernity, but for that very reason it is not thereby the best medium for comprehending it. On the contrary; it is an impediment to understanding modernity. When we come to recognize that the world is not ontologically divided into nature on the one hand and culture on the other – the distinction that we thought we alone had grasped, and that constituted the dividing line between us moderns and the premoderns – then we also come to realize, as Latour signals in the provocative title of his book, that *We Have Never Been Modern*.

While the separation between Nature and Culture is undoubtedly essential to our sense of ourselves as modern, it is not the sole or defining feature of that sense. There are other sources and features of modernity, and the idea of modernity cannot be conjured away by showing Nature to be an idea that moderns need(ed), rather than a fact that they unearthed. Modernity is real, even if it is not what we thought it was. What I find most stimulating in Latour's book is not, however, its details, but rather the attempt to show that while modern thought has played an important role in constituting modernity, it is not thereby a privileged medium for comprehending it. In Latour's argument, more sharply than in Taylor's, modern thought is not the modern grasped reflexively; indeed, it is in important ways a bad guide to the modern, even if it is the only one we have. The arguments of Latour, Taylor, and others – including those critics of Reason who draw their inspiration from Nietzsche and Heidegger, and who have provided the intellectual background to this project, even though I have referred to them sparingly in the preceding pages – help me to clarify the implications of my own arguments in this book.

Our knowledge is not the privileged bearer of universal insights. Knowledge is not necessarily a relation between a knowing subject and an object known; we are not even all subjects; the world is not disenchanted. These are not truths that are finally grasped by modern knowledge, but rather what it has helped to bring into being. Yet from this it does not follow that modern knowledge is homologous with modernity, or even (a more modest claim) with the western variant thereof. Thought can be out of alignment with the world that it purports to describe, and that it has brought into being. This is not something we can know by stepping outside modern knowledge and gaining unmediated access to the real, since we would still have to explain how we are able to gain such access, and would in any case still be trapped within the representational epistemology that I have sought to render problematic. But it is something we can seek to explore by other means.

I have sought to do this by examining how knowledge traveled. Western knowledge arrived in India through the coercive agency of colonialism. We were told, most forthrightly by Macaulay, that this knowledge was true and that our own knowledges, like our gods, were false. I have read the discourses that western education generated as perturbations on the surface of this knowledge, half-acknowledgments that the "foundational assumptions" underpinning and enabling modern knowledge could not in fact be assumed. Nonetheless, that knowledge has now become global. There is no easy point outside it, no escape from it other than by engaging with and through it; thus I write as one of Macaulay's misbegotten offspring, working with this knowledge to contribute to the self-questioning that renews intellectual traditions and keeps them alive. There are myriad ways of doing so, and I do not claim any privilege for the tack I have taken. But if those who were once "subject to pedagogy" can, long after they are gone, be studied in a fashion that subjects modern western knowledge to critical scrutiny, there is a pleasing irony in the thought that Macaulay's bastard children will have contributed to the critical appropriation of a knowledge that was once imposed upon them.

Notes

Introduction

1. Minute recorded by Macaulay, law member of the Governor-General's Council, 2 February 1835, reprinted in Zastoupil and Moir, eds., *The Great Indian Education Debate*, 166.

2. Despatch from the Court of Directors of the East India Company to the Governor General of India, 19 July 1854, section 7, reprinted in Richey, ed., *Selections from Educational Records*, 366. The reasoning behind this, the Court of Directors went on to explain, was that "the systems of science and philosophy which form the learning of the East abound with grave errors, and eastern literature is at best very deficient as regards all modern discovery and improvements" (section 8, 366).

3. The universities of Punjab and Allahabad were established in 1882 and 1887, and by 1929 thirteen further universities had been established.

4. Lee-Warner, *The Citizen of India*, 1897.

5. *Report of the [Young] Committee on Educational Hygiene*, 6.

6. The Maitland Prize Essay at Cambridge in 1886 distinguished between "education in its widest sense," namely "all that tends to revolutionize thought in India, and to make it conform to the developments of Western civilization," and "the system of education" instituted by the colonial government. Haines, *Education and Missions in India and Elsewhere*, 32. Sir Richard Temple, recalling his career as a senior colonial official in India, distinguished between that education imparted through "contemplation of the example set by the British Government in India in its wise legislation" and that imparted through "definite instruction." *Men and Events of My Time in India*, 494. Sir Narayan G. Chandarvarkar, the distinguished vice chancellor of Bombay University, told a conference that "the very presence of the British with their traditions of liberty . . . [was] an education to the people," one fortunately supplemented by the decision in 1835 to provide western education to Britain's Indian subjects. Sir Narayan G. Chandarvarkar, "Presidential Address," *Report on the First Bombay Educational Conference*, ed. Jamnadas M. Mehta (Bombay, 1917), 12.

7. The system of education was top-heavy, with a disproportionate emphasis on colleges and universities. But the numbers involved at this level of the educational system, as a proportion of the total population, were of course minuscule. At the primary level enrollment figures remained abysmal: fewer than one-fifth of boys eligible to attend classes 1–4 of elementary school were enrolled in an educational

institution by the turn of the century. *Lord Curzon in India*, 331; by 1921–22 that proportion had increased to 31.5 percent and by 1936–37 had just passed the halfway
mark. Sargent, *Progress of Education in India, 1932–37*, 125, table lvi. However, even
these figures are highly misleading. The percentages were calculated on the assumption that 15 percent of the population was of elementary school–going age, the figure
widely used in Europe; but in India, as was often pointed out, the true figure was
certainly much higher than this. Officialdom in the princely state of Travancore
estimated that 25 percent was a more likely figure (*Report of the Administration for
Travancore for 1915–16*, quoted in "Percentage of Persons of School-Going Age," *Modern
Review*, December 1917, 626–27). The Government of India continued to use 15 percent, which made the numbers enrolled appear artificially high, but in-house official
correspondence acknowledged that the figure was misleading (Letter from Government of India to Government of United Provinces, 4 January 1907, Home Education,
January 1907, 13(A), National Archives of India). Moreover, the figures on numbers
actually enrolled did not convey much information – they did not reveal how many
of those enrolled in educational institutions actually attended them regularly; and
"wastage rates" were extremely high, meaning that a large number of those who enrolled in elementary school did not proceed as far as the fourth grade, conventionally
calculated as the minimum level of schooling necessary to achieve literacy.

8. Trevelyan, *On the Education of the People of India*, 13.

9. *Pioneer*, 10 January 1888.

10. Mahmood, *A History of English Education in India*, 1.

11. K.V.A., "Calcutta University Reform," 10.

12. Among them Chakrabarty, *Provincializing Europe*; Mignolo, *The Darker Side of
the Renaissance*; Mitchell, *Colonizing Egypt*; and Nandy, *The Intimate Enemy*.

13. Foucault, "About the Beginnings of a Hermeneutics of the Self," 223 n. 4.

14. "The fate of an epoch which has eaten of the tree of knowledge," Weber wrote,
"is that it must know that we cannot learn the *meaning* of the world from the results of its analysis, be it ever so perfect; it must rather be in a position to create this
meaning itself." "Objectivity in Social Science and Social Policy," 57.

15. Taylor, *Hegel*, 5.

16. He writes, "the transcendental presupposition of any *cultural science* lies in the
fact that we are *cultural beings*, endowed with the capacity and the will to take a deliberate attitude towards the world and to lend it significance." Weber, "Objectivity in
Social Science and Social Policy," 81. I will consider this passage and the claim made
in it in much greater detail in chapter 3.

17. "The world picture does not change from an earlier medieval one into a modern one, but rather the fact that the world becomes picture at all is what distinguishes
the essence of the modern age." Heidegger, "The Age of the World Picture," 130.

18. Heidegger, *Nietzsche*, 17.

19. Heidegger was aware that drawing attention to what is different about the
modern situation can lend itself to historicist readings. His insistence that man be-

comes subject only with modernity "might give rise," he writes, "to the notion that the innermost history of metaphysics and of the change in its basic positions is simply a history of the alteration in man's self-conception. This opinion would correspond completely to contemporary anthropological modes of thought. But it would be an erroneous notion . . . in fact *it would be the one error it is necessary to overcome.*" Nietzsche, 138, emphasis added.

20. Poovey, "The Liberal Civil Subject and the Social," 130.

21. The classic account and critique of this conception is Rorty, *Philosophy and the Mirror of Nature.*

22. Chatterjee, *The Nation and Its Fragments*, chapter 6.

Chapter 1: Changing the Subject

1. *Report of the General Committee of Public Instruction for the Presidency of Fort William in Bengal for 1838-39*, 7, 8, 9.

2. *General Report on Public Instruction in the Lower Provinces of the Bengal Presidency for 1844-45*, ccviii.

3. "On the Disadvantage of an Education Exclusively in English," essay reprinted in "Annual Report of the Elphinstone Institution for the Year 1850," appendix to *Report of the Bombay Board of Education from January 1, 1850, to April 30, 1851*, 265.

4. *Essays and Discourses by Professor Prafulla Chandra Ray*, 203.

5. "Address to Convocation of Delhi University, 1927," *Indian Problems: Speeches by Lord Irwin*, 184.

6. *General Report on Public Instruction in the Lower Provinces of the Bengal Presidency for 1856-57*, appendix A, 123 [each appendix separately paginated].

7. Quoted in Chaturvedi, *The History of Rural Education in the United Provinces of Agra and Oudh*, 178 (my translation).

8. *General Report on Public Instruction in the Lower Provinces of the Bengal Presidency for 1856-57*, appendix A, 123 (inspector of schools for South Bengal) and 153 (inspector of schools for northeast Bengal and Assam); see similar remarks by other officials at 40, 74; and in *General Report on Public Instruction in the Lower Provinces of Bengal for 1857-58*, appendix A, 43. For similar remarks for Bombay see *Report of the [Bombay] Board of Education for the Year 1849*, 18; and *Report of the Director for Public Instruction, Bombay, for the Year 1863-64*, 22. The Despatch of 1859 (acknowledging that according to the reports from its officers in Bengal as well as Bombay the grant-in-aid policy was not proving at all effective in promoting the establishment of vernacular schools) was compelled to authorize local authorities to look into imposing a land tax or rate to fund the creation of vernacular schools in rural areas. Despatch of 1859, sections 37, 50-53 (reprinted in Richey, ed., *Selections from Educational Records*, 426-50).

9. "Education in Bengal," *Calcutta Review*, reproduced (as appendix E) in Lethbridge, *High Education in India*, 199, 200. According to an inspector of schools for East Bengal, in Anglo-Vernacular schools – schools where English was taught as a lan-

guage but was not to be used as the medium of instruction – this requirement was widely flouted, for parents wished their sons "to speak English as much as possible, and they grudge every hour in which instruction is imparted in the Vernacular language." At least one Anglo-Vernacular school had a sign up in class warning boys that they would be caned if they spoke any language other than English. *General Report on Public Instruction in the Lower Provinces of Bengal for 1860–61*, appendix A, 31–32 [each appendix separately paginated].

10. *General Report on Public Instruction in the Lower Provinces of the Bengal Presidency for 1856–57*, appendix A, 122. See also *General Report on Public Instruction in Bengal, 30 September 1852–27 January 1855*, lii.

11. As was often observed – see for instance Subrahmanyam, "National Education: Literary or Technical?," 15; Cornelius, *A Study of Tagore's Experiment in the Indianization of Education in the Light of India's History*, pt 2, 117; Mayo, *Mother India*, 186. When marriage advertisements began to appear in the newspapers, for a long while "matriculation failed" was something worthy of mention, among the prospective groom's other assets.

12. *Short Essays and Reviews on the Educational Policy of the Government of India*, 88.

13. *Report of the [Bombay] Board of Education for the Year 1846*, 5. In another story a group of students admitted that they only believed what they had been taught, namely that the earth went round the sun, "as long as we are in the class-room." Archer, *India and the Future*, 240 n. In a variant of this story a schoolteacher states in response to a query from a government official that he teaches that the earth goes round the sun, but adds, "I believe that the sun goes round the earth." Sharp, *Rural Schools in the Central Provinces*, 101.

14. When the Sapru Commission came to investigate the issue, it complained that no reliable statistics had been collected by either government or educational institutions, making it difficult to estimate how many Indians did in fact end up in government employ. However it did conclude, "Upon the evidence before us, the vast majority of the products of our universities – and their parents share the feeling – aim at securing some appointment or other in the Government service." *Report of the Unemployment [Sapru] Committee*, 92. An attempt was made in 1882 to compute where graduates of the University of Calcutta had gone in the twenty-odd years since the first graduation. It found that for those whose subsequent steps could be tracked, 528 were in government service, 547 self-employed (but almost all of these were pleaders, or else attorneys or articled clerks), 187 in private service (but a large number of these were teachers in private schools), and 88 still studying. That is, almost all graduates were in government service or the law, or were teachers in private schools. Roy, *High Education and the Present Position of Graduates in Arts and Law of the Calcutta University*. In Madras the director of public instruction estimated that of the thousand or so graduates in the previous decade, probably 350 joined the government service, over half of these in the educational service. *Report on Public Instruction in the Madras Presidency for 1881–82*, 183.

15. The *Native Review* compared Indians to the Russians, for whom "all occupations not immediately connected with the State are comparatively mean and despicable." "Loyalty and Disloyalty," 355. See also *Constitution of India under the British Rule* (Montagu-Chelmsford Report, 1918), section 181, which summarizes some of the explanations commonly given for the premium that students and parents placed upon government employment.

16. In the educational system introduced by the British, wrote Sasadhar Sinha, "utility was, as it still continues to be, its chief test and justification. Education . . . in so far as it leads to knowledge for its own sake has been sacrificed to fruitbearing at its lowest level-administrative employment." "The Past, Present and Future of Indian Education," 58.

17. Mehta, *The Problem of Our Young Men After Leaving Schools and Colleges*, 12.

18. Holmes, "University Education in Bengal," 256. "A Native Philomath" confirmed that graduates "sell more dearly in the marriage market." *High Education in Bengal and the University of Calcutta*, 13.

19. Quoted in "Watchman," *Higher Education and Control* [i].

20. Examples include *The Bombay University Convocation Address of 1894*; Ghosh, *Higher Education in Bengal Under British Rule*, 151; and Wood, *Selected Articles on National Education*, 50.

21. *An Address by S. C. Roy*, 4.

22. *Proceedings of the Punjab Educational Conference and Exhibition*, 13–14. An inspector of schools in Bihar similarly reported that neither parents nor pupils had much regard for what they were being taught, "but they consider the acquisition of our language as necessary for the advancement of their children in this life, and therefore overcome their suspicions as to what may be the effect of this mode of Education upon their prospects in the next." *General Report on Public Instruction in the Lower Provinces of the Bengal Presidency for 1855–56*, appendix A, 122.

23. *Presidential Address at 26th Annual Session of the All India Muhammadan Educational Conference*, 25.

24. Convocation Address, Madras University, 1873, *Convocation Addresses of the Universities of Bombay and Madras*, ed. Rao, 88.

25. *Calcutta University Commission Report*, vol. 2, 154.

26. *Lord Curzon in India*, 485. "Memory," Curzon declared in an address delivered the year before, "is not mind, though it is a faculty of the mind." *Lord Curzon in India*, 317.

27. "A Native Philomath," *High Education in Bengal and the University of Calcutta*, 18.

28. On other matters to do with education, there were differences between the princely states and British India, some of which are explored in Bhagavan, *Sovereign Spheres*.

29. *Indian Universities [Raleigh] Commission Report*, vol. 2: Abstract of Evidence [unpaginated].

30. See for instance C. B. Rama Row, "Condition of Public Examinations," *Re-*

port of the Madras Educational Conference, 24. The system of payment by results came under criticism in Britain also, as did external examinations: the "Report of the Consultative Committee of the Board of Education on the Subject of Examinations in Secondary Schools in Great Britain" (1911) advised against allowing a "proliferation" of external exams – extracts in Maclure, ed., Educational Documents, 164–66.

31. Premchand, "Gorakhpur me Shiksha Sammelan," 212.

32. Indian Educational Policy . . . 1904, sections 11–12.

33. Indian Educational Policy . . . 1913, section 26.

34. Day, "Recollections of My School-Days," Bengal Peasant Life, Folktales of Bengal, Recollections of My School-Days, 510.

35. Welinkar, Our Young Men.

36. Calcutta University Commission Report, vol. 2, 224–25.

37. Mukerjee, An Examination into Present System of University Education in India and A Scheme of Reform, 11.

38. "1908 Convocation Address," University of Calcutta Convocation Addresses, 2nd edn, vol. 4, 1105. The Raleigh Commission similarly pronounced: "It is beyond doubt that the greatest evil from which the system of university education suffers in India is that teaching is subordinated to examination, not examination to teaching." Indian Universities [Raleigh] Commission Report, vol. 1, section 156 [p. 43].

39. Sarkar, "Confessions of a History Teacher," 663.

40. Rama Row, "Condition of Public Examinations," Report of the Madras Educational Conference, 24.

41. Shrivastava, "Some Aspects of our Present Educational System," 580.

42. "It was found that the abolition of texts obviated cramming methods in one direction, [but] it tended to make the examinations, and hence the teaching, centre upon grammatical niceties and to lead to the neglect of all reading, and thus conduced to cramming of another kind" (director of public instruction, Madras, quoted in Orange, Progress of Education in India, 1902–1907, 72). See also the testimony of C. A. Patterson, registrar of Madras University, reporting that the Madras University Senate had voted to reintroduce a textbook for English after the failure of the experiment in abolishing it. Indian Universities [Raleigh] Commission Report, vol. 2, Abstract of Evidence [unpaginated].

43. Reminiscences, Speeches and Writings of Sir Gooroo Dass Banerjee, 193. However, the proposal was adopted, and thus Calcutta University abolished a textbook for English at the very time Madras University reintroduced it. That thirty years later the Anderson Committee was still lamenting the effects of textbooks gives some indication of how ineffective such measures were; see Punjab University Enquiry [Anderson] Committee Report, 23.

44. J. R. Barrow, officiating principal of Presidency College, in Calcutta University Commission Report, vol. 10, 122. An unsuccessful product of this system even went so far as to say that university examinations were held "to patronise the key-makers." Chowdhury, A Humble Appeal of a Humble Heart, 10–11.

45. *Calcutta University Commission Report,* vol. 10, 197.

46. It was widely felt that European college teachers were those who could not achieve any distinction in their own country. An unsigned essay on "The Public Services Commission and the Educational Service," for instance, calculated that the forty-six Europeans appointed to the Indian Educational Service between 1912 and 1914 had an average academic achievement of only a Third Class Oxford Honours degree. *Modern Review,* August 1917, 181. Yet they were virtually assured of higher income than their Indian colleagues, because the Indian Educational Service was reserved mostly for Europeans and the second-rung Provincial Education Service for Indians, in fact if not in name. This inequality was compounded when the Public Services Commission added distinctions of rank and nomenclature to the existing racially based inequalities of income.

47. This did not make for easy interaction with their Indian students. Rabindranath Tagore wrote, "every European teacher carries about with him on his person the emblems of sovereign power, and so the throne takes the place of the *guru's* seat . . . the European professor does not look upon his vocation simply as that of teacher. He feels himself also to be a king of the country. He is a European and a Professor of an Imperial service to boot – a fragment of royalty. Often, also, he suffers from the conviction that he has come out to 'do us some good.'" "Indian Students and Western Teachers," 418.

48. L. C. Williams, "Status of Primary Teachers," *Report of the Madras Educational Conference,* 2.

49. The schoolteacher, wrote R. Rangaswami Aiyar, is "held in contempt . . . the butt of social ridicule." "Is the Teaching Profession Calculated to Attract the Best Type of Men?," 403. Schoolteaching was respectively described as "one of the least respected professions in society," "the last refuge of the incompetent and the despairing," and an occupation which "may be truly regarded as the forlorn hope of a hungry humanity" by Miss N. Ghose [Head Mistress of the Victoria Institution], "How to Make the Teaching Profession Attractive," *Report of the Bengal Women's Educational Conference,* 64; C. H. Barry, principal of Aitchison College in a radio talk (?1945), typescript in Barry Papers, 2; and Day, *Primary Education in Bengal,* 10.

50. "Report of the Committee of the Central Advisory Board Appointed to Consider the Question of Training, Recruitment and Conditions of Service of Teachers," Bureau of Education, *Reports of the Committees Appointed by the Central Advisory Board of Education in India,* 99. The *Educational Record,* a monthly issued from Madras, carried regular reports from officials of teacher's associations, documenting the appalling rates of pay and conditions.

51. Until the eve of Independence, having passed the Vernacular Final Exam – that is, having completed eight years of education – constituted a qualification for teaching at primary level. Only 54 percent of primary teachers in the public school sector had received any teacher training. The *Report of the [More] Committee on the Training of Primary Teachers,* from which these figures are drawn, concluded that "half the

teachers charged with the responsible task of imparting primary education are those who have had inadequate general training and no [teacher] training at all, and the remaining, though trained, have had unsatisfactory general education and a [teacher] training of an intermittent character" (18).

52. Answers of Hariprasad Ghosal to questions of the Hartog Committee [typescript] in Hartog Papers, MSS Eur. 221/45b, pp. 10, 11, India Office Library and Records, British Library.

53. Address to Calcutta Convocation, 1866, in University of Calcutta Convocation Addresses, vol. 1, 148.

54. Setalvad, Indian University Commission, vi.

55. Curzon, Principles and Methods of University Reform, 116.

56. Thus "A Native Philomath" described cramming as "the most serious intellectual malady of the present age throughout the civilised world," but added that "no where is it more dangerous than in Bengal." High Education in Bengal and the University of Calcutta, 18. Similarly, Lord Curzon acknowledged that cramming was a "universal" problem, but added that it appeared in its worst form in India and China. Opening Address to Educational Conference, Simla, September 1901, Lord Curzon in India, 317.

57. H. Dippie, "Principles of Education and Class Teaching," Instruction in Indian Primary Schools, 5.

58. Prasad, Teaching the Teacher, 6.

59. I refer of course to "An Answer to the Question: What Is Enlightenment." See also Kant's essay "What Does Orientation in Thinking Mean?" (1786) and also Anthropology from a Pragmatic Point of View, trans. Victor Dowdell, S 42 [pp. 91–92], in which Kant contrasts memory with genuine "understanding."

60. Quoted in John H. Zammito, Kant, Herder, and the Birth of Anthropology, 72.

61. Reminiscences, Speeches and Writings of Sir Gooroo Dass Banerjee, 155, 171.

62. Pal, Memories of My Life and Times, 21.

63. Verma, Shiksha-Samhar, 1921.

64. Fisher, India's Silent Revolution, 148.

65. Dippie, "Principles of Education and Class Teaching," 7.

66. Lord Curzon in India, 485.

67. Chanda, "Future of Education in Bengal," 316.

68. Quoted in Chaturvedi, The History of Rural Education in the United Provinces of Agra and Oudh, 174.

69. Calcutta University Commission Report, vol. 2, 150.

70. Report of the [Bombay] Board of Education for the Year 1845, 15–16.

71. Saiyidain, "Experiments in Education," 617. Twenty-five years later again, it was still being argued that "the indigenous systems of education helped to fix the character which was to be assumed by western education in India." Sinha, Problem of Education in Bengal, 103.

72. Brown, States of Injury, 22.

73. William Adam provided a revealing snapshot of the diversity of learning practices even in a single administrative unit, the *thana* of Nattore in Rajshahi district. See *Reports on the State of Education in Bengal*, second report and third report, 221 passim.

74. The discussion of *svadhyaya* in this paragraph draws upon Muller, *Lectures on the Origin and Growth of Religion* (especially the postscript to the third lecture); Staal, *Nambudiri Veda Recitation*; and Staal, *Ritual and Mantras*.

75. In his scholarly and nationalist work *Education in Ancient India* (which appeared first in the 1930s and then in subsequent editions) A. S. Altekar acknowledged that many pandits did not know the meaning of what they recited, but explained this as a consequence of a division of labor initiated when the number of texts became too large for any one body of persons to both commit them to memory and to understand and interpret them. At this point, he speculates, some pandits were assigned the task of interpreting, while others were required to "devote their energies to the mechanical memorizing of this extensive literature with a view to prevent its loss," an arrangement which "no doubt exposed some Brahmanas to the taunt of being mere parrot-like reciters of the Vedic hymns." "It is gratifying to find," Altekar goes on to observe, "that they did not mind it in the wider interests of the preservation of the national literature and culture" (150).

76. Staal, *Nambudiri Veda Recitation*, 16.

77. On the importance accorded to memory learning see inter alia Muller, *Lectures on the Origin and Growth of Religion*; Altekar, *Education in Ancient India*; Achyuthan, *Educational Practices in Manu, Panini and Kautilya*; Ghurye, *Preservation of Learned Tradition in India*; Venkateswara, *Indian Culture through the Ages*; Michaels, ed., *The Pandit*.

78. Carruthers, *The Book of Memory*.

79. Carruthers, *The Book of Memory*. See also Jaffee, *Torah in the Mouth*.

80. Sharp, *Rural Schools in the Central Provinces*, 69–70. Another European observer commented: "A large number of these naked little children would astound our most practised city clerks by running on with the multiplication table up to one hundred times one hundred." Fredrick Pincot, quoted in Chaturvedi, *The History of Rural Education in the United Provinces of Agra and Oudh*, 60.

81. "Education in Bengal," reproduced in Lethbridge, *High Education in India*, 194.

82. Mitchell, *Colonizing Egypt*, 85.

83. *Report of the Indian Education [Hunter] Commission*, vol. 1, 72, 66.

84. Williams, "Status of Primary Teachers," *Report of the Madras Educational Conference*, 3.

85. M. G. Ranade observed in 1882 that "the grown-up men of this generation have all been taught in their young days by indigenous school masters." "Primary Education and Indigenous Schools" (1882), *The Miscellaneous Writings of the Late Hon'ble Mr. Justice M. G. Ranade*, 265. For the reminiscences of some elderly men on the indigenous education which they had received around the turn of the century in Kerala see Wood, *Knowledge before Printing and After*.

86. Chaturvedi, *The History of Rural Education*. My summary of Chaturvedi's account of his school days is drawn from pp. 40–66.

87. Chaturvedi, *The History of Rural Education*, 41.

88. Chaturvedi, *The History of Rural Education*, 61.

89. Chaturvedi, *The History of Rural Education*, 64–65.

90. Chaturvedi, *The History of Rural Education*, 66.

91. The very richness of the Greek idea of freedom, it has been argued, is intimately connected to the absolute subjection implied by slavery in ancient Greece; see for instance Anderson, *Passages from Antiquity to Feudalism*, 23.

Chapter 2: Diagnosing Moral Crisis

1. Bengal Government Resolution establishing the General Committee of Public Instruction, 17 July 1823, reprinted in Zastoupil and Moir, eds., *The Great Indian Education Debate*, 108 (emphasis added).

2. *Indian Educational Policy . . . 1913*, section 5.

3. Ratcliffe, "The Teaching of Morals and Religion," 456.

4. Reddy, *An Address to Students*, 8.

5. Though they were partially mollified by the Despatch of 1854, which introduced a system of grant-in-aid for private schools, including missionary schools, as long as they provided instruction in secular subjects and submitted to government inspection and regulation.

6. Quoted in Clive, *Macaulay*, 411. Similarly, Charles Trevelyan told a Select Committee of the House of Lords that conversions "will take place at last wholesale . . . The country will have Christian instruction infused into it in every way by direct missionary education, and indirectly through books of various kinds, through the public papers, through conversations with Europeans, and in all the conceivable ways in which knowledge is communicated. Then at last, when society is completely saturated with Christian knowledge, and public opinion has taken a decided turn that way, they will come over by thousands." Quoted in Smith, *The Life of Alexander Duff*, vol. 2, 244–45. See similarly Richter, *A History of Missions in India*, 367; Elphinstone, *Selections from the Minutes and the Official Writings of the Honourable Mountstuart Elphinstone, Governor of Bombay*, 185–86; and a communication from the Madras Council of Education to the Board of Control, 29 July 1847, in "Papers Relating to Public Instruction," cclvi.

7. On missionary involvement in education see Laird, *Missionaries and Education in Bengal*; Viswanathan, *Masks of Conquest*, chapter 2; and Seth, "Which Good Book?"

8. Duff, *India and India Missions*, 560.

9. Duff, *India and India Missions*, 563.

10. The alarm this raised was genuine, but "Young Bengal" soon assumed almost mythical status as a warning-to-hand of the evils of freethinking. Lal Behari Day, a student and success story of Duff's educational endeavours—he converted and be-

came a Christian minister – wrote of "the revolution" which the intellectual youth of Calcutta were undergoing as a result of their contact with western education, and of the "wildness of their views; the reckless innovations they were introducing; the infidel character of their religious sentiments; and the spirit of unbounded liberty, or rather of lawless licentiousness, which characterised their speculations." Day, *Bengal Peasant Life, Folktales of Bengal, Recollections of My School-Days*, 472. Addressing the Muhammadan Educational Conference, Abdul Karim gave expression to what had become a sort of commonplace: "Not being grounded in their ancestral theology and traditions these men were infected with scepticism; and the morals of educated Bengalis suffered in consequence. Indeed the Hindu society of the time presented the appearance of chaos." Karim, *Muhammedan Education in Bengal*, 4.

11. Letter, 15 October 1830, Church of Scotland Foreign Mission Papers, MS 7530, National Library of Scotland.

12. Duff, *Missionary Addresses*, 88. Duff himself acknowledged the "service" that Hindu College had rendered his cause when he rhetorically asked, "Have all the efforts of the missionaries given a tithe of that shock to the superstitions of the people which has been given by the Hindu College?" *New Era of English Language and English Literature in India*, 39.

13. Bryce, *The Schoolmaster and the Missionary in India*, 8.

14. Bryce, *The Schoolmaster and the Missionary in India*, 9.

15. See Jordens, "Reconversion to Hinduism"; and Oddie, "Anti-missionary Feeling and Hindu Revivalism in Madras." With this self-assertion also came a new self-confidence. In 1932 Lajpat Rai could declare that while missionaries would make some converts, India would always remain Hindu, because it had developed many defensive ramparts, including the Brahmo Samaj, the Arya Samaj, the Theosophists, and the Vivekenanda mission. Rai, *The Arya Samaj*, 308.

16. Keane, *A Letter to the Late Honourable J. E. D. Bethune, Esq.*, 10, 12.

17. Sherring, *The History of Protestant Missions in India*, 114. The Duke of Marlborough, inveighing against the exclusion of the Bible from government schools in the House of Lords, warned that the corrosive effects of secular learning left the native student "a man without a creed, and without a faith." *Speech of the Duke of Marlborough upon the Exclusion of the Bible from Government Schools*, 12. The indefatigable John Murdoch, speaking in one of his many avatars as the bringer of light to the natives (this time as secretary to the Madras branch of the Christian Vernacular Education Society), warned that "the natives are in great danger of passing from superstition to scepticism." "Papers Relating to Discipline and Moral Training in Schools and Colleges of India," 64.

18. *Report of the Indian Education [Hunter] Commission*, vol. 1, 303–7.

19. "Letter from the Government of India to all Local Governments and Administrations," Calcutta, 31 December 1887, "Papers Relating to Discipline and Moral Training in Schools and Colleges of India," 11, 18.

20. The minutes of the discussions held in Simla are in Home Education, November 1901, 47–61(A), National Archives of India.

21. *Indian Educational Policy . . . 1904*, para. 25.

22. Chirol, *Indian Unrest*, 207.

23. Chirol, *Indian Unrest*, 239.

24. Chirol, *Indian Unrest*, 240–41.

25. "Papers Regarding the Educational Conference, Allahabad, February 1911," 86.

26. *Report of the Proceedings of a Conference on Moral, Civic and Sanitary Instruction*, 2.

27. As was noted by the director general for education in 1910. Education Department, September 1911, 74–76(A), 10, National Archives of India.

28. It was observed that these textbooks were often used by schools to provide reading lessons, rather than for their moral content; see "Papers Regarding the Educational Conference, Allahabad, February 1911," 87. And Curzon observed, "If people can cram Euclid, there is nothing to prevent them from cramming ethics." *Lord Curzon in India*, 337. Scepticism was also expressed about the quality of the textbooks; for instance, J. L. Jenkins, Home Member of the Government of India, commented, "All the moral text-books I have seen are either dreadfully dull or intolerably mawkish and priggish. To a boy of sound healthy mind they would only afford matter for scoffing." Education Department, September 1911, 74–76(A), 11, National Archives of India. An inspector of schools wrote, "It is a question whether some of the moral stories now read by school children do not tend to make moral instruction ridiculous." Quoted in Orange, *Progress of Education in India, 1902–1907*, 81. See also Ghosh, *National Education*, 7.

29. Quoted in Kumar, "Religion and Ritual in Indian Schools," 139.

30. Education Department, September 1911, 74–76(A), National Archives of India.

31. Education Department, September 1911, 74–76(A), National Archives of India.

32. A resolution was drafted on the question of religious and moral education and sent to the secretary of state in December 1919; the draft and the introductory comments of the education member are in Education Department, December 1919, 18(A), National Archives of India.

33. "Papers Relating to Discipline and Moral Training in Schools and Colleges of India," 107.

34. "Papers Relating to Discipline and Moral Training in Schools and Colleges of India," 73.

35. Quoted in Satthianadhan, *History of Education in the Madras Presidency*, 89.

36. See for instance the convocation address in 1874 of E. C. Bayley, vice-chancellor of Calcutta University, in *University of Calcutta Convocation Addresses*, vol. 1; the address in 1898 of the lieutenant-governor of Punjab, Sir William Mackworth Young, to the Punjab University in Thapar, ed., *Convocation Addresses of the University of the Punjab*; and the convocation address in 1893 of the chancellor of Allahabad University, Sir Charles Crosthwaite, in Thapar, ed., *Convocation Addresses of the Universities of Allahabad and Punjab*.

37. "Minute recorded by Kashinath Telang," *Report of the Indian Education [Hunter] Commission*, vol. 1, 606–19.

38. Gupta, *Addresses on Educational Matters*, 3.

39. *Calcutta University Commission Report*, vol. 12, 60.

40. *Calcutta University Commission Report*, vol. 12, 65.

41. *An Appeal to the British Nation for the Promotion of Education in India*, 5, 4.

42. Sen, *Letters on Educational Measures to Lord Northbrook*, 40. These open letters to the viceroy of India were first published in the *Indian Mirror* in 1872.

43. Quoted in Murdoch, *India's Greatest Educational Need*, 3.

44. In his estimation, "The vast majority of the newly-educated classes were condemned to live in an agonising mental and moral conflict ... not a few of them [were driven] to an openly irreligious and immoral life." Pal, *Memories of My Life and Times*, 400. Pal was not writing as a propagandist for the Brahmo cause, however. He went on to argue that Hindu revivalism was another way out of this dilemma, for it allowed Hindus to make their peace with their traditions, reject British critiques of them, and yet pursue modernizing agendas upon other fronts.

45. Malaviya, *The Hindu University of Benares*, 29. Similarly, Lala Hansraj (head of the Arya Samaj's Dayanand Anglo-Vedic College in Lahore) denounced the "godless education of Government Schools and Colleges" for cutting educated Hindus off from their spiritual and moral moorings, consequences only preventable by an education which reinforced their religious and spiritual values; cited in Rai, *The Arya Samaj*, 283–85.

46. *The Hindu University*, 9. The movement to establish a Hindu university was successful. When in 1915 Sir Harcourt Butler, education member of the Government of India, introduced a bill to establish a Hindu university to the Imperial Legislative Council, he acknowledged that ten years previously such a bill would not have been supported by the government. One reason for acting now was the perceived need for religious instruction. Reflecting upon the colonial government's newfound enthusiasm for instruction even in the tenets of Hinduism, he told another audience, "I would far rather see religious instruction conveyed in a faith alien and even hostile to my own than to see children brought up on non-religious instruction." Butler, *Collection of Speeches*, 4–5, 23.

47. Home Education, November 1905, 80–81(A), National Archives of India. The government responded by assuring the memorialists that it was conscious of the "supreme importance" of the issue, and that it was "strenuously" exerting itself with the hope that in time "a progressive elevation of the character and conduct of the race" would become apparent.

48. Home Education, August 1920, 1–3(A), National Archives of India. See also Ratcliffe, "The Teaching of Morals and Religion."

49. Fuller, *The Empire of India*, 179.

50. Fuller, *The Empire of India*, 179.

51. Archer, *India and the Future*, 240.

52. K.V.A., "Calcutta University Reform," 10–11.

53. *The Pioneer*, 10 January 1888, 2.

54. Banerji, "Discipline," 37.

55. Ghosh, *Higher Education in Bengal under British Rule*, 161.

56. Response of VD Ghate to questionnaire of Hartog Commission, 29 Sept 1928, in Hartog Collection, MSS Eur E221/406, unpaginated, Indian Office Library and Records.

57. Marx, *Capital*, vol. 1, 174.

58. Quoted in Godlove, *Religion, Interpretation, and Diversity of Belief*, 40.

59. Harrison, *"Religion" and the Religions in the English Enlightenment*, 2. See also Asad, *Genealogies of Religion*; Wittgenstein, *Remarks on Frazer's Golden Bough*; Byrne, *Natural Religion and the Nature of Religion*; Pailin, *Attitudes to Other Religions*; Needham, *Belief, Language, and Experience*; Balagangadhara, *"The Heathen in His Blindness . . ."*; and Puillon, *"Remarks on the Verb 'To Believe.' "* Wilfred Cantwell Smith argues that unlike most other religions Christianity has required a "belief" in certain things as evidence of faith. He also traces the etymology of the word "believe," showing that "a shift has taken place from the verb's designating an interpersonal relation to its naming a theoretical judgment . . . Between believing a person, in the sense of trusting him or her, having faith in him or her . . . and believing a proposition." *Faith and Belief*, 118.

60. King, *Orientalism and Religion*, 40.

61. John Hick, Foreword vii. Jonathan Z. Smith goes further, suggesting that "man has had his entire history in which to imagine deities and modes of interaction with them. But man, more precisely western man, has had only the last few centuries in which to imagine religion . . . Religion is solely the creation of the scholar's study. It is created for the scholar's analytic purposes by his imaginative acts of comparison and generalization. Religion has no independent existence apart from the academy." *Imagining Religion*, xi.

62. Marshall, Introduction, *The British Dictionary of Hinduism in the Eighteenth Century*, 43.

63. Marshall, Introduction, *The British Dictionary of Hinduism in the Eighteenth Century*, 20.

64. L. S. S. O'Malley, for instance, writes, "The higher and the lower forms of religion still coexist side by side. At one end of the scale, therefore, is the cultured monotheist or the eclectic pantheist for whom no mysticism is too subtle . . . At the bottom of the scale is a great multitude of people in a low scale of religious development, some of whom have scarcely risen above mere fetishism." *Popular Hinduism*, 2. See similarly Henry Whitehead, *The Village Gods of South India*, 12.

65. For instance, Lawrence Babb, author of an ethnographic study of popular Hinduism in Central India, finds: "There is practically nothing to be gained in questioning Chattisgarhi informants about what they believe, for this is simply not the

primary context in which religious matters are understood." *The Divine Hierarchy*, 31. See similarly Balagangadhara, "*The Heathen in his Blindness . . . ,*" 16.

66. Muller, *Anthropological Religion*, 155.

67. Quoted in Jones, "The Concept of Belief in *The Elementary Forms*," 55.

68. Nandy, "A Report on the Present State of Health of the Gods and Goddesses in South Asia," 126.

69. Fuller, *The Camphor Flame*, 31. Similarly, Nandy writes, "the human inferiority to gods is not absolute; no wide chasm separates the goals and motivations of gods and humans . . . There is continuity between the divine and the earthly." Nandy, "A Report on the Present State of Health of the Gods and Goddesses in South Asia," 130.

70. Luke Scrafton, *Reflections on the Government etc of Indostan; and a Short Sketch of the History of Bengal, from the Year 1739 to 1756* (1761), quoted in Trautmann, *Aryans and British India*, 65. O'Malley similarly writes that "cultured and enlightened" Hindus, for whom the many gods are all faces of one God, sanctioned idolatry as "permissible or even expedient for those who are incapable of transcendental thought and require external aids to worship." *Popular Hinduism*, 23.

71. Quoted in Freedberg, *The Power of Images*, 162.

72. Richard Davis marks the difference in the following terms: "Medieval Christian images . . . are instrumental and representational. Aquinas and Bonaventure locate them within a semiotic aesthetics, where the image is seen as conveying a message separate from the image itself." By contrast, "Vaisnava and Saiva theologians locate their holy icons within an aesthetics of presence. As an instantiation of the godhead, the image is ultimately the message." *Lives of Indian Images*, 32, 33.

73. On these see among others Davis, *Lives of Indian Images*, esp. chapter 1; and the essays in Waghorne and Cutler, eds., *Gods of Flesh, Gods of Stone*. Such consecration ceremonies, preparing statues to come to "life," were common in ancient Egypt, Babylonia, Sumer, and Assyria; see Freedberg, *The Power of Images*, 84–87.

74. Eck, *Darsan*, 38. See also the essays in Waghorne and Cutler, eds., *Gods of Flesh, Gods of Stone*.

75. On this see my "Reason or Reasoning? Clio or Siva?"

76. Fuller, *The Camphor Flame*.

77. McDougall, *Lamps in the Wind*, 79.

78. Hegel, *Lectures on the Philosophy of Religion*, 289. In a similar vein Hegel refers to the "shocking inconsistency" of a religion which has a concept of totality, of a singular god, but which at the same time particularizes that Oneness into numerous gods, "a wild particularity in which there is no system . . . no understandable totality or systematization, much less a rational one" (272).

79. Fuller, for instance, whose study of popular Hinduism I draw upon above, writes, "This fluidity—which means that one deity can become many and many deities can become one—is a supremely important characteristic of Hindu polytheism." *The Camphor Flame*, 30.

80. "It is at a later stage of social evolution that what we call a natural phenomenon tends to become the sole content of perception to the exclusion of other elements, which then assume the aspect of beliefs, and finally appear as superstitions." Lévy-Bruhl, How Natives Think, 44–45.

81. Lévy-Bruhl, How Natives Think, 68.

82. Lévy-Bruhl, How Natives Think, 363.

83. Needham, Belief, Language, and Experience, 183.

84. Mitchell, Colonizing Egypt, 61.

85. Mitchell, Colonizing Egypt, 60. Extracts from Bourdieu's original essay are reprinted in English as "The Berber House" in Douglas, ed., Rules and Meaning.

86. The idea that there is a different logic at work—a "Hindu" way of thinking, for instance, in which "inconsistency" does not appear as a problem—is one that has been speculated upon by anthropologists and others. A. K. Ramanujan adapts the linguistic concept of "context sensitivity" to explain the reasons for Indian inconsistency in "Is There an Indian Way of Thinking?," 44. In a somewhat similar fashion, Sheryl Daniel has explained inconsistency in terms of the "tool box" approach of the Tamil, whose culture, she explains, "enjoins a certain relativistic and consequently an inconsistent pattern of choosing among the various options available within the culture. It legitimizes a "contextualized" approach to decision making and discourages trans-contextual, consistent preferences." Daniel, "The Tool Box Approach of the Tamil to the Issues of Moral Responsibility and Human Destiny." Bernard Cohn has wondered aloud whether the question itself might not be misplaced—whether the presumption that consistency is the norm and inconsistency something in need of explanation might simply reflect a modern prejudice. Cohn, "The Pasts of an Indian Village," An Anthropologist among the Historians and Other Essays, 98.

87. See for instance Mohanty, Reason and Tradition in Indian Thought, esp. 198.

88. On this see Collins, Selfless Persons.

89. Marriot, "Hindu Transactions," 111. See also Strathern, The Gender of the Gift.

90. Marriot, "Hindu Transactions," 109–10.

91. Thus Valentine Daniel titles his study Fluid Signs: Being a Person the Tamil Way.

92. Quoted in Winch, The Idea of a Social Science.

93. Here I am of course drawing upon Ricoeur's well-known characterization of Marx, Nietzsche, and Freud as masters of a "hermeneutics of suspicion." See Freud and Philosophy.

94. Singer's study is a product of a time when "tradition" and "modernity" were the two poles around which many studies of the nonwestern world were organized, and his argument seeks to problematize the antithetical nature of these two organizing categories by showing that the "transition" from one to another is not a complete effacement of tradition by modernity. As he puts it, his study is an argument against "the tendency to misinterpret this relationship as a temporal succession of mutually incompatible types of society." Singer, When a Great Tradition Modernizes, 365.

95. Singer, When a Great Tradition Modernizes, 343.

96. Singer, *When a Great Tradition Modernizes*, 321.

97. Singer, *When a Great Tradition Modernizes*, 348.

98. Singer, *When a Great Tradition Modernizes*, 385.

99. Chakrabarty, *Provincializing Europe*, 22; the discussion of KK is from 218–23.

100. Chakrabarty, *Provincializing Europe*, 220.

101. Chakrabarty, *Provincializing Europe*, 221.

102. Žižek, "Is There a Cause of the Subject?," 102.

103. See for instance Sarkar, " 'Kaliyuga,' 'Chakri' and 'Bhakti.' "

Chapter 3: Which Past? Whose History?

1. Guha, *Dominance without Hegemony*, 193.

2. Guha, *Dominance without Hegemony*, 195.

3. For discussions of the early historical writings by Indians see Chatterjee, *The Nation and Its Fragments*, chapters 4–5; Kaviraj, *The Unhappy Consciousness*, chapter 4; Nandy, *The Intimate Enemy*; Guha, *Dominance without Hegemony*; Mallick, "Modern Historical Writing in Bengali"; and Majumdar, "Nationalist Historians." There was at least one "history" written in this period in the "Puranic" mode: Mrityunjay Vidyalankar's *Rajabali* (1808), which spans a period from the kings of the *Mahabharata* to early colonial times.

4. Appleby, Hunt, and Jacob, *Telling the Truth about History*, 259.

5. "An Introduction to the Study of the Human Sciences," Dilthey, *Selected Writings*, 159.

6. "Understanding ranges from the apprehension of scientific patter to understanding *Hamlet* or the *Critique of Pure Reason*. The same human spirit speaks to us from stone, marble, musical compositions, gestures, words and writings, from actions, economic arrangements and constitutions, and has to be interpreted." "The Development of Hermeneutics," Dilthey, *Selected Writings*, 248.

7. "The Construction of the Historical World in the Human Sciences," Dilthey, *Selected Writings*, 221.

8. "An Introduction to the Study of the Human Sciences," Dilthey, *Selected Writings*, 162.

9. "The Construction of the Historical World in the Human Sciences," Dilthey, *Selected Writings*, 207.

10. "Drafts for a Critique of Historical Reason," Dilthey, *Selected Writings*, 207.

11. Gadamer, *Truth and Method*, 204.

12. "The Construction of the Historical World in the Human Sciences," Dilthey, *Selected Writings*, 193. Thus Dilthey "demotes" art, religion, and philosophy to the position of objective mind rather than absolute mind.

13. Gadamer, *Truth and Method*, 204.

14. Bambach, *Heidegger, Dilthey, and the Crisis of Historicism*, 181. Or as Gadamer puts it, "Dilthey ultimately conceives the investigation of the historical past as a de-

ciphering and not as an historical experience . . . epistemological Cartesianism domi-nated . . . so that in Dilthey the historicity of historical experience did not become a truly determining element." *Truth and Method*, 213.

15. Gadamer, *Truth and Method*, 339.

16. Gadamer, *Truth and Method*, 245.

17. Gadamer, *Truth and Method*, 245.

18. Gadamer writes, "Even the most genuine and solid tradition does not per-sist by nature because of the inertia of what once existed. It needs to be affirmed, embraced, cultivated. It is, essentially, preservation . . . But preservation is an act of reason, though an inconspicuous one . . . preservation is as much a freely-chosen action as revolution and renewal." *Truth and Method*, 250.

19. Gadamer, *Truth and Method*, 246.

20. Indeed, it is precisely through an encounter with an object from the past that our prejudices can be "stimulated" and thus recognized as prejudices that have to be reexamined afresh. *Truth and Method*, 266.

21. Warnke, *Gadamer*, 103.

22. Ricoeur, "The Task of Hermeneutics," 150. Or as Gadamer himself puts it, "only the vivid thematization of human existence as 'being-in-the-world' discloses the full implications of *Verstehen* as an existential possibility and structure." "The Problem of Historical Consciousness," 84.

23. Heidegger, "Annotations," quoted in Barash, *Martin Heidegger and the Problem of Historical Meaning*, 143.

24. Gadamer, *Truth and Method*, 232.

25. Gadamer, *Truth and Method*, 264.

26. Gadamer, *Truth and Method*, 261.

27. Gadamer, *Truth and Method*, 268.

28. Palmer, ed. and trans., *Gadamer in Conversation*, 46.

29. Ricoeur, *Time and Narrative*, vol. 3, 80.

30. Heidegger, *Being and Time*, s72 [pp. 427–28].

31. Heidegger, *Being and Time*, s74 [p. 434].

32. Heidegger, *Being and Time*, s74 [p. 438].

33. Heidegger writes, "I can very well admit that if, in a certain way, one takes the analysis of *Dasein* in *Being and Time* as an investigation of people, and then asks the question how, on the basis of this understanding of people, it might be possible to understand culture and the realms of culture; that when one asks this question in such a way, it is impossible to say something from what is given here." Quoted in Barash, *Martin Heidegger and the Problem of Historical Meaning*, 225 n. 29.

34. Ricoeur, "The Task of Hermeneutics," 156.

35. Ricoeur, *Time and Narrative*, vol. 3, 79. See similarly Carr, *Time, Narrative and History*.

36. Ricoeur, *Time and Narrative*, vol. 3, 241.

37. Ricoeur, *Time and Narrative*, vol. 3, 247.

38. Ricoeur, *Time and Narrative*, vol. 3, 248.

39. Heidegger, *Being and Time*, esp. s76 [pp. 446–47]. On this see also Hoy, "History, Historicity, and Historiography in *Being and Time*," 345–46.

40. Veyne, *Writing History*, 80.

41. Veyne, *Writing History*, 72. See also Michael Oakeshott, "Three Essays on History," *On History and Other Essays*.

42. Lévi-Strauss, *The Savage Mind*, 258.

43. Constantine Fasolt provides an admirably lucid description of the "basic principles" that the practice of history encodes: "That the past is gone; that it can nonetheless be turned into an object of scholarly examination by means of evidence; that the evidence was produced by some specific agent at some specific time and place for a specific purpose; that scholarly examination can take advantage of the agent's responsibility for the evidence to reconstruct its meaning; that evidence must therefore be interpreted in the context of its time and place; and above all, that things do have a time and place that may be called their own." *The Limits of History*, 222.

44. Koselleck, *Futures Past*, 200.

45. On which see Baker, "Enlightenment and the Institution of Society"; Polanyi, *The Great Transformation*, esp. chapter 10; and Joyce, ed., *The Social in Question*.

46. Koselleck, *Futures Past*, 296.

47. Ludwig Feuerbach, "Principles of the Philosophy of the Future," *The Fiery Brook*, 177 [para./aphorism 1].

48. James Clifford, "On Ethnographic Authority," *The Predicament of Culture*, 39–40. See also Asad, "The Concept of Cultural Translation in British Social Anthropology," 155.

49. Bloch, *The Historian's Craft*, 26.

50. Bloch, *The Historian's Craft*, 55.

51. In Oakeshott's elegant formulation, "a record never lies; even if it does not mean what it says it may be made to say what it means." "Three Essays on History," *On History and Other Essays*, 52.

52. Weber, "Objectivity in Social Science and Social Policy," 81. Earlier in the same essay Weber makes clear that what he defines as the cultural sciences encompass what are traditionally defined as social sciences (67).

53. Weber, "Objectivity in Social Science and Social Policy," 57.

54. Kolb, *The Critique of Pure Modernity*, 9–10.

55. From *The Will to Power*, quoted in Heidegger, *Nietzsche*, 81.

56. Martin Heidegger, "The Age of the World Picture," 133.

57. Foucault, *The Archaeology of Knowledge*, 12.

58. Foucault, *The Archaeology of Knowledge*, 14.

59. Lévi-Strauss, *The Savage Mind*, 262.

60. Certeau, *The Writing of History*, 138. The two paragraphs quoted here appear in the reverse order in the original, but the emphasis is in the original.

61. Certeau, *The Writing of History*, 138.

62. Certeau, *The Writing of History*, 36.

63. Certeau, *The Writing of History*, 36.

64. This book was published under Conring's name, possibly by one of his students (it is the text of a "dissertation" submitted by one of Conring's students to the University of Helmstedt, in 1841), a practice not unusual at the time; Conring disowned the work, but Fasolt suggests that the ideas in it are Conring's, for they are a reprise of a work he had written earlier.

65. Fasolt, *The Limits of History*, 199.

66. Fasolt, *The Limits of History*, 218.

67. Fasolt, *The Limits of History*, 223. In Fasolt's presentation this form of understanding was promoted by the Renaissance humanists for a particular purpose: to invalidate the claims to authority of the Holy Roman Emperor and the church, and thereby to secure and legitimate the claims of the emergent sovereign, territorial states. What was a novel mode of argumentation congealed into common sense once that mode of reasoning and the political cause that it served had triumphed: "History was no longer recognized as the tool that a particular party had deployed in order to advance its cause. History was thought to be no tool at all but an impartial form of understanding, capable of encompassing all forms of humanity . . . History seemed no longer humanist but human" (27).

68. Arguably he overstates this incommensurability – see the interesting review essay by Hunter, "The State of History and the Empire of Metaphysics."

69. Fasolt, *The Limits of History*, 213.

70. As Walter Mignolo observes, "The understanding of 'our' tradition, in which the foundation of philosophical discursive hermeneutics rests, implies that the tradition to be understood and the understanding subject are one and the same." *The Darker Side of the Renaissance*, 11. This presumption does not obtain in the colonies, and Mignolo, who labels it a "monotopic" understanding of hermeneutics, goes on to advocate and practice "plurotopic hermeneutics."

71. For a brief but illuminating comment on this see Guha, "The Authority of Vernacular Pasts."

72. Foucault, *The Archaeology of Knowledge*, 203.

73. In much the same way, the free, equal, and autonomous individual presumed by liberalism is a historical product, not a "natural" premise. But this does not disqualify this premise; to posit and presume such an individual may be a useful way of analyzing liberal societies, and of engaging in debates within them.

74. Jacques Derrida, "White Mythology: Metaphor in the Text of Philosophy," *Margins of Philosophy*.

Chapter 4: Governmentality and Identity

1. Hacking, "Making Up People," 223.

2. Hacking, "Making Up People," 228.

3. Anderson, *Imagined Communities*, 169. See also his "Nationalism, Identity, and the Logic of Seriality" in *The Specter of Comparisons*.

4. Bernard Cohn, "The Census, Social Structure and Subjectification in South Asia," *An Anthropologist among the Historians and Other Essays*.

5. On this see the essays in Barrier, ed., *The Census in British India*; Pandey, *The Construction of Communalism in Colonial North India*; Bernard Cohn, "Notes on the History of the Study of Indian Society and Culture" and "The Census, Social Structure and Objectification in South Asia," both in *An Anthropologist among the Historians and Other Essays*; Smith, "Rule-by-Records and Rule-by-Reports"; Pant, "The Cognitive Status of Caste in Colonial Ethnography"; Dirks, *Castes of Mind*; Nigam, "Disciplining and Policing the 'Criminals by Birth.'" Accounts which contest or seek to radically qualify this proposition include Peabody, "Cents, Sense, Census"; and Guha, "The Politics of Identity and Enumeration in India."

6. Appadurai, "Number in the Colonial Imagination," 335.

7. Appadurai, "Number in the Colonial Imagination," 335.

8. *General Report on Public Instruction in Bengal, 1851–52*, xliv. See also *General Report on Public Instruction in the Lower Provinces of the Bengal Presidency for 1844–45*, appendix 5.

9. W. S. Seton-Karr in *University of Calcutta Convocation Addresses*, vol. 1, 18.

10. Hunter is here quoting E. C. Bayley, secretary to the government of India. Hunter, *The Indian Musalmans*, 112.

11. A resolution issued by Governor-General Hardinge in October 1844 declared that preference should be given in government employment to those who had been educated in institutions established by the government. However, it was to be many years before western education in fact became necessary for government employ, occasioning persistent complaint by those who had urged the resolution – see for example Kerr, *A Review of Public Instruction in the Bengal Presidency from 1835 to 1851*, pt I, chapter xv.

12. Hunter, *The Indian Musalmans*, 132.

13. Hunter, *The Indian Musalmans*, 137. What is implicit here – the suggestion that the "conservatism" of Muslims, responsible for their tardy embrace of western education, nonetheless reflected to their credit – was sometimes made explicit. A senior civil servant and former director of public instruction in Bengal declared that Muslim students were much superior in character to Hindus, precisely because their parents insisted that the education of their sons include religious instruction. This insistence had proved a barrier to Muslim participation in western education, and Muslims had suffered "in that they have not secured the loaves and fishes" which followed upon western education; but "their staunchness has been worthy of the greatest admiration." Note by A. Earle, 28 August 1910, Education Department 74–76(A), 1911, National Archives of India.

14. Hunter, *The Indian Musalmans*, 124–25.

15. In fact the evolution of government policy and the publication of Hunter's book were not entirely unconnected. Viceroy Mayo had asked Hunter to write a book

on the question of whether Muslims were likely to rebel against British rule, and the book was written at the same time that government policy on the issue was evolving – see Hardy, *The Muslims of British India*, 85, 88.

16. Quoted in Hunter, *A Life of the Earl of Mayo*, 307.

17. *Report of the Indian Education [Hunter] Commission*, vol. 1, 505.

18. In his review of Hunter's *The Indian Musalmans*, reprinted in abridged form in Mohammad, ed., *Writings and Speeches of Sir Syed Ahmad Khan*, 65–82.

19. "Correspondence on the Subject of the Education of the Muhammadan Community in British India and Their Employment in the Public Service Generally," 237, 239.

20. Huque, *History and Problems of Moslem Education in Bengal*, 2–3.

21. Huque, *History and Problems of Moslem Education in Bengal*, 25, 26.

22. "Memorial of the Central National Muhammadan Association," 2.

23. For instance, the claim that Muslims in the Bombay presidency were more likely to attend school if Urdu was the language of instruction was repeatedly disputed – see *Report of the Director of Public Instruction in the Bombay Presidency for the Year 1872-73*, appendixes A3–A4; *The Problem of Urdu Teaching in the Bombay Presidency*; and Education Department, July 1917, 12–13(A), National Archives of India.

24. "Report of the Members of the Select Committee for the Better Diffusion and Advancement of Learning among the Muhammadans of India," Muhammad, ed., *The Aligarh Movement*, 340–43. This report is discussed at some length in Lelyveld, *Aligarh's First Generation*, esp. 121–30, and also Malik, *Sir Sayyid Ahmad Khan and Muslim Modernization in India and Pakistan*, 126–36.

25. *Report of the Committee Appointed by the Bengal Government to Consider Questions Connected with Muhammadan Education*, 3. The authorities in the princely state of Travancore also concluded that "the question of the provision of religious education had stood in the way of an extension of education for Muslims." *Report of the Travancore Education Reforms Committee*, 283.

26. Government of Bengal Resolution, 3 August 1916, reprinted in *Muslim Education, with Special Reference to the Madrasa-i-Azam*, 9. A few years later the Calcutta University Commission drew a similar conclusion: *Calcutta University Commission Report*, vol. 1, 37.

27. Anderson, *Progress of Education in India, 1927-32*, vol. 1, 242.

28. *Report of the Indian Education [Hunter] Commission*, vol. 1, 483.

29. H. N. B. Erskine, commissioner for Sind, declared, "so far as Sind is concerned . . . Mahomedans have no ground for complaining that they do not get a fair share of valuable appointments." "Correspondence on the Subject of the Education of the Muhammadan Community in British India and Their Employment in the Public Service Generally," 264.

30. "Correspondence on the Subject of the Education of the Muhammadan Community in British India and Their Employment in the Public Service Generally," 264, 280.

31. "Correspondence on the Subject of the Education of the Muhammadan Community in British India and Their Employment in the Public Service Generally," 373.

32. "Report of the Members of the Select Committee for the Better Diffusion and Advancement of Learning among the Muhammadans of India."

33. Mahmood, *A History of English Education in India*, iv. The eighth annual meeting of the Muhammadan Educational Conference, held in 1893 after some two decades of government efforts to address the problem, passed a resolution declaring: "The Conference is of the opinion that whatever has been done up to this time for the education and instruction of the Mussalmans is entirely insufficient . . . As long as united exertions are not made to impart to them the highest education and culture, we must despair of the advancement of the Mussalmans, either in education or in their general condition." Report by the *Bombay Gazette* on the Eighth Muhammadan Educational Conference, 1893, reprinted in Muhammad, ed., *The Aligarh Movement*, vol. 3, 837.

34. For instance, a circular from the Government of India to local governments, dated 3 April 1913, observed that while there had been considerable improvement in the proportion of Muslims enrolled at the lower rungs of the educational ladder, they continued to be underrepresented at the higher rungs. The circular attributed this fact to the poverty of the community, the special linguistic needs of Muslims, the absence of religious instruction in government high schools and colleges, and the underrepresentation of Muslims on educational bodies. Provincial governments were asked to appoint committees to enquire into the problem and make recommendations for alleviating it. Education Department, May 1913, 106(3), National Archives of India.

35. These included scholarships specifically for Muslim students, separate institutions for Muslims (such as Islamia colleges and secondary schools, and *maktabs* and *madrassas* adapted to combine "traditional" and western learning), the appointment of special inspectors in education departments to oversee and encourage Muslim education, a requirement that educational appointments include a minimum number of Muslims, and after 1911 a relaxation of the rule that no religious instruction should take place in government schools. For a more complete list see Basu, *The Growth of Education and Political Development in India*, 156–61.

36. Lelyveld, *Aligarh's First Generation*, 86.

37. A senior educational official was to echo the Hunter Commission some twenty years after its report: "the most powerful factors which have up to now held them back will probably be found in their pride of race, memory of by-gone superiority, religious fears, a deep-rooted attachment to the religion of Islam, and the question of language . . . When the control of the country passed from the Muhammadan conquerors to the British . . . [Muslims] sat apart, wrapped in the memory of their traditions and in the contemplation of their ancient literature and bygone systems of science." H. Sharp, quoted in Orange, *Progress of Education in India, 1902–1907*, 295. See also the *Calcutta University Commission Report*, vol. 1, chapter 6.

38. Ronaldshay, *India*, 235; Sen, *History of Elementary Education in India.*

39. For instance, in the Madras census of 1871 the tables on education and literacy lumped together Hindus, Jains, and Christians, to allow a comparison of how Muslims were faring vis-à-vis "the rest." Conlon, "The Census of India as a Source for the Historical Study of Religion and Caste," 106.

40. Quoted in Mahmood, *History of English Education*, 175.

41. "The Mahomedan Educational Congress: Aims and Objectives," reprinted in Muhammad, ed., *The Aligarh Movement*, vol. 3, 767–69.

42. Beck reported on the results of this to the 1893 session of the conference; this "Report of the Muhammadan Educational Census" is reprinted in Muhammad, ed., *The Aligarh Movement*, vol. 3, 842–45.

43. See for instance Latour and Woolgar, *Laboratory Life.*

44. Canguilhem, *The Normal and the Pathological*, esp. 76, 89.

45. Hunter, *Rethinking the School*, 45.

46. For an interesting study of the relation between "traditional" education and Islam in a very different setting see Eickelman, *Knowledge and Power in Morocco.*

47. Foucault, *The History of Sexuality*, 138, 139.

48. Foucault, "Governmentality," 101.

49. Barry, Osborne, and Rose, Introduction, *Foucault and Political Reason*, 8.

50. Hunter, *Culture and Government*, 38.

51. Hunter, *Culture and Government*, 38.

52. Hunter, *Culture and Government*, 39.

53. Hunter, *Culture and Government*, 266.

54. Chatterjee, *The Nation and Its Fragments*, 19–20.

55. See for instance Prakash, *Another Reason*, chapter 5, and Chatterjee, *The Nation and Its Fragments*, chapter 2.

56. Hindess, "The Liberal Government of Unfreedom," 101.

57. Hindess, "The Liberal Government of Unfreedom," 101.

58. Report dated 8 September 1824 in Parulekar, ed., *Survey of Indigenous Education in the Province of Bombay*, 9, 7.

59. From a report dated June 1853 in "Correspondence Relating to Education in the Lower Provinces of Bengal," 9–10.

60. A debate that continues to the present—Rafiuddin Ahmed, for instance, accepts the claim that Muslims were educationally backward in his *The Bengal Muslims*, 132–40. By contrast, Aparna Basu argues that Muslim educational backwardness was a "myth"; a phenomenon true principally for Bengal was illegitimately generalized because it "suited the Muslims as well as the government after the 1870s." *The Growth of Education and Political Development in India*, 155. For a recent, careful assessment of the evidence see Murshid, *The Sacred and the Secular*, 54–88.

61. Lelyveld, *Aligarh's First Generation*, 7.

62. Kaviraj, "The Imaginary Institution of India," 26.

63. See for instance Lelyveld's finely drawn picture of Sayyid Khan's life, and the

life of north Indian *ashraf* more generally, in *Aligarh's First Generation*, chapter 2. See also Russell and Islam, *Ghalib*, which provides a richly textured account of the social and cultural mileu of the great nineteenth-century poet.

64. Jalal, *Self and Sovereignty*, 142.

65. Lelyveld, *Aligarh's First Generation*, 317–18.

Chapter 5: Gender and the Nation

1. *Report of the Indian Education [Hunter] Commission*, vol. 1, 530.

2. *Report of the Indian Education [Hunter] Commission*, vol. 1, 530.

3. *Report of the National Committee on Women's Education*, 17.

4. Orange, *Progress of Education in India, 1902–1907*, 254.

5. Orange, *Progress of Education in India, 1902–1907*, 255.

6. Anderson, *Progress of Education in India, 1927–32*, vol. 1, 172; *Report of the [Piggot] Committee on Primary Education*, 23.

7. *Indian Educational Policy . . . 1913*, section 16 [p. 15].

8. On which see my "Rewriting Histories of Nationalism."

9. I address the ways a modernizing nationalism like Nehru's sought to construct the "unity of India" – as well as the difficulties it encountered – in "Nationalism, National Identity and 'History.'" On the charged imagery of India as Mother see Bagchi, "Representing Nationalism."

10. For accounts of Naoroji's position and its implications see Ganguli, *Dadabhai Naoroji and the Drain Theory*, and Chandra, *The Rise and Growth of Economic Nationalism in India*. Sudhir Chandra has shown that "economic nationalism" is too narrow a description of this strand of nationalism in "The Cultural Component of Economic Nationalism."

11. Nehru would write, for instance, "The British take credit for having first opened India's window to the West and brought her . . . Western industrialization and science. But having done so they throttled the further industrial growth of the country . . . They prevented our industrial growth and thus delayed our political growth, and preserved all the out-of-date feudal and other relics they could find in the country." *Towards Freedom*, 276.

12. Inden, *Imagining India*, 45.

13. Mill, *The History of British India*, vol. 1, 280, 281. John Millar had argued that as societies progressed "from ignorance to knowledge, and from rude to civilized manners," the position of women improved accordingly, from being virtual slaves of men to being their "friends and companions." Millar's contrasts were not, however, organized around an East-West axis: his examples of societies where the lot of women was a degraded one were drawn principally from Greece, Rome, and Africa. See *The Origin of the Distinction of Ranks*, chapter 1.

14. See Ramusack, "Cultural Missonaries, Maternal Imperialists, Feminist Allies"; Jayawardena, *The White Woman's Other Burden*; and Burton, *Burdens of History*.

15. For some further examples see Forbes, *Women in Modern India*, 13–14.

16. Banerjea, *A Prize Essay on Native Female Education*, 41–42.

17. Reproduced as appendix K to *General Report on Public Instruction in the Bengal Presidency for 1842–43*, xcvi.

18. Mittra, "A Few Desultory Remarks," 294.

19. Chakravarti, "Whatever Happened to the Vedic Dasi?," 46. This is an important essay in a collection of essays (Sangari and Vaid, eds., *Recasting Women*) which have shaped much of the subsequent writing on the woman question in colonial India.

20. Quoted in Tharu, "Tracing Savitri's Pedigree," 259.

21. Besant, *Wake Up, India*, 54.

22. Banerji, *The Ideal of Swaraj in Education and Government*, 29.

23. Sarkar, *Hindu Wife, Hindu Nation*, 120.

24. Chatterjee, *The Nation and Its Fragments*, 6.

25. Quoted in Raman, *Getting Girls to School*, 170.

26. Dutt, *A Woman of India*, 48.

27. Chatterjee, *The Nation and Its Fragments*, 121.

28. Banerji, "Attired in Virtue," 71.

29. On missionary efforts in Bengal see Laird, *Missionaries and Education in Bengal*, chapter 5; and Bagal, *Women's Education in Eastern India*.

30. Letter from Government of India to the Government of Bengal in Richey, ed., *Selections from the Educational Records*, 58–60. The Despatch of 1854 finally allowed for some public funding of girl's schools.

31. *Calcutta University Commission Report*, vol. 2, 1–2.

32. *Report of the Indian Education [Hunter] Commission*, vol. 1, 542.

33. *Report of the Indian Education [Hunter] Commission*, vol. 1, 521.

34. Women's autobiographies sometimes tell of strong opposition from older women in the family, even where the men were keen to educate their wives; see Ghosh, "'Birds in a Cage,'" 88.

35. Perhaps the first pamphlet urging female education was Gourmohan Vidya-lanker's Bengali text *Strisiksha bidhayak* (1822), which cited precedents from ancient times to argue that female education was not foreign to the Hindu tradition, and suggested that its benefits included a mother's being able to instruct her children, and a wife's being able to better manage household accounts and correspond with an absent husband; see Borthwick, *The Changing Role of Women in Bengal*, 62–64. This pamphlet was soon translated into Hindi: there is a Hindi (khari boli) version in the British Library (*Strisikshavidhayaka*) dated 1823, along with subsequent Hindi versions.

36. In western India the circles around the reformist Prarthana Samaj, for instance, all sought to educate their child wives; and in Bengal, small but growing numbers of *bhadralok* similarly began to educate their child wives from the 1840s. See O'Hanlon, Introduction, 15; Borthwick, *The Changing Role of Women in Bengal*, 120; and Murshid, *Reluctant Debutante*, 36–40. There were of course exceptions, such as the

remarkable Rashsundari Debi, who secretly taught herself how to read and later to write, and who went on to write the first autobiography in Bengali; see Sarkar, *Words to Win*.

37. See Forbes, "In Search of the 'Pure Heathen' "; and Chakraborty, *Condition of Bengali Women around the 2nd Half of the 19th Century*, chapters 3 and 4.

38. Borthwick writes that "by 1900 attending a public school had become an accepted part of a [middle-class or *bhadralok*] girl's life"; *The Changing Role of Women in Bengal*, 108. Gail Minault finds that by the beginning of the twentieth century the same was true for Muslim girls of the respectable classes; *Secluded Scholars*, 215.

39. There is a growing literature which explores and draws on these women's magazines, including Borthwick, *The Changing Role of Women in Bengal*; Banerji, "Fashioning a Self"; Shukla, "Cultivating Minds"; Talwar, "Women's Journals in Hindi"; Ramakrishna, "Women's Journals in Andhra during the Nineteenth Century"; and Minault, *Secluded Scholars*, chapter 3.

40. For a study focused on two of these "advice for women" texts see Walsh, "The Virtuous Wife and the Well-Ordered Home."

41. The claim that women had their views disregarded because they were uneducated was a common one. The male author of a work addressed to women, advocating female education, writes, "my dear sisters . . . What disrespect and unhappiness you have had to suffer because of your ignorance! We women receive no respect." Vankelal, *Nari Sudasha Pravartak*, pt 4, p. 5.

42. [Pannalala of Sujangarh,] *Vanitabodhini*; the author's name does not appear on the pamphlet but is identified in the catalogue of the British Library, where this item was consulted.

43. Reproduced in Sharma and Sharma, eds., *Women [sic] Education in British India*, 80, 81–82.

44. Quoted in Chatterjee, *The Nation and its Fragments*, 129.

45. Quoted in Karlekar, *Voices from Within*, 96. As Karlekar notes and documents, educated women "were active agents in the construction of the new femininity" (68).

46. Quoted in Borthwick, *The Changing Role of Women in Bengal*, 116. See also Chakrabarti, "Changing Notions of Conjugal Relations in Nineteenth Century Bengal."

47. For a small number of élite men, having a wife who could take part in public society, such as by hosting her husband's British superiors, was a career asset; in 1901 one of the leading women's magazines in Bengal published a series of articles on the lives of (European) women who had helped their husband's careers. See Borthwick, *The Changing Role of Women in Bengal*, 122–24.

48. During this trip he appealed to Englishwomen to come out to India and provide their Indian sisters with an education "calculated to make Indian women good wives, mothers, sisters and daughters"; quoted in Karlekar, *Voices from Within*, 84.

49. Basu, *The Introduction of English and its Effects on Bengalee Society*, 14–15.

50. Besant, *Wake Up, India*, 228.

51. The essay is reproduced in the appendix to the *Report of the [Bombay] Board of Education from January 1 1850, to April 30, 1851,* 267.

52. Quoted in Borthwick, *The Changing Role of Women in Bengal,* 65.

53. Borthwick, *The Changing Role of Women in Bengal,* 184.

54. See Karlekar, *Voices from Within,* chapter 1; and Minault, "Other Voices, Other Rooms."

55. On which see Sumanta Banerjee's essay "Marginalization of Women's Popular Culture in Nineteenth Century Bengal."

56. Minault, *Secluded Scholars,* 55. See similarly Amin, *The World of Muslim Women in Colonial Bengal,* 210.

57. Especially in the ranks of the Brahmo Samaj – see Karlekar, "Kadambani and the Bhadralok."

58. Dayal, *Female Education,* 4.

59. Over and above the difference already noted – namely, that the champions of female education were at great pains to insist that the educated woman would not only be a better wife but also a better daughter-in-law, and thus that this new femininity would not in any way undermine the joint family. For example, see Walsh, "The Virtuous Wife and the Well-Ordered Home," and for an important discussion see Chakrabarty, *Provincializing Europe,* 224–32.

60. Haridas Goswamy, headmaster of East India Railway High School, Asanol, in *Calcutta University Commission Report,* vol. 12, 426.

61. Besant, *Wake Up, India,* 219.

62. Besant, *Wake Up, India,* 219.

63. Quoted in Sarkar, *Hindu Wife, Hindu Nation,* 265.

64. See Chatterjee, *The Nation and Its Fragments,* 121–24.

65. Though of course it also emanated from these quarters: a self-described "old man" expressing "the views of the old section of the Brahmin community" wrote, "If our females also betake themselves to the habit of taking early morning tea or coffee with bread and butter, of spending the morning in reading English books and newspapers, the afternoon in attending to games, lectures, clubs, and the evening in visits to friends and drives or walks for fresh air and exercise, then adieu to the peace and economy of the house and the comfort and solvency of the household." Anuntharow, *Female Education,* 22c.

66. Quoted in Gupta, "Portrayal of Women in Premchand's Stories." See also Pandey, "How Equal?"

67. Rabindra Mohan Datta in *Calcutta University Commission Report,* vol. 12, 422.

68. Datta, *What English Education Has Made of Us,* 58, 62.

69. Bhatt, "Striyan," 25.

70. Sanat Kumar Roy Choudhuri in *Report of the All-India Educational Conference,* 12.

71. Cited in Orsini, *The Hindi Public Sphere,* 253–54 (Tandon made this remark in 1916).

72. These other areas were never entirely left to be addressed in the future. Part of the significance of Gandhism is precisely Gandhi's insistence that successful reform of social evils was the moral and political precondition for Independence, and hence his campaigns against untouchability and for "constructive programmes" of village reform. However, while the nationalist leadership deferred to Gandhi's moral authority on such issues, the dominant strand of nationalism saw these as matters which could only be effectively addressed through state action, presupposing the nationalist seizure of state power.

73. Francesca Orsini notes: "The contrast between the large number of articles in favour of women's education . . . and the small number of pupils shows that girls' education was far from being an accepted or widespread practice." Orsini, *The Hindi Public Sphere*, 254.

74. Mayo, *Slaves of the Gods*, 211–12.

75. Quoted in Editor's Introduction to Mayo, *Selections from Mother India*, 25.

76. On this see Singer, *When a Great Tradition Modernizes*, 11–38; Rosenthal, "Mother India Thirty Years Later"; and William Emilsen, "Gandhi and Mayo's Mother India," an article useful for information but painfully poor in analysis.

77. These are listed in Harry Field's *After Mother India*, 10–11. Some additional book-length responses are listed in Sinha, Editor's Introduction, 34, 43.

78. World-Citizen, *Sister India*, 104. The author describes Mayo as "an old maiden of 49, [who] has all along, been absorbed in the attempt to understand the mystery of sex. If she was a married lady, she would have easily understood what the mystery was" (103–4). Natarajan described Mayo as "a shameless woman, herself too obviously suffering from the sex-complex"; *Miss Mayo's Mother India*, 80.

79. And Mayo did in fact receive active, though covert, support and guidance from British officialdom, a fact widely suspected at the time, denied by Mayo and the colonial authorities, but since definitively proved through the researches of Manoranjan Jha in his *Katherine Mayo and India*.

80. See Field, *After Mother India*, 9.

81. See Mayo, *Volume Two*, 198–99.

82. See Mayo, *Volume Two*, 200.

83. Sinha, Editor's Introduction, 36–39.

84. Sinha, Editor's Introduction, 33.

85. This is some seven pages in length; all references in the following discussion are from this introduction to *Mother India* (New York: Greenwood, 1969), without page reference. All other references to *Mother India* give the page reference in brackets in the text.

86. In his famous response, "Drain Inspector's Report."

87. What little progress had occurred was the result of the efforts of the British government and dedicated missionaries, and of Indian converts to Christianity (frequently of the despised low castes), who provided the vast majority of teachers at

female schools. The chapter concludes: "one beholds a curious spectacle: the daughters of rich landlords; of haughty Brahman plutocrats; of militant nationalist politicians, ferocious denouncers of the white man and all his works, fed and lodged by the dimes and sixpences of dear old ladies in Illinois and Derbyshire, and taught the a-b-c of responsible living by despised Christians and outcaste apostates" (140–41).

88. Most notably Kanhaya Lal Gauba's *Uncle Sham* (reviewed by the *New Yorker* as "the best comic volume of the year"), written, according to the author, so that "the truth about American life be made known as fearlessly and as fully as Miss Mayo has made known what she only believed to be the truth about India" (ix). See also Iyer, *Father India.*

89. Gandhi, "Drain Inspector's Report," 310–11. Gandhi even went so far as to declare that the agitation against her book was "in danger of being overdone" (311).

90. Sinha, Editor's Introduction.

91. "What the earlier abolition of *sati* represented for the project of a colonialist modernity, the Child Marriage Restraint Act now represented for the project of a nationalist modernity in late colonial India," Mrinalini Sinha concludes. For "If the abolishing of *sati* allowed the colonial state to stake the claims of British colonialism as the modernizers of indigenous patriarchy in India, then the Child Marriage Restraint Act of 1929 wrested that claim away from colonialism for modern Indian nationalism." "The Lineage of the 'Indian' Modern," 207.

92. Sargent, *Progress of Education in India, 1932–37*, vol. 1, 158. "Wastage rates," as the dropout rate between grades was termed, were in general extraordinarily high: the corresponding figure for boys was 27.7 percent (for statistical tables on wastage rates in boys' education see 131). A detailed survey of an educational district in the United Provinces found that only 4 percent of girls enrolled continued to complete the fourth grade. Chaturvedi, *An Educational Survey of a District*, 213. By the eve of Independence wastage rates had improved but continued to be extremely high: only 27 percent of girls and 39 percent of boys who enrolled in class 1 (first grade) continued to class 4 (fourth grade). Sargent, *Progress of Education in India, 1937–47*, vol. 1, table 5 [p. 61].

93. Sargent, *Progress of Education in India, 1937–47*, vol. 1, table 18 [p. 89]. If one includes middle schools, the (total) figure for girls enrolled in secondary education becomes 600,000. *Report of the National Committee on Women's Education*, 26.

94. See for instance Anderson, *Progress of Education in India, 1927–32*, vol. 1, 170, 173; Sargent, *Progress of Education in India, 1932–37*, vol. 1, 150ff.

95. Anderson, *Progress of Education in India, 1927–32*, vol. 1, 165.

96. Sargent, *Progress of Education in India, 1932–37*, vol. 1, 154; Bureau of Education, *Education in India in 1935–36*, 56.

97. Anderson, *Progress of Education in India, 1927–32*, vol. 1, 170.

98. Orsini, *The Hindi Public Sphere*, 259–60.

99. Sinha, Editor's Introduction, 38.

Chapter 6: Vernacular Modernity

1. For a socioeconomic profile of the leaders of what proved to be the most important and long-lived of these organizations, the Indian National Congress, see McLane, *Indian Nationalism and the Early Congress*, chapter 2.

2. "1897 Presidential Address," Zaidi, ed., *Congress Presidential Addresses*, vol. 1, 366–67; "1902 Presidential Address," Zaidi, ed., *Congress Presidential Addresses*, vol. 2, 366; "1911 Presidential Address," Zaidi, ed., *Congress Presidential Addresses*, vol. 2, 464.

3. The fourth annual session of the congress in 1888 declared that "it is the first duty of the British government in India to foster and encourage education," and went on to "respectfully" urge upon the government "the extreme importance of increasing, or at any rate not decreasing, the present expenditure on education." Resolution of Fourth [Allahabad] Session of the Congress, December 1888, Zaidi and Zaidi, eds., *The Encyclopaedia of the Indian National Congress*, vol. 1, 310. Four years later the congress was no longer "respectfully" urging but rather "affirm[ed] in the most emphatic manner, the importance of increasing the public expenditure on all branches of Education." Resolution of the Eighth [Allahabad] Session of the Congress, December 1892, Zaidi and Zaidi, eds., *The Encyclopaedia of the Indian National Congress*, vol. 2, 233.

4. "Watchman," *Higher Education and Popular Control*, 27.

5. "Presidential Address," *Report of the First Bombay Educational Conference*, 23.

6. "Address to a Conference of Directors of Public Instruction" (Simla, 1905), *Lord Curzon in India*, 355. Some thirty years later the *Report of the Unemployment [Sapru] Committee* was still noting that Indians regarded every proposal for educational reform as "calculated to retard the political or educational progress of the country" (186).

7. Of course there was always something contradictory about demanding more education, and yet at the same time denouncing it for being denationalizing. The ambiguity surfaced sharply when the history of western education was written from a nationalist point of view. In Basu's *The History of Education in India under the Rule of the East India Company* the British are accused of selfishly neglecting the education of India, but also of introducing education merely to equip themselves with cheap native civil servants. Bentinck, the governor-general who introduced the "Anglicist" policy, is accused of wanting to anglicize Indians and thus preventing the formation of a national consciousness, at the same time as Raja Rammohan Roy is described as the "prophet of his race" for the very same thing – that is, for petitioning the government to provide modern, scientific education in English rather than Oriental education. The Anglicists are accused of deliberately neglecting education in the vernaculars for fear that it might be detrimental to continued British dominance, but only after the Orientalists have been denounced for seeking to deny Indians the dignity that goes with English education.

8. See for instance *Indian Educational Policy . . . 1904*, section 8.

9. R. C. Majumdar, vice-chancellor's speech at the Convocation of Dacca University (1938), *Dacca University Convocation Speeches, 1929-46*, 11 [each speech separately

paginated]. Similarly, in 1936 the principal of Central Hindu College of Benares Hindu University noted that "almost every glaring evil of the day has been ascribed to our Universities." K. V. Rangaswami Aiyangar, Foreword, Tandon, ed., *Messages to Indian Students*, ii.

10. Wanchoo, *Studies in Indian Education*, 21–22. The 1938 session of the Congress, held in Haripura, declared: "The existing system of education in India is admitted to have failed. Its objectives have been anti-national and anti-social, its methods have been antiquated, and it has been confined to a small number of people and has left the vast majority of our people illiterate." Zaidi and Zaidi, eds., *The Encyclopaedia of the Indian National Congress*, vol. 11, 431.

11. As Tagore put it, "trams ply between our homes and our schools but the mind refuses to travel the distance." "The Diffusion of Education," 28. Less poetically, Jadunath Sarkar adjudged: "The chasm between the (English) school and the (Oriental) home remains unbridged." "The Vernacular Medium," 2.

12. *An Address by S. C. Roy*, 4.

13. Lal Behari Day, "Recollections of My School-Days" (1873), *Bengal Peasant Life, Folktales of Bengal, Recollections of My School-Days*, 510.

14. Satishchandra Mukherjee in *Dawn*, September 1898, quoted in Mukherjee and Mukherjee, *The Origins of the National Education Movement*, 10.

15. Mukherjee, *An Examination into the Present System of University Education in India and a Scheme of Reform*, 11.

16. Lajpat Rai, Introduction, i.

17. Dayal, "The Social Conquest of the Hindu Race," 247.

18. Coomaraswamy, "Education in India," 42, 43.

19. Ahmad, *Present Day Problems of Indian Education*, 33.

20. Tagore, "The Diffusion of Education," 28.

21. Pal, *Memories of My Life and Times*, 88.

22. See Jones, *Arya Dharm*, esp. chapter 3. There were other experiments seeking to combine western knowledge with Hindu traditions, including Annie Besant's Central Hindu College (founded 1898), and the Arya Mahila School (founded 1926); on these see Kumar, "Religion and Ritual in Indian Schools."

23. Established to "bring into more intimate relation with one another, through patient study and research, the different cultures of the East on the basis of their underlying unity," and to "approach the West from the standpoint of such a unity of the life and thought of Asia." "Visva-Bharati Memorandum of Association: Objects," reproduced as an appendix in Sinha, *Social Thinking of Rabindranath Tagore*, 157.

24. Tagore, "My School," 501.

25. Tagore, "The Schoolmaster," 370. This thought was developed allegorically in Tagore's story "The Parrot's Training," in which a Raja decides to have his pretty but "ignorant" parrot educated. The "educational authorities" confine the parrot in a gilded cage, and subject it to textbooks and lessons. All are impressed and pleased at

the thoroughness and professionalism of the venture, except the bird, which ends up – dead.

26. Tagore, "To the Child," 500.

27. For a detailed study of Tagore's educational ideas and practices see Mukherjee, *Education for Fulness*.

28. On Aligarh Muslim University see Minault and Lelyveld, "The Campaign for a Muslim University." On Benares Hindu University see the collection of documents in Sundaram, ed., *Benares Hindu University*.

29. See Lelyveld, *Aligarh's First Generation*.

30. See Kumar, *Political Agenda of Education*.

31. Missionary institutions suffered from the same constraints – the principal of the Women's Christian College, Madras, ruefully observed, "There can be no doubt that any Missionary College which wishes to attract students must give them what they ask for – the ordinary University course." McDougall, *Women's Christian College, Madras*, 2.

32. Quoted in Mukherjee and Mukherjee, *The Origins of the National Education Movement*, 421.

33. Quoted in Jones, *Arya Dharm*, 220.

34. On this see Fischer-Tine, "The Only Hope for Fallen India"; and Datta, "The 'Subalternity' of Education."

35. Letter dated 19 December 1937 in Elmhirst, *Rabindranath Tagore*, 37–38.

36. Gooroo Dass Banerjee, speech at a meeting to inaugurate the National Council of Education, 15 August 1906, in Banerjee, *Reminiscences, Speeches and Writings of Sir Gooroo Dass Banerjee*. For a history of these educational endeavors see Mukkerjee and Mukherjee, *The Origins of the National Education Movement*.

37. Sarkar, *The Swadeshi Movement in Bengal*, 181.

38. Quoted in Basu, "National Education in Bengal," 65.

39. Tagore, "The Poet's Anxiety," *Young India*, 1 June 1921, reprinted in R. K. Prabhu and R. Kelekar, eds., *Truth Called Them Differently (Tagore-Gandhi Controversy)*, 38.

40. Gandhi, "The Function of National Schools and Colleges," *Young India*, 10 October 1929, reprinted in Gandhi, *The Problem of Education*, 182.

41. "An Account of our Works," *Navajivan*, 3 August 1924, reprinted in Gandhi, *The Problem of Education*, 91.

42. "The Non-Cooperating Students," *Navajivan*, 21 December 1924, reprinted in Gandhi, *The Problem of Education*, 36.

43. "Essentials of National Education," *Navajivan*, 10 August 1924, reprinted in Gandhi, *The Problem of Education*, 105.

44. "The Non-Cooperating Students," *Navajivan*, 21 December 1924, reprinted in Gandhi, *The Problem of Education*, 33.

45. "Address to Maha Vidyalaya," *Navajivan*, 21 June 1928, reprinted in Gandhi, *The Problem of Education*, 145.

46. "Address to Maha Vidyalaya," *Navajivan*, 21 June 1928, reprinted in Gandhi, *The Problem of Education*, 145.

47. Rai, *The Problem of National Education in India*, 75–76.

48. Gandhi, *The Collected Works of Mahatma Gandhi*, vol. 48, 199–200.

49. Hartog had been academic registrar of the University of London for over a decade, before serving as a member of the Calcutta University (Sadler) Commission, then as first vice-chancellor of Dacca University, and then as chairman of the Auxiliary Committee on Education of the Indian Statutory (Simon) Commission.

50. The correspondence is reprinted in Dharampal, *The Beautiful Tree*, 355–90.

51. Das, *The Educational System of the Ancient Hindus*, 1. By the time of the second edition of his book in 1938, Keay noted that there had been a good deal of research and a number of books published on the subject by "competent Indian scholars." Keay, *Indian Education in Ancient and Later Times*, ix (the book changed its title between the first and second editions).

52. Thompson and Garrat, *Rise and Fulfilment of British Rule in India*, 312.

53. Dayal, "The Social Conquest of the Hindu Race," 244. See also his *Thoughts on Education*.

54. Sarkar, *The Pedagogy of the Hindu*, 36–45.

55. Bose, *National Education and Modern Progress*.

56. Only a few years later the unpredictable Har Dayal was castigating the proponents of a Hindu University, asking: "are the future leaders of India to chew the cud of old Hindu thought for all time without daring to think for themselves?" Dayal, "Some Phases of Contemporary Thought in India," 473. For biographies of this remarkable if unstable personality see Brown, *Har Dayal*, and (though it is more hagiography than biography) Dharmavira, *Lala Har Dayal and Revolutionary Movements of His Times*. Benoy Kumar Sarkar's advocacy of a specifically Hindu pedagogy was nonetheless one which included instruction in science and technology.

57. Rai, *The Problem of National Education in India*, 55.

58. Rai, *The Problem of National Education in India*, 80.

59. Reproduced in *Papers Connected with the Punjab University Question*, 37–91.

60. *Papers Connected with the Punjab University Question*, 27.

61. "The Brahmo Public Opinion" (21 July 1881), *Papers Connected with the Punjab University Question*, 29. For a history of this episode see Perrill, "Punjab Orientalism."

62. These reasons are set out in Duncan's letter to the governor-general, dated 1 January 1792, reproduced in Zastoupil and Moir, eds., *The Great Indian Education Debate*, 77–80.

63. Schwab, *The Oriental Renaissance*.

64. Bernard Cohn, "The Command of Language and the Language of Command," *Colonialism and its Forms of Knowledge*, 48. See also Kumar, *Lessons from Schools*, chapter 2.

65. *Report of the [Bombay] Board of Education from May 1, 1851, to April 30, 1852*, 119.

66. *Report of the Indian Education [Hunter] Commission*, vol. 1, 259.

67. Quoted in Young, *Resistant Hinduism*, 53.

68. To be sure, the standard on offer was not very high, the medium of instruction was English, and in the judgment of one scholar, the education provided was "devoid of the main and basic ideals of . . . [the] traditional Sanskrit system." Sharma, *Linguistic and Educational Aspirations under a Colonial System*, 192.

69. Kejariwal, *The Asiatic Society of Bengal and the Discovery of India's Past*, 232. A recent, uncritical study goes so far as to say, "The widespread movement of Western education which was apparently a curse for the traditional education proved a boon in disguise for Sanskrit. Sanskrit was rid of its obsolete, antiquated character and came to be included in the main stream of Indian education." Bhate, "Position of Sanskrit in Public Education and Scientific Research in Modern India," 389.

70. Quoted in Deshpande "Pandit and Professor," 142.

71. Pollock, "New Intellectuals in Seventeenth-Century India," 5.

72. Pollock, "The Death of Sanskrit," 393.

73. Pollock, "New Intellectuals in Seventeenth-Century India," 3.

74. Quoted in Dalmia, "Sanskrit Scholars and Pandits of the Old School," 328–29. I draw upon this essay for its material as well as some of its analyses.

75. Quoted in "Politicus," "A Peep into the History of Sanskrit Education in British India," 173.

76. Quoted in Dalmia, "Sanskrit Scholars and Pandits of the Old School," 330–31.

77. *Indian Educational Policy . . . 1913*, sections 58–59.

78. The most important contemporary institute for the study of Sanskrit in India bears his name: the Bhandarkar Oriental Research Institute, established in 1917.

79. Quoted in Deshpande, "Pandit and Professor," 134. Pandits in turn sometimes were (and are) dismissive of the "superficial" learning of "Indologists," as Deshpande notes (139–40).

80. Minute recorded by Macaulay, law member of the governor-general's council, 2 February 1835, reprinted in Zastoupil and Moir, eds., *The Great Indian Education Debate*, 170.

81. Pollock, "New Intellectuals in Seventeenth-Century India," 24.

82. Rai, *The Problem of National Education in India*, 75.

83. Chakrabarty, "The Difference-Deferral of a Colonial Modernity," 50–51.

84. Chatterjee, *The Nation and Its Fragments*, 5.

85. Chatterjee, *The Nation and Its Fragments*, 9.

86. "Evil Wrought by English Education," *Young India*, 27 April 1921, reprinted in Prabhu and Kelekar, eds., *Truth Called Them Differently*, 24.

87. *Navajivan*, 30 December 1920, reprinted in Gandhi, *The Problem of Education*, 20.

88. Gandhi declared, "my plan to impart Primary Education through the medium of village handicrafts . . . [is] conceived of as the spearhead of a silent social revolution fraught with the most far-reaching consequences." *Harijan*, 9 October 1937, reprinted in Gandhi, *The Problem of Education*, 275. For a highly suggestive interpretation of the social and educational implications of the Wardha Scheme see Kumar, *Political Agenda of Education*, 167–77.

89. The Haripura Congress of 1938 adopted a resolution to this effect; see Zaidi and Zaidi, eds., *The Encyclopaedia of the Indian National Congress*, vol. 11, 431–32.

90. "Higher Education," *Harijan*, 9 July 1938, reprinted in Gandhi, *The Problem of Education*, 59.

91. Reprinted in Engl. trans. in *University of Calcutta Convocation Addresses*, vol. 7, as appendix A [pp. 113–30]. Page references given in text.

92. "Higher Education," *Harijan*, 9 July 1938, reprinted in Gandhi, *The Problem of Education*, 59–60.

93. The incident is recounted in Sastri, *A History of the Renaissance in Bengal*, 31–32.

94. *The Selected Works of Maulana Abul Kalam Azad*, ed. Kumar, vol. 3, 98–99.

Epilogue: Knowing Modernity, Being Modern

1. Burckhardt, *The Civilization of the Renaissance in Italy*, 121.

2. Marx and Engels, *Manifesto of the Communist Party*, 36.

3. I borrow this phrase from Fabian, *Time and the Other*.

4. See Taussig, *The Devil and Commodity Fetishism in South America*.

5. See Muecke, *Ancient and Modern*.

6. Chakrabarty, *Habitations of Modernity*, 28.

7. Taylor, "Two Theories of Modernity," 154.

8. Taylor, "Two Theories of Modernity," 170.

9. Taylor writes: "when the old metaphysical and religious beliefs crumble, we find as a matter of neutral fact that we are instrumental individuals, and we need to draw from elsewhere our values and acceptable grounds for association with others." "Two Theories of Modernity," 173. This could serve as a summary of Weber's position, though in fact Taylor is offering a summary of what is entailed by the acultural theory of modernity.

10. Taylor, "Two Theories of Modernity," 161–62.

11. Taylor, "Two Theories of Modernity," 171.

12. Here I am paraphrasing Latour, *We Have Never Been Modern*, 115–16.

13. Taylor, "Two Theories of Modernity," 159.

14. Taylor, "Two Theories of Modernity," 170.

15. As Brian Massumi points out, "Social constructivism easily leads to a cultural solipsism . . . In this worst case solipsist scenario, nature appears as immanent to culture (as its construct). At best, when the status of nature is deemed unworthy of attention, it is simply shunted aside . . . Theoretical moves at ending Man end up making human culture the measure and meaning of all things, in a kind of unfettered anthropomorphism." "The Autonomy of Affect," 231.

16. Daston, "The Nature of Nature in Early Modern Europe," 154. Daston shows that the invention of nature, as we now understand the term, had as much to do with changes in jurisprudence and theology as with the disenchantment of nature allegedly brought about by the Scientific Revolution, and thus emerges much later

than the conventional account suggests. See also her "Marvelous Facts and Miraculous Evidence in Early Modern Europe."

17. Shapin and Schaffer, *Leviathan and the Air-Pump*.

18. Latour, *We Have Never Been Modern*, 71.

19. Adas, *Machines as the Measure of Men*, 7.

20. Latour, *We Have Never Been Modern*, 98–99.

21. See also Rorty, *Philosophy and the Mirror of Nature*, 351–52, 379–89; and Toulmin, *Cosmopolis*, chapter 3.

Bibliography

Unpublished Sources

Barry Papers, Cambridge South Asia Centre Library
Church of Scotland Foreign Mission Papers, MS 7530, National Library of Scotland
Government of India, Education Proceedings, 1911–1920, National Archives of India
Hartog Papers, MSS Eur E 221, India and Oriental Research Collection, British
    Library
Hicks Papers, Cambridge South Asia Centre Library
Government of India, Home Department (Education) Proceedings, 1869–1910,
    National Archives of India
Orange Papers, Cambridge South Asia Centre Library

Published Works Cited
Enquiries and Reports

Anderson, George. *Progress of Education in India, 1927–32.* Delhi: Manager of
    Publications, 1934.
Bureau of Education. *Education in India in 1935–36.* Delhi: Manager of Publications,
    1938.
———. *Reports of the Committees Appointed by the Central Advisory Board of Education in
    India (1938–43).* New Delhi, 1944.
Calcutta University Commission Report. Calcutta: Superintendent of Government
    Printing, 1919.
Constitution of India under the British Rule (Montagu-Chelmsford Report, 1918). New
    Delhi: Sumit, 1992 [repr.].
General Report on Public Instruction in Bengal, 1851–52. Calcutta, 1852.
General Report on Public Instruction in Bengal, 30 September 1852–27 January 1855.
    Calcutta, 1855.
General Report on Public Instruction in the Bengal Presidency for 1842–43. Calcutta:
    Military Orphan Press, 1843.
*General Report on Public Instruction in the Lower Provinces of the Bengal Presidency for
    1855–56.* Calcutta, 1857.
*General Report on Public Instruction in the Lower Provinces of the Bengal Presidency for
    1856–57.* Calcutta, 1857.

General Report on Public Instruction in the Lower Provinces of Bengal for 1857–58. Calcutta, 1859.

General Report on Public Instruction in the Lower Provinces of the Bengal Presidency for 1844–45. Calcutta: Sanders and Cone, 1845.

General Report on Public Instruction in the Lower Provinces of the Bengal Presidency for 1859–60. Calcutta, 1861.

General Report on Public Instruction in the Lower Provinces of Bengal for 1860–61. Calcutta, 1862.

Indian Educational Policy, Being a Resolution Issued by the Governor-General in Council on the 21st February, 1913. Calcutta: Superintendent of Government Printing, 1913.

Indian Educational Policy: Resolution of the Government of India in the Home Department, 11th March, 1904. Calcutta: Superintendent of Government Printing, 1904.

Indian Universities [Raleigh] Commission Report. Simla, 1902.

Orange, H. W. Progress of Education in India, 1902–1907. Calcutta: Superintendent of Government Printing, 1909.

Punjab University Enquiry [Anderson] Committee Report. Lahore: Superintendent of Government Printing, 1933.

Report of the [Bombay] Board of Education for the Year 1845. Bombay: Government Press, 1847.

Report of the [Bombay] Board of Education for the Year 1846. Bombay: American Mission Press, 1847.

Report of the [Bombay] Board of Education for the Year 1849. Bombay: Bombay Education Society, 1851.

Report of the [Bombay] Board of Education from Jan 1, 1850, to April 30, 1851. Bombay: Bombay Education Society, 1851.

Report of the [Bombay] Board of Education from May 1, 1851, to April 30, 1852. Bombay: Bombay Education Society, 1852.

Report of the Committee Appointed by the Bengal Government to Consider Questions Connected with Muhammadan Education. Calcutta, 1915.

Report of the [Young] Committee on Educational Hygiene. Naini Tal, 1913.

Report of the [Piggot] Committee on Primary Education. United Provinces, 1913.

Report of the [More] Committee on the Training of Primary Teachers. Bombay: Government Central Press, 1938.

Report of the Director for Public Instruction, Bombay, for the Year 1863–64. Bombay: Bombay Education Society, 1865.

Report of the Director of Public Instruction in the Bombay Presidency for the Year 1872–73. Bombay, 1874.

Report of the General Committee of Public Instruction for the Presidency of Fort William in Bengal for 1838–39. Calcutta: Military Orphan Press, 1840.

Report of the Indian Education [Hunter] Commission. Calcutta: Superintendent of Government Printing, 1883.

Report of the National Committee on Women's Education (May 1958 to January 1959).
Ministry of Education, 1959.

Report of the Travancore Education Reforms Committee. Trivandrum: Superintendent,
Government Press, 1934.

Report of the Unemployment [Sapru] Committee. Allahabad, 1936.

Report on Public Instruction in the Madras Presidency for 1881–82. Madras: Government
Press, 1883.

Sargent, John. Progress of Education in India, 1932–37. Delhi: Manager of Publications,
1940.

———. Progress of Education in India, 1937–47: Decennial Review. Ministry of
Education, n.d. [1948].

Contemporary Sources

Adam, William. Reports on the State of Education in Bengal (1835 and 1838), ed.
Anathnath Basu. Calcutta: University of Calcutta, 1941.

Ahmad, M. M. Zuhurrudin. Present Day Problems of Indian Education (with Special
Reference to Muslim Education). Bombay, 1935.

Aiyangar, Rangaswami. Foreword. Messages to Indian Students (An Anthology of
Famous Convocation Addresses), ed. Purushottam Das Tandon. Allahabad:
Students' Friends, 1936.

Aiyar, R. Rangaswami. "Is the Teaching Profession Calculated to Attract the Best
Type of Men?" Educational Review, June 1920.

An Address by S. C. Roy, Delivered on the Anniversary of the Students Weekly Service.
Cuttack: Star, 1911.

An Appeal to the British Nation for the Promotion of Education in India. Calcutta:
Calcutta Printing and Publishing, n.d. [1861].

"A Native Philomath." High Education in Bengal and the University of Calcutta.
Calcutta: Imperial Victoria, 1888.

Anuntharow, V. Female Education. N.p., 1916.

Archer, William. India and the Future. London: Hutchinson, 1917.

Banerjea, K. M. A Prize Essay on Native Female Education. Calcutta: Bishops College,
1841.

Banerjee, Gooroo Dass. Reminiscences, Speeches and Writings of Sir Gooroo Dass Banerjee,
comp. Upendra Chandra Banerjee. Calcutta: Narkeldanga, 1927.

Banerji, Nripendra Chandra. The Ideal of Swaraj in Education and Government.
Madras: Ganesh, 1921.

Banerji, Sasadhar. "Discipline." Educational Review, January 1920.

Basu, Amrita Krishna. The Introduction of English and Its Effects on Bengalee Society:
A Paper Read in a Meeting of the Simla Literary Society on 10th July 1871. Calcutta:
Local, 1873.

Basu, B. D. *The History of Education in India under the Rule of the East India Company.* Calcutta: Modern Review Office, n.d.

Besant, Annie. *Wake Up, India.* Madras: Theosophical Publishing, 1913.

Bhandarkar, Ramakrishna Gopal. *The Bombay University Convocation Address of 1894, Delivered by Ramakrishna Gopal Bhandarkar, Vice-Chancellor of Bombay University.* Bombay: Indian Printing, 1894.

Bhatt, Balkrishna. *Bhatt Nibandhamala* [Collected Essays]. Kashi [Benares]: Nagari Pracharani Sabha, 1947.

———. "Striyan" [Women] [1891]. *Bhatt Nibandhamala* [Collected Essays]. Kashi [Benares]: Nagari Pracharani Sabha, 1947.

Bilgrami, Syed. *Presidential Address at 26th Annual Session of the All India Muhammadan Educational Conference, Lucknow, Dec 28, 1912.* Delhi, 1913.

Bose, Pramatha Nath. *National Education and Modern Progress.* Calcutta: Kar, Majumdar, n.d. [?1921].

Bryce, James. *The Schoolmaster and the Missionary in India.* Edinburgh, 1856.

Butler, Harcourt. *Collection of Speeches.* Rangoon: Government Press, n.d. [1927].

Chanda, Ramaprasad. "Future of Education in Bengal." *Modern Review,* September 1917.

Chattopadhyaya, Goutam, ed. *Awakening in Bengal in Early Nineteenth Century (Selected Documents).* Calcutta: Progressive, 1965.

Chaturvedi, S. N. *The History of Rural Education in the United Provinces of Agra and Oudh (1840–1926).* Allahabad: Indian Press, 1930.

———. *An Educational Survey of a District, Being a Quantitative Study of Vernacular Primary and Secondary Education in the District of Etawah in the United Provinces of Agra and Oudh.* Allahabad: Indian Press, 1935.

Coomaraswamy, A. K. "Education in India." *National Education,* ed. H. V. Dugvekar. Benares, 1917.

Cornelius, John J. *A Study of Tagore's Experiment in the Indianization of Education in the Light of India's History.* Madras, 1930.

"Correspondence on the Subject of the Education of the Muhammadan Community in British India and Their Employment in the Public Service Generally." *Selections from the Records of the Government of India: Home Department.* Calcutta, 1886.

"Correspondence Relating to Education in the Lower Provinces of Bengal." *Selections from the Records of the Bengal Government,* vol. 22. Calcutta, 1855.

Curzon, Lord. *Lord Curzon in India, Being a Selection from His Speeches as Viceroy and Governor-General of India, 1898–1905.* London: Macmillan, 1906.

———. *Principles and Methods of University Reform, Being a Letter Addressed to the University of Oxford.* Oxford: Clarendon, 1909.

Dacca University Convocation Speeches, 1929–46. N.p., n.d.

Das, Santosh Kumar. *The Educational System of the Ancient Hindus.* Calcutta: Mitra, 1930.

Datta, T. K. *What English Education Has Made of Us*. Lahore: Doaba House, n.d. [1939].

Day, Lal Behari. *Bengal Peasant Life, Folktales of Bengal, Recollections of My School-Days*, ed. Mahadevprasad Saha. Calcutta: Editions Indian, 1969.

———. *Primary Education in Bengal: A Lecture Delivered at the Bethune Society on 10 December 1868*. Calcutta: Barham, Hill, 1869.

Dayal, Har. "The Social Conquest of the Hindu Race." *Modern Review*, September 1909.

———. "Some Phases of Contemporary Thought in India." *Modern Review*, November 1912.

———. *Thoughts on Education*. New Delhi: Rajdhani Granthagar, n.d. [1908].

Dayal, Sibeswar. *Female Education: How It Can Be Best Effected in Behar*. Bankipore: Behar Bandhu, 1908.

Dippie, H. "Principles of Education and Class Teaching." *Instruction in Indian Primary Schools*. Bombay: Oxford University Press, 1936.

Duff, Alexander. *India and India Missions*. Edinburgh: John Johnstone, 1839.

———. *Missionary Addresses*. Edinburgh: Johnstone and Hunter, 1850.

———. *New Era of English Language and English Literature in India*. Edinburgh, 1839.

Dugvekar, H. V., ed. *National Education*. Benares, 1917.

Dutt, G. S. *A Woman of India, Being the Life of Saroj Nalini*. London, 1929 [orig. pubd in Bengali, 1926].

Elphinstone, Mountstuart. *Selections from the Minutes and the Official Writings of the Honourable Mountstuart Elphinstone, Governor of Bombay*, ed. George W. Forrest. London: Richard Bentley and Son, 1884.

Fuller, Bampfylde, *The Empire of India*. London: Isaac Pitman and Sons, 1913.

Gandhi, M. K. *The Collected Works of Mahatma Gandhi*, vol. 48. Ahmedabad: Navajivan Trust, 1958–2000.

———. "Drain Inspector's Report." *Young India, 1919–1931*, vol. 9. Ahmedabad: Navajivan, 1981.

———. *The Problem of Education*. Ahmedabad: Navajivan, 1962.

———. *Young India: 1919–1931*, vol. 9. Ahmedabad: Navajivan, 1981.

Gauba, Kanhaya Lal. *Uncle Sham: The Strange Tale of a Civilization Run Amuck*. New York: Claude Kendall, 1929.

Ghosh, Aurobindo. *National Education*. Allahabad: Leader, 1918.

Ghosh, J. *Higher Education in Bengal under British Rule*. Calcutta: Book Company, 1926.

Gupta, K. C. *Addresses on Educational Matters*. Cuttack, 1901.

Haines, C. R. *Education and Missions in India and Elsewhere*. Cambridge: Deighton, Bell and Sons, 1886 [Maitland Prize Essay, 1886].

The Hindu University: The Deputation in Calcutta. Calcutta, 1911.

Holmes, W. H. G. "University Education in Bengal." *Hindustan Review* 23 (March–April 1911).

Hunter, W. W. *The Indian Musalmans*. Lahore: Premier Book House, 1964 [1871].

———. *A Life of the Earl of Mayo*, 2nd edn, vol. 2. London: Smith, Elder, 1876.

Huque, M. Azizul. *History and Problems of Moslem Education in Bengal.* Calcutta: Thacker, Spink, 1917.

Indian Problems: Speeches by Lord Irwin. London: George Allen and Unwin, 1932.

Instruction in Indian Primary Schools. Bombay: Oxford University Press, 1936.

Iyer, C. S. Ranga. *Father India.* London: Selwyn and Blount, 1927.

Karim, Abdul. *Muhammedan Education in Bengal.* Calcutta, 1900.

Keane, William. *A Letter to the Late Honourable J. E. D. Bethune, Esq., on the Present State, and Results of Government Public Instruction in Bengal.* Madras, 1851.

Keay, F. E. *Indian Education in Ancient and Later Times.* Oxford University Press, 1938.

Kerr, J. *A Review of Public Instruction in the Bengal Presidency from 1835 to 1851,* pt 1. Calcutta, 1852.

K.V.A. "Calcutta University Reform." *Modern Review,* July 1918.

Lee-Warner, William. *The Citizen of India.* London: Macmillan, 1897.

Lethbridge, Roper. *High Education in India: A Plea for the State Colleges.* London: W. H. Allen, 1882.

"Loyalty and Disloyalty." *Native Review,* 8 June 1873.

Mahmood, Syed. *A History of English Education in India.* Delhi: Idarah-I Adabiyat-I Delli, 1981 [1895].

Malaviya, Madan Mohan. *The Hindu University of Benares: Why It Is Wanted and What It Aims at.* Allahabad, 1911.

Mayo, Katherine. *Mother India.* New York: Greenwood, 1969 [1927].

——. *Slaves of the Gods.* London: Jonathan Cape, 1929.

——. *Volume Two.* London: Jonathan Cape, 1931.

McDougall, Eleanor. *Lamps in the Wind: South Indian College Women and Their Problems.* London: Edinburgh House, 1943 [1940].

——. *Women's Christian College, Madras, 1919–1925.* Madras: Madras Diocesan, n.d.

Mehta, Nagindas P. *The Problem of Our Young Men after Leaving Schools and Colleges.* Bombay, 1915.

"Memorial of the Central National Muhammadan Association," presented to Chelmsford and Montagu. *Addresses Presented to Lord Chelmsford and Montagu,* unpublished collation, Nehru Memorial Museum and Library.

Mill, James. *The History of British India.* New Delhi: Atlantic, 1990 [1817].

The Miscellaneous Writings of the Late Hon'ble Mr. Justice M. G. Ranade. Bombay: Manoranjan, 1915.

Mittra, Baboo Peary Chand. "A Few Desultory Remarks on . . . Reverend K. M. Banerjea's Prize Essay on Native Female Education" [January 1842]. *Awakening in Bengal in Early Nineteenth Century (Selected Documents),* ed. Goutam Chatto-padhyaya. Calcutta: Progressive, 1965.

Mohammad, Shan, ed. *Writings and Speeches of Sir Syed Ahmad Khan.* Bombay: Nachiketa, 1972.

Muhammad, Shan, ed. *The Aligarh Movement: Basic Documents, 1864–1898,* vol. 3. Meerut: Meenakshi Prakashan, 1978.

Mukerjee, Satischandra. *An Examination into the Present System of University Education in India and a Scheme of Reform*. Calcutta, 1902.

Muller, Max. *Anthropological Religion*. London: Longmans, Green, 1892.

———. *Lectures on the Origin and Growth of Religion*. Varanasi: Indological Book House, 1964.

Murdoch, John. *India's Greatest Educational Need: The Adequate Recognition of Ethics in Her Present Transition State*. London, 1904.

Muslim Education, with Special Reference to the Madrasa-i-Azam. Madras, 1916.

Natarajan, K. *Miss Mayo's Mother India*, 3rd edn. Madras: G. A. Nateson, 1928.

Nehru, Jawaharlal. *Towards Freedom*. New York: John Day, 1941.

O'Malley, L. S. S. *Popular Hinduism: The Religion of the Masses*. New York: Johnson Reprint, 1970 [1935].

Pal, Bipan Chandra. *Memories of My Life and Times*. Calcutta: Bipanchandra Pal Institute, 1973.

[Pannalala of Sujangarh.] *Vanitabodhini*, 2nd edn. Bombay: Karnatak, 1896.

Papers Connected with the Punjab University Question, Collected and Published by the Executive Committee of the Indian Association. Lahore, 1881.

"Papers Regarding the Educational Conference, Allahabad, February 1911." *Selections from the Records of the Government of India*, vol. 448. Calcutta, 1911.

"Papers Relating to Discipline and Moral Training in Schools and Colleges of India." *Selections from the Records of the Government of India (Home Department)*, vol. 265. Calcutta: Superintendent of Government Printing, 1890.

"Papers Relating to Public Instruction." *Selections from the Records of the Madras Government*, vol. 2. Madras, 1855.

Parulekar, R. V., ed. *Survey of Indigenous Education in the Province of Bombay (1820–1830)*. Bombay: Asia Publishing, 1945.

"Percentage of Persons of School-Going Age." *Modern Review*, December 1917.

Pioneer, 10 January 1888.

"Politicus." "A Peep into the History of Sanskrit Education in British India." *Modern Review*, August 1916.

Prabhu, R. K., and R. Kelekar, eds. *Truth Called Them Differently (Tagore-Gandhi Controversy)*. Ahmedabad: Navajivan, 1961.

Prasad, Ram. *Teaching the Teacher*. Allahabad, 1915.

Premchand. "Gorakhpur me Shiksha Sammelan" [Education Conference in Gorakhpur, 1933]. *Premchand ke Vicar* [Thoughts of Premchand]. Allahabad: Saraswati, 1988.

The Problem of Urdu Teaching in the Bombay Presidency. Government of Bombay, 1914.

Proceedings of the Punjab Educational Conference and Exhibition, Held in December 1926, ed. J. E. Parkinson and R. H. Whitehouse. N.p., n.d.

"The Public Services Commission and the Educational Service." *Modern Review*, August 1917.

Rai, Lajpat. *The Arya Samaj*. Lahore: Uttar Chand Kapur and Sons, 1932.

———. Introduction. *Thoughts on Education*, by Har Dayal. New Delhi: Rajdhani Granthagar, n.d. [1908].

———. *The Problem of National Education in India*. London: Allen and Unwin, 1920.

Ranade, M. G. *The Miscellaneous Writings of the Late Hon'ble Mr. Justice M. G. Ranade*. Bombay: Manoranjan, 1915.

Rao, K. Subba, ed. *Convocation Addresses of the Universities of Bombay and Madras*. Madras: Lawrence Asylum, 1892.

Ratcliffe, S. K. "The Teaching of Morals and Religion." *Modern Review* 4 (1908).

Ray, Prafulla Chandra. *Essays and Discourses by Professor Prafulla Chandra Ray*. Madras: G. A. Nateson, 1918.

Reddy, C. Ramalinga. *An Address to Students*. Madras, 1910.

Reminiscences, Speeches and Writings of Sir Gooroo Dass Banerjee. Calcutta: Narkeldanga, 1927.

Report of the All-India Educational Conference, Calcutta, Dec 26–30, 1937, ed. R. M. Roy. Calcutta, 1938.

Report of the Bengal Women's Educational Conference. N.p., 1927.

Report of the First Bombay Educational Conference, ed. Jamnadas M. Mehta. Bombay, 1917.

Report of the Madras Educational Conference, Held on 21st and 22nd December, 1896. Madras: Varodochari, 1897.

Report of the Proceedings of a Conference on Moral, Civic and Sanitary Instruction, Held on 6th and 7th April, 1910. Bombay: Bombay Guardian Mission, 1910.

Richey, J. A., ed. *Selections from Educational Records*. Calcutta: Superintendent Government Printing, 1922.

Richter, Julius. *A History of Missions in India*, trans. Sydney Moore. Edinburgh: Oliphant, Anderson and Ferrier, 1908.

Ronaldshay, Lord. *India: A Bird's-Eye View*. London: Constable, 1924.

Roy Chowdhury, M. N. *A Humble Appeal of a Humble Heart*. N.p., n.d.

Roy, Krishna Chandra. *High Education and the Present Position of Graduates in Arts and Law of the Calcutta University*. Calcutta, 1882.

Saiyidain, K. G. "Experiments in Education." *Indian Review*, November 1915.

Sarkar, Benoy Kumar. *The Pedagogy of the Hindu*. Calcutta: Chuckerverty Chatterjee, 1912.

Sarkar, Jadunath. "Confessions of a History Teacher." *Modern Review*, December 1915.

Sarkar, Jadunath. "The Vernacular Medium: Views of an Old Teacher." *Modern Review*, January 1918.

Sastri, Sivanath. *A History of the Renaissance in Bengal: Ramtanu Lahiri, Brahman and Reformer*. Calcutta: Editions Indian, 1972 [1904].

Satthianadhan, S. *History of Education in the Madras Presidency*. Madras: Srinivasa, Varadachari, 1894.

Selected Papers Read at Divisional Conferences Held in 1896. N.p., n.d.

The Selected Works of Maulana Abul Kalam Azad, ed. Ravindra Kumar, vol. 3. New Delhi: Atlantic, 1991–92.

Sen, J. M. *History of Elementary Education in India*. Calcutta: Book Company, 1933.

Sen, Keshub Chunder. *Letters on Educational Measures to Lord Northbrook*, ed. G. C. Banerjee. N.p., 1936.

Setalvad. *Indian University Commission: Letters Addressed to "The Times of India" on the Vice-Chancellor's Vindication of Its Recommendations*. Bombay, 1903.

Sharp, H. *Rural Schools in the Central Provinces*. Calcutta: Office of the Director-General of Education in India, 1904.

Sherring, M. A. *The History of Protestant Missions in India*. London: Trübner, 1875.

Short Essays and Reviews on the Educational Policy of the Government of India, Reprinted from the "Englishman." Calcutta, 1866.

Shrivastava, S. N. L. "Some Aspects of Our Present Educational System." *Indian Review*, September 1940.

Sinha, Prabodh Chandra. *Problem of Education in Bengal*. Calcutta: Thacker, Spink, 1941.

Sinha, Sasadhar. "The Past, Present and Future of Indian Education." *Modern Review*, January 1936.

Smith, George. *The Life of Alexander Duff*. London: Hodder and Stoughton, 1879.

Speech of the Duke of Marlborough upon the Exclusion of the Bible from Government Schools, House of Lords, 2nd July 1860. London: W. H. Dalton.

Subrahmanyam, S. "National Education: Literary or Technical?" *Educational Review*, January 1921.

Sundaram, V. A., ed. *Benares Hindu University, 1905 to 1935*. Benares: Tata, 1936.

Tagore, Rabindranath. "Calcutta University Convocation Address, 1937." *University of Calcutta Convocation Addresses*, vol. 7 (1935–38).

———. "The Diffusion of Education." *Modern Review*, July 1939.

———. "Indian Students and Western Teachers." *Modern Review*, April 1916.

———. "My School." *Modern Review*, May 1925.

———. "The Parrot's Training." *Modern Review*, March 1918 [repr. in Elmhirst, *Rabindranath Tagore*; and *Rabindranath Tagore: An Anthology*, ed. Krishna Dutta and Andrew Robinson (London: Picador, 1997)].

———. "The Schoolmaster." *Modern Review*, October 1924.

———. "To the Child." *Modern Review*, May 1925.

Tandon, Purushottam Das, ed. *Messages to Indian Students (An Anthology of Famous Convocation Addresses)*. Allahabad: Students' Friends, 1936.

Temple, Richard. *Men and Events of My Time in India*. Delhi: BR, 1985 [1882].

Thapar, K. B., ed. *Convocation Addresses of the Universities of Allahabad and Punjab*. Lahore, 1895.

———. *Convocation Addresses of the University of the Punjab*. Lahore: Addison, 1903.

Thompson, Edward, and G. T. Garrat. *Rise and Fulfilment of British Rule in India*. Allahabad: Central Book Depot, 1966 [repr.].

Trevelyan, C. E. *On the Education of the People of India*. London: Longman, Orme, Brown Green and Longman, 1838.

University of Calcutta Convocation Addresses, University of Calcutta, 1914; 2nd edn. 1936.

Vankelal. *Nari Sudasha Pravartak* [Foundations of Women's Welfare]. Allahabad, 1893–95.

Venkateswara, S. V. *Indian Culture through the Ages*. London: Longmans, Green, 1928.

Verma, Vishveshvar Nath. *Shiksha-Samhar* [Destruction of Education]. N.p., 1921.

Wanchoo, H. N. *Studies in Indian Education*. Allahabad: Allahabad Law Journal, 1934.

"Watchman." *Higher Education and Popular Control*. Calcutta, 1916.

Welinkar. *Our Young Men: Two Lectures*. Bombay: Bombay Guardian Mission, n.d. [?1909].

Whitehead, Henry. *The Village Gods of South India*. Madras: Asian Educational Series, 1988 [1921].

Wood, Ernest. *Selected Articles on National Education*. Hyderabad, Sind: Sind, 1917.

World-Citizen. *Sister India*. Bombay: Sister India Office, n.d.

Zaidi, A. M., ed. *Congress Presidential Addresses*. New Delhi: Indian Institute of Applied Political Research, 1985–.

Zaidi, A. M., and S. G. Zaidi, eds. *The Encyclopaedia of the Indian National Congress*. New Delhi: S. Chand.

Other Works

Achyuthan, Mavelikara. *Educational Practices in Manu, Panini and Kautilya*. Trivandrum: College Book House, 1974.

Adas, Michael. *Machines as the Measure of Men*. Ithaca: Cornell University Press, 1989.

Ahmed, Rafiuddin. *The Bengal Muslims, 1871–1906: A Quest for Identity*. Delhi: Oxford University Press, 1981.

Allen, N. J., W. S. F. Pickering, and W. Watts Miller, eds. *On Durkheim's Elementary Forms of Religious Life*. London: Routledge, 1998.

Altekar, A. S. *Education in Ancient India*, 5th edn. Varanasi: Nand Kishore and Bros., 1965.

Amin, Sonia Nishat. *The World of Muslim Women in Colonial Bengal, 1876–1939*. Leiden: E. J. Brill, 1996.

Anderson, Benedict. *Imagined Communities*, 2nd edn. London: Verso, 1991.

———. *The Specter of Comparisons*. New York: Verso, 1998.

Anderson, Perry. *Passages from Antiquity to Feudalism*. London: Verso, 1978.

Appadurai, Arjun. "Number in the Colonial Imagination." *Orientalism and the Postcolonial Predicament*, ed. Carol Breckenridge and Peter van der Veer. Philadelphia: University of Pennsylvania Press, 1993.

Appleby, Joyce, Lynn Hunt, and Margaret Jacob. *Telling the Truth about History*. New York: W. W. Norton, 1994.

Archer, William. *India and the Future*. London: Hutchinson, 1917.

Arnold, David, and David Hardiman, eds. *Subaltern Studies VIII*. Delhi: Oxford University Press, 1994.

Asad, Talal. "The Concept of Cultural Translation in British Social Anthropology." *Writing Culture*, ed. James Clifford and G. E. Marcus. Berkeley: University of California Press, 1986.

———. *Genealogies of Religion*. Baltimore: Johns Hopkins University Press, 1993.

Austin, Granville. *The Indian Constitution: Cornerstone of a Nation*. Delhi: Oxford University Press, 1999.

Babb, Lawrence. *The Divine Hierarchy: Popular Hinduism in Central India*. New York: Columbia University Press, 1975.

Bagal, Jogesh Chandra. *Women's Education in Eastern India: The First Phase*. Calcutta: World Press, 1956.

Bagchi, Jasodhara. "Representing Nationalism: Ideology of Motherhood in Colonial Bengal." *Economic and Political Weekly*, 20 October 1990, 27 October 1990.

Baker, Keith Michael. "Enlightenment and the Institution of Society: Notes for a Conceptual History." *Civil Society: History and Possibilities*, ed. S. Kaviraj and S. Khilnani. Cambridge: Cambridge University Press, 2001.

Balagangadhara, S. N. *"The Heathen in His Blindness . . .": Asia, the West and the Dynamic of Religion*. Leiden: E. J. Brill, 1994.

Bambach, Charles. *Heidegger, Dilthey, and the Crisis of Historicism*. Ithaca: Cornell University Press, 1995.

Banerjee, Sumanta. "Marginalization of Women's Popular Culture in Nineteenth Century Bengal." *Recasting Women*, ed. Kumkum Sangari and Sudesh Vaid. New Brunswick: Rutgers University Press, 1990.

Banerji, Himani. "Attired in Virtue: The Discourse on Shame (lajja) and Clothing of the Bhadramahila in Colonial Bengal." *From the Seams of History: Essays on Indian Women*, ed. Bharati Ray. Delhi: Oxford University Press, 1995.

———. "Fashioning a Self." *Economic and Political Weekly*, 26 October 1991.

Barash, Jeffrey. *Martin Heidegger and the Problem of Historical Meaning*. Dordrecht: Martinus Nijhoff, 1988.

Barrier, N. Gerald, ed. *The Census in British India*. New Delhi: Manohar, 1981.

Barry, Andrew, Thomas Osborne, and Nikolas Rose. Introduction. *Foucault and Political Reason*. Chicago: University of Chicago Press, 1996.

———, eds. *Foucault and Political Reason*. Chicago: University of Chicago Press, 1996.

Basu, Aparna. *The Growth of Education and Political Development in India, 1898–1920*. Delhi: Oxford University Press, 1974.

———. "National Education in Bengal: 1905–1912." *The Contested Terrain: Perspectives on Education in India*, ed. Sabyasachi Bhattacharya. New Delhi: Orient Longman, 1998.

Berkemer, G., et al., eds. *Explorations in the History of South Asia: Essays in Honour of Dieter Rothmund*. New Delhi: Manohar, 2001.

Bhagavan, Manu. *Sovereign Spheres: Princes, Education and Empire in Colonial India.* New Delhi: Oxford University Press, 2003.

Bhate, Saroja. "Position of Sanskrit in Public Education and Scientific Research in Modern India." *Ideology and Status of Sanskrit*, ed. Jan E. M. Houben. Leiden: E. J. Brill, 1996.

Bhattacharya, Sabyasachi, ed. *The Contested Terrain: Perspectives on Education in India.* New Delhi: Orient Longman, 1998.

Bloch, Marc. *The Historian's Craft*, trans. P. Putnam. Manchester: Manchester University Press, 1979.

Borthwick, Meredith. *The Changing Role of Women in Bengal, 1849–1905.* Princeton: Princeton University Press, 1984.

Bourdieu, Pierre. "The Berber House." *Rules and Meaning*, ed. Mary Douglas. New York: Penguin, 1973.

Breckenridge, Carol, and Peter van der Veer, eds. *Orientalism and the Postcolonial Predicament.* Philadelphia: University of Pennsylvania Press, 1993.

Brown, Emily C. *Har Dayal: Hindu Revolutionary and Rationalist.* Tucson: University of Arizona Press, 1975.

Brown, Wendy. *States of Injury.* Princeton: Princeton University Press, 1995.

Burchell, Graham, Colin Gordon, and Peter Miller, eds. *The Foucault Effect.* Chicago: University of Chicago Press, 1991.

Burckhardt, Jacob. *The Civilization of the Renaissance in Italy*, trans. S. C. G. Middlemore. New York: Mentor, 1960.

Burton, Antoinette. *Burdens of History: British Feminists, Indian Women, and Imperial Culture, 1865–1915.* Chapel Hill: University of North Carolina Press, 1994.

———, ed. *Gender, Sexuality and Colonial Modernities.* London: Routledge, 1999.

Byrne, Peter. *Natural Religion and the Nature of Religion: The Legacy of Deism.* London: Routledge, 1989.

Canguilhem, Georges. *The Normal and the Pathological*, trans. Carolyn Fawcett. New York: Zone, 1989.

Carr, David. *Time, Narrative and History.* Bloomington: Indiana University Press, 1986.

Carruthers, Mary J. *The Book of Memory: A Study of Memory in Medieval Culture.* Cambridge: Cambridge University Press, 1990.

Certeau, Michel de. *The Writing of History*, trans. Tom Conley. New York: Columbia University Press, 1988.

Chakrabarti, Sambuddha. "Changing Notions of Conjugal Relations in Nineteenth Century Bengal." *Mind, Body and Society: Life and Mentality in Colonial Bengal*, ed. Rajat Kanta Ray. Calcutta: Oxford University Press, 1995.

Chakrabarty, Dipesh. "The Difference-Deferral of a Colonial Modernity: Public Debates on Domesticity in British Bengal." *Subaltern Studies VIII*, ed. David Arnold and David Hardiman. Delhi: Oxford University Press, 1994.

———. *Habitations of Modernity.* Chicago: University of Chicago Press, 2002.

————. *Provincializing Europe: Postcolonial Thought and Historical Difference*. Princeton: Princeton University Press, 2000.

Chakraborty, Usha. *Condition of Bengali Women around the 2nd Half of the 19th Century*. Calcutta: K. L. Mukhopadhyaya, 1963.

Chakravarti, Uma. "Whatever Happened to the Vedic Dasi? Orientalism, Nationalism and a Script for the Past." *Recasting Women*, ed. Kumkum Sangari and Sudesh Vaid. New Brunswick: Rutgers University Press, 1990.

Chandra, Bipan. *The Rise and Growth of Economic Nationalism in India*. New Delhi: People's Publishing House, 1966.

Chandra, Sudhir. "The Cultural Component of Economic Nationalism: R. C. Dutt's *Lake of Palms*." *Indian Historical Review* 12, nos. 1–2 (July 1985–January 1986).

Chatterjee, Partha. *The Nation and Its Fragments*. Delhi: Oxford University Press, 1995.

Chatterjee, Partha, and Gyan Pandey, eds. *Subaltern Studies VII*. Delhi: Oxford University Press, 1994.

Chaudhuri, Nupur, and Margaret Strobel, eds. *Western Women and Imperialism: Complicity and Resistance*. Bloomington: Indiana University Press, 1992.

Chirol, Valentine. *Indian Unrest*. London: Macmillan, 1910.

Clifford, James. *The Predicament of Culture*. Cambridge: Harvard University Press, 1988.

Clifford, James, and G. E. Marcus, eds. *Writing Culture*. Berkeley: University of California Press, 1986.

Clive, John. *Macaulay: The Shaping of the Historian*. Cambridge: Harvard University Press, 1987.

Clothey, F., ed. *Images of Man: Religion and Historical Process in South Asia*. Madras: New Era, 1982.

Cohn, Bernard S. *An Anthropologist among the Historians and Other Essays*. New Delhi: Oxford University Press, 1988.

————. *Colonialism and Its Forms of Knowledge*. Princeton: Princeton University Press, 1996.

Collins, Steven. *Selfless Persons: Imagery and Thought in Theravada Buddhism*. Cambridge: Cambridge University Press, 1982.

Conlon, Frank. "The Census of India as a Source for the Historical Study of Religion and Caste." *The Census in British India*, ed. N. Gerald Barrier. New Delhi: Manohar, 1981.

Copjec, Joan, ed. *Supposing the Subject*. London: Verso, 1994.

Crook, Nigel, ed. *The Transmission of Knowledge in South Asia*. Delhi: Oxford University Press, 1996.

Dalmia, Vasudha. "Sanskrit Scholars and Pandits of the Old School: The Benares Sanskrit College and the Constitution of Authority in the Late Nineteenth Century." *Journal of Indian Philosophy* 24 (1996).

Daniel, Sheryl B. "The Tool Box Approach of the Tamil to the Issues of Moral

Responsibility and Human Destiny." *Karma: An Anthropological Inquiry*, ed. Charles F. Keyes and E. Valentine Daniel. Berkeley: University of California Press, 1983.

Daniel, Valentine. *Fluid Signs: Being a Person the Tamil Way*. Berkeley: University of California Press, 1984.

Daston, Lorraine. "Marvelous Facts and Miraculous Evidence in Early Modern Europe." *Critical Inquiry* 18, no. 1 (autumn 1991).

———. "The Nature of Nature in Early Modern Europe." *Configurations* 6, no. 2 (1998).

Datta, Nonica. "The 'Subalternity' of Education: Gurukuls in Rural Southeast Punjab." *Knowledge, Power and Politics*, ed. Mushirul Hasan. New Delhi: Roli, 1998.

Davis, Richard. *Lives of Indian Images*. Princeton: Princeton University Press, 1997.

Derrida, Jacques. *Margins of Philosophy*, trans. Alan Bass. Brighton, Sussex: Harvester, 1982.

Deshpande, Madhav M. "Pandit and Professor: Transformations in the 19th Century Maharashtra." *The Pandit: Traditional Scholarship in India*, ed. Axel Michaels. New Delhi: Manohar, 2001.

Dharampal. *The Beautiful Tree: Indigenous Education in the Eighteenth Century*. New Delhi: Biblia Impex, 1983.

Dharmavira. *Lala Har Dayal and Revolutionary Movements of His Times*. New Delhi: Indian Book, 1970.

Dilthey, W. W. *Selected Writings*, ed. and trans. H. P. Rickman. Cambridge: Cambridge University Press, 1976.

Dirks, Nicholas. *Castes of Mind*. Princeton: Princeton University Press, 2001.

Douglas, Mary, ed. *Rules and Meaning*. Penguin, 1973.

Dutta, Krishna, and Andrew Robinson, eds. *Rabindranath Tagore: An Anthology*. London: Picador, 1997.

Eck, Diana L. *Darsan: Seeing the Divine Image in India*, 3rd edn. New York: Columbia University Press, 1998.

Eickelman, Dale F. *Knowledge and Power in Morocco: The Education of a Twentieth-Century Notable*. Princeton: Princeton University Press, 1985.

Elmhirst, L. K. *Rabindranath Tagore: Pioneer in Education*. London: John Murray, 1961.

Emilsen, William. "Gandhi and Mayo's Mother India." *South Asia* 10, no. 1 (June 1987).

Fabian, Johannes. *Time and the Other: How Anthropology Makes Its Object*. New York: Columbia University Press, 1983.

Fasolt, Constantine. *The Limits of History*. Chicago: University of Chicago Press, 2004.

Feuerbach, Ludwig. *The Fiery Brook: Selected Writings of Ludwig Feuerbach*, trans. Zawar Hanfi. New York: Anchor, 1972.

Field, Harry. *After Mother India*. New York: Harcourt, Brace, 1929.

Fischer-Tine, H. "The Only Hope for Fallen India: The Gurukul Kangri as an

Experiment in National Education." *Explorations in the History of South Asia: Essays in Honour of Dieter Rothmund*, ed. G. Berkemer et al. New Delhi: Manohar, 2001.

Fisher, Fred B. *India's Silent Revolution*. New York: Macmillan, 1919.

Forbes, Geraldine. "In Search of the 'Pure Heathen': Missionary Women in Nineteenth Century India." *Economic and Political Weekly*, 26 April 1986.

———. *Women in Modern India*. Cambridge: Cambridge University Press, 1996.

Foucault, Michel. "About the Beginnings of a Hermeneutics of the Self." *Political Theory* 21, no. 2 (May 1993).

———. *The Archaeology of Knowledge*. New York: Harper Colophon, 1972.

———. "Governmentality." *The Foucault Effect*, ed. Graham Burchell, Colin Gordon, and Peter Miller. Chicago: University of Chicago Press, 1991.

———. *The History of Sexuality: An Introduction*. New York: Pantheon, 1968–86.

Freedberg, Daniel. *The Power of Images*. Chicago: University of Chicago Press, 1989.

Fuller, C. J. *The Camphor Flame: Popular Hinduism and Society in India*. Princeton: Princeton University Press, 1992.

Gadamer, Hans-Georg. "The Problem of Historical Consciousness." *Interpretive Social Science: A Second Look*, ed. Paul Rabinow and William Sullivan. Berkeley: University of California Press, 1987.

———. *Truth and Method*. London: Sheed and Ward, 1975.

Ganguli, Birendranath N. *Dadabhai Naoroji and the Drain Theory*. New Delhi, 1965.

Ghosh, Srabashi. " 'Birds in a Cage': Bengali Social Life as Recorded in Autobiographies by Women." *Economic and Political Weekly*, 25 October 1986.

Ghurye, K. G. *Preservation of Learned Tradition in India*. Bombay: Popular Book Depot, 1950.

Godlove, Terry F. *Religion, Interpretation, and Diversity of Belief*. Cambridge: Cambridge University Press, 1989.

Guha, Ranajit. "The Authority of Vernacular Pasts." *Meanjin*, winter 1992.

———. *Dominance without Hegemony*. Cambridge: Harvard University Press, 1997.

Guha, Sumit. "The Politics of Identity and Enumeration in India c. 1600–1990." *Comparative Studies in Society and History* 45, no. 1 (2003).

Gupta, Charu. "Portrayal of Women in Premchand's Stories: A Critique." *Social Scientist* 19, nos. 5–6 (May–June 1991).

Hacking, Ian. "Making Up People." *Reconstructing Individualism*, ed. Thomas Heller, Morton Sosna, and David Wellbery. Stanford: Stanford University Press, 1986.

Hardy, Peter. *The Muslims of British India*. Cambridge: Cambridge University Press, 1972.

Harrison, Peter. *"Religion" and the Religions in the English Enlightenment*. Cambridge: Cambridge University Press, 1990.

Hasan, Mushirul, ed. *Knowledge, Power and Politics*. New Delhi: Roli, 1998.

Hegel, G. W. F. *Lectures on the Philosophy of Religion* [The Lectures of 1827], ed. Peter C. Hodgson. Berkeley: University of California Press, 1988.

Heidegger, Martin. "The Age of the World Picture." *The Question concerning Technology and Other Essays*, trans. William Lovitt. New York: Harper Torchbooks, 1977.

———. *Being and Time*, trans. John Macquarrie and Edward Robinson. Oxford: Blackwell, 2000.

———. *Nietzsche*, vol 4, *Nihilism*, ed. David F. Krell, trans. Frank A. Capuzzi. San Francisco: Harper and Row, 1982.

Heller, Thomas, Morton Sosna, and David Wellbery, eds. *Reconstructing Individualism*. Stanford: Stanford University Press, 1986.

Hick, John. Foreword. *The Meaning and End of Religion*, by Wilfred Cantwell Smith. Minneapolis: Fortress, 1991.

Hindess, Barry. "The Liberal Government of Unfreedom." *Alternatives* 26, no. 2 (2001).

Houben, Jan E. M., ed. *Ideology and Status of Sanskrit*. Leiden: E. J. Brill, 1996.

Hoy, David Couzens. "History, Historicity, and Historiography in *Being and Time*." *Heidegger and Modern Philosophy: Critical Essays*, ed. Michael Murray. New Haven: Yale University Press, 1978.

Hunter, Ian. *Culture and Government: The Emergence of Literary Education*. Houndsmill, Basingstoke, Hampshire: Macmillan, 1988.

———. *Rethinking the School*, New York: St. Martins, 1994.

———. "The State of History and the Empire of Metaphysics." *History and Theory* 44 (May 2005).

Inden, Ronald. *Imagining India*. Oxford: Basil Blackwell, 1990.

Izard, Michael, and P. Smith, eds. *Between Belief and Transgression*. Chicago: University of Chicago Press, 1982.

Jaffee, Martin S. *Torah in the Mouth: Writing and Oral Tradition in Palestinian Judaism 200 BCE–400 CE*. New York: Oxford University Press, 2001.

Jalal, Ayesha. *Self and Sovereignty: Individual and Community in South Asian Islam Since 1850*. London: Routledge, 2000.

Jayawardena, Kumari. *The White Woman's Other Burden: Western Women and South Asia during British Colonial Rule*. New York: Routledge, 1995.

Jha, Manoranjan. *Katherine Mayo and India*. New Delhi: People's Publishing, 1971.

Jones, Kenneth W. *Arya Dharm: Hindu Consciousness in 19th Century Punjab*. New Delhi: Manohar, 1989.

Jones, Sue Stedman. "The Concept of Belief in *The Elementary Forms*." *On Durkheim's Elementary Forms of Religious Life*, ed. N. J. Allen, W. S. F. Pickering, and W. Watts Miller. London: Routledge, 1998.

Jordens, J. T. F. "Reconversion to Hinduism: The *Shuddhi* of the Arya Samaj." *Religion in South Asia*, 2nd edn, ed. Geoff A. Oddie. New Delhi: Manohar, 1991.

Joyce, Patrick, ed. *The Social in Question*. London: Routledge, 2002.

Kabir, Humayun. *Education in New India*. London: Allen and Unwin, 1956.

Kant, Immanuel. *Anthropology from a Pragmatic Point of View*, trans. Victor Dowdell. Carbondale: Southern Illinois University Press, 1978.

Kapferer, Bruce, ed. *Transaction and Meaning*. Philadelphia: Institute for the Study of Human Issues, 1976.

Karlekar, Malavika. "Kadambani and the Bhadralok: Early Debates over Women's Education in Bengal." *Economic and Political Weekly*, 26 April 1986.

———. *Voices from Within: Early Personal Narratives of Bengali Women*. Delhi: Oxford University Press, 1991.

Kaviraj, Sudipta. "The Imaginary Institution of India." *Subaltern Studies VII*, ed. Partha Chatterjee and Gyan Pandey. Delhi: Oxford University Press, 1994.

———. *The Unhappy Consciousness*. Delhi: Oxford University Press, 1998.

Kaviraj, Sudipta, and Sunil Khilnani, eds. *Civil Society: History and Possibilities*. Cambridge: Cambridge University Press, 2001.

Kejariwal, O. P. *The Asiatic Society of Bengal and the Discovery of India's Past, 1784–1838*. Delhi: Oxford University Press, 1988.

Keyes, Charles F., and Daniel E. Valentine, eds. *Karma: An Anthropological Inquiry*. Berkeley: University of California Press, 1983.

King, Richard. *Orientalism and Religion: Postcolonial Theory, India and "The Mystic East."* London: Routledge, 1999.

Kolb, David. *The Critique of Pure Modernity*. Chicago: University of Chicago Press, 1986.

Koselleck, Reinhart. *Futures Past*, trans. Keith Tribe. Cambridge: MIT Press, 1985.

Kumar, Krishna. *Political Agenda of Education*. New Delhi: Sage, 1991.

Kumar, Nita. *Lessons from Schools: The History of Education in Banaras*. New Delhi: Sage, 2000.

———. "Religion and Ritual in Indian Schools: Benaras from the 1880s to the 1940s." *The Transmission of Knowledge in South Asia*, ed. Nigel Crook. Delhi: Oxford University Press, 1996.

———, ed. *Women as Subjects: South Asian Histories*. Charlottesville: University Press of Virginia, 1994.

Laird, M. A. *Missionaries and Education in Bengal, 1793–1837*. Oxford: Clarendon, 1972.

Latour, Bruno. *We Have Never Been Modern*, trans. Catherine Porter. Cambridge: Harvard University Press, 1993.

Latour, Bruno, and Steve Woolgar. *Laboratory Life: The Construction of Scientific Facts*, 2nd edn. Princeton: Princeton University Press, 1986.

Lelyveld, David. *Aligarh's First Generation: Muslim Solidarity in British India*. Delhi: Oxford University Press, 1996.

Lévi-Strauss, Claude. *The Savage Mind*. London: Weidenfeld and Nicolson, 1972.

Lévy-Bruhl, Lucien. *How Natives Think*, trans. Lilian Clare. London: George Allen and Unwin, 1926 [1910].

Maclure, J. Stuart, ed. *Educational Documents: England and Wales, 1816–1963*. London: Chapman and Hall, 1965.

Majumdar, R. C. "Nationalist Historians." *Historians of India, Pakistan and Ceylon,* ed. C. H. Philips. London: Oxford University Press, 1961.
———. *Renascent India: First Phase.* Calcutta: G. Bharadwaj, 1976.
Malik, Hafeez. *Sir Sayyid Ahmad Khan and Muslim Modernization in India and Pakistan.* New York: Columbia University Press, 1980.
Mallick, A. R. "Modern Historical Writing in Bengali." *Historians of India, Pakistan and Ceylon,* ed. C. H. Philips. London: Oxford University Press, 1961.
Marriot, McKim. "Hindu Transactions: Diversity without Dualism." *Transaction and Meaning,* ed. Bruce Kapferer. Philadelphia: Institute for the Study of Human Issues, 1976.
———, ed. *India through Hindu Categories.* New Delhi: Sage, 1990.
Marshall, P. J. Introduction. *The British Discovery of Hinduism in the Eighteenth Century.* Cambridge: Cambridge University Press, 1970.
———, ed. *The British Discovery of Hinduism in the Eighteenth Century.* Cambridge: Cambridge University Press, 1970.
Marx, Karl. *Capital,* vol. 1. Moscow: Progress, 1978.
Marx, Karl, and Frederick Engels. *Manifesto of the Communist Party.* Peking: Foreign Languages Press, 1968.
Massumi, Brian. "The Autonomy of Affect." *Deleuze: A Critical Reader,* ed. Paul Patton. Oxford: Blackwell, 1996.
McLane, John R. *Indian Nationalism and the Early Congress.* Princeton: Princeton University Press, 1977.
Michaels, Axel, ed. *The Pandit: Traditional Scholarship in India.* New Delhi: Manohar, 2001.
Mignolo, Walter. *The Darker Side of the Renaissance,* 2nd edn. Ann Arbor: University of Michigan Press, 2003.
Millar, John. *The Origin of the Distinction of Ranks.* Bristol: Thoemmes Antiquarian, 1990 [1806].
Minault, Gail. "Other Voices, Other Rooms: The View from the Zenana." *Women as Subjects: South Asian Histories,* ed. Nita Kumar. Charlottesville: University Press of Virginia, 1994.
———. *Secluded Scholars: Women's Education and Muslim Social Reform in Colonial India.* Delhi: Oxford University Press, 1998.
Minault, Gail, and David Lelyveld. "The Campaign for a Muslim University, 1898–1920." *Modern Asian Studies* 8, no. 2 (1974).
Mitchell, Timothy. *Colonizing Egypt.* Cambridge: Cambridge University Press, 1988.
Mohanty, Jitendra Nath. *Reason and Tradition in Indian Thought.* Oxford: Clarendon, 1992.
Muecke, Stephen. *Ancient and Modern: Time, Culture and Indigenous Philosophy.* Sydney: UNSW, 2004.
Mukherjee, Haridas, and Uma Mukherjee. *The Origins of the National Education*

Movement (1905-1910), 2nd edn. Calcutta: National Council of Education, Bengal, 2000.

Mukherjee, Himangshu B. *Education for Fulness: A Study of the Educational Thought and Experiment of Rabindranath Tagore*. Bombay: Asia Publishing, 1962.

Murray, Michael, ed. *Heidegger and Modern Philosophy: Critical Essays*. New Haven: Yale University Press, 1978.

Murshid, Ghulam. *Reluctant Debutante: Response of Bengali Women to Modernization, 1849-1905*. Rajshahi: Rajshahi University, 1983.

Murshid, Tazeen M. *The Sacred and the Secular: Bengal Muslim Discourses, 1871-1971*. Calcutta: Oxford University Press, 1995.

Nandy, Ashis. *The Intimate Enemy*. Delhi: Oxford University Press, 1983.

———. "A Report on the Present State of Health of the Gods and Goddesses in South Asia." *Postcolonial Studies* 4, no. 2 (July 2001).

Needham, Rodney. *Belief, Language, and Experience*. Chicago: University of Chicago Press, 1972.

Nigam, Sanjay. "Disciplining and Policing the 'Criminals by Birth.'" *Indian Economic and Social History Review* 27 nos. 2-3 (1990).

Oakeshott, Michael. *On History and Other Essays*. Oxford: Basil Blackwell, 1983.

Oddie, Geoff A. "Anti-missionary Feeling and Hindu Revivalism in Madras: The Hindu Preaching and Tract Societies, C. 1886-91." *Images of Man: Religion and Historical Process in South Asia*, ed. F. Clothey. Madras: New Era, 1982.

———, ed. *Religion in South Asia*, 2nd edn. New Delhi: Manohar, 1991.

O'Hanlon, Rosalind. Introduction. *A Comparison between Women and Men*, by Tarabai Shinde. Madras: Oxford University Press, 1994.

Orsini, Francesca. *The Hindi Public Sphere, 1920-1940*. New Delhi: Oxford University Press, 2002.

Pailin, David A. *Attitudes to Other Religions: Comparative Religion in Seventeenth and Eighteenth-Century Britain*. Manchester: Manchester University Press, 1984.

Palmer, Richard, ed. and trans. *Gadamer in Conversation*. New Haven: Yale University Press, 2001.

Pandey, Geetanjali. "How Equal? Women in Premchand's Writings." *Economic and Political Weekly*, 13 December 1986.

Pandey, Gyan. *The Construction of Communalism in Colonial North India*. New Delhi: Oxford University Press, 1992.

Pant, Rashmi. "The Cognitive Status of Caste in Colonial Ethnography: A Review of Some Literature on the North West Provinces and Oudh." *Indian Economic and Social History Review* 24, no. 2 (1987).

Patton, Paul, ed. *Deleuze: A Critical Reader*. Oxford: Blackwell, 1996.

Peabody, Norbert. "Cents, Sense, Census: Human Inventories in Late Precolonial and Early Colonial India." *Comparative Studies in Society and History* 43 (2001).

Perrill, Jeffrey. "Punjab Orientalism: the Anjuman-I-Punjab and Punjab University, 1865-1888." PhD diss., University of Missouri, Columbia, 1976.

Philips, C. H., ed. *Historians of India, Pakistan and Ceylon*. London: Oxford University Press, 1961.

Polanyi, Karl. *The Great Transformation*. Boston: Beacon, 1965.

Pollock, Sheldon. "The Death of Sanskrit." *Comparative Studies in Society and History* 43, no. 2 (2001).

———. "New Intellectuals in Seventeenth-Century India." *Indian Economic and Social History Review* 38, no. 1 (2001).

Poovey, Mary. "The Liberal Civil Subject and the Social." *Public Culture* 14, no. 1 (winter 2002).

Prakash, Gyan. *Another Reason: Science and the Imagination of Modern India*. Princeton: Princeton University Press, 1999.

Puillon, Jean. "Remarks on the Verb 'To Believe,' " trans. John Leavitt. *Between Belief and Transgression*, ed. Michael Izard and P. Smith. Chicago: University of Chicago Press, 1982.

Rabinow, Paul, and William Sullivan, eds. *Interpretive Social Science: A Second Look*. Berkeley: University of California Press, 1987.

Ramakrishna, V. "Women's Journals in Andhra during the Nineteenth Century." *Social Scientist* 19, nos. 5–6 (May–June 1991).

Raman, Sita Anantha. *Getting Girls to School: Social Reform in the Tamil Nadu Districts, 1870–1930*. Calcutta: Stree, 1996.

Ramanujan, A. K. "Is There an Indian Way of Thinking? An Informal Essay." *India through Hindu Categories*, ed. McKim Marriot. New Delhi: Sage, 1990.

Ramusack, Barbara N. "Cultural Missonaries, Maternal Imperialists, Feminist Allies: British Women Activists in India, 1865–1945." *Western Women and Imperialism: Complicity and Resistance*, ed. Nupur Chaudhuri and Margaret Strobel. Bloomington: Indiana University Press, 1992.

Ray, Bharati, ed. *From the Seams of History: Essays on Indian Women*. Delhi: Oxford University Press, 1995.

Ray, Rajat Kanta, ed. *Mind, Body and Society: Life and Mentality in Colonial Bengal*. Calcutta: Oxford University Press, 1995.

Ricoeur, Paul. *Freud and Philosophy: An Essay on Interpretation*, trans. David Savage. New Haven: Yale University Press, 1970.

———. "The Task of Hermeneutics." *Heidegger and Modern Philosophy: Critical Essays*, ed. Michael Murray. New Haven: Yale University Press, 1978.

———. *Time and Narrative*, vol. 3, trans. K. Blamey and D. Pellauer. Chicago: University of Chicago Press, 1988.

Rorty, Richard. *Philosophy and the Mirror of Nature*. Princeton: Princeton University Press, 1979.

Rosenthal, A. M. "Mother India Thirty Years Later." *Foreign Affairs* 35, no. 4 (July 1957).

Russell, Ralph, and Khurshidul Islam. *Ghalib: Life and Letters*. Delhi: Oxford University Press, 1994.

Sangari, Kumkum, and Sudesh Vaid, eds. *Recasting Women*. New Brunswick: Rutgers University Press, 1990.

Sarkar, Sumit. " 'Kaliyuga,' 'Chakri' and 'Bhakti': Ramakrishna and His Times." *Economic and Political Weekly*, 18 July 1992.

Sarkar, Sumit. *The Swadeshi Movement in Bengal, 1903-1908*. New Delhi: People's Publishing, 1973.

Sarkar, Tanika. *Hindu Wife, Hindu Nation*. Bloomington: Indiana University Press, 2001.

———. *Words to Win: The Making of Amar Jiban: A Modern Autobiography*. New Delhi: Kali for Women, 1999.

Schwab, Raymond. *The Oriental Renaissance*, trans. G. Patterson-Black and V. Reinking. New York: Columbia University Press, 1984 [1950].

Seth, Sanjay. "Nationalism, National Identity and 'History': Nehru's Search for India." *Thesis Eleven* 32 (1992).

———. "Reason or Reasoning? Clio or Siva?" *Social Text* 78 (2004).

———. "Rewriting Histories of Nationalism: The Politics of 'Moderate Nationalism' in India, 1870-1905." *American Historical Review* 104, no. 1 (February 1999).

———. "Which Good Book? Missionary Education and Conversion in Colonial India." *Semeia* 88 (2001).

Shapin, Steven, and Simon Schaffer. *Leviathan and the Air-Pump*. Princeton: Princeton University Press, 1985.

Sharma, Narinder Kumar. *Linguistic and Educational Aspirations under a Colonial System*. Delhi: Concept, 1976.

Sharma, Usha, and B. M. Sharma, eds. *Women [sic] Education in British India*. New Delhi: Commonwealth, 1995.

Shils, Edward, and Henry Finch, eds. *The Methodology of the Social Sciences: Max Weber*. New York: Free Press, 1949.

Shukla, Sonal. "Cultivating Minds: 19th Century Gujarati Women's Journals." *Economic and Political Weekly*, 26 October 1991.

Singer, Milton. *When a Great Tradition Modernizes*. New York: Praeger, 1972.

Sinha, Mrinalini. Editor's Introduction. *Selections from Mother India*, by Katherine Mayo, ed. Mrinalini Sinha. New Delhi: Kali for Women, 1998.

———. "The Lineage of the 'Indian' Modern." *Gender, Sexuality and Colonial Modernities*, ed. Antoinette Burton. London: Routledge, 1999.

Sinha, Sasadhar. *Social Thinking of Rabindranath Tagore*. Bombay: Asia Publishing, 1961.

Smith, Jonathan Z. *Imagining Religion: From Babylon to Jonestown*. Chicago: University of Chicago Press, 1982.

Smith, Richard S. "Rule-by-Records and Rule-by-Reports: Complementary Aspects of the British Imperial Rule of Law." *Contributions to Indian Sociology* 19, no. 1, new series (1985).

Smith, Wilfred Cantwell. *Faith and Belief*. Princeton: Princeton University Press, 1979.

———. *The Meaning and End of Religion*. Minneapolis: Fortress, 1991.

Staal, J. F. *Nambudiri Veda Recitation*. The Hague: Mouton, 1961.

———. *Ritual and Mantras: Rules without Meaning*. Delhi: Motilal Banarsidass, 1996.

Strathern, Marilyn. *The Gender of the Gift*. Berkeley: University of California Press, 1988.

Talwar, Vir Bharat. "Women's Journals in Hindi, 1910–1920." *Recasting Women*, ed. Kumkum Sangari and Sudesh Vaid. New Brunswick: Rutgers University Press, 1990.

Taussig, Michael. *The Devil and Commodity Fetishism in South America*. Chapel Hill: University of North Carolina Press, 1980.

Taylor, Charles. *Hegel*. Cambridge: Cambridge University Press, 1975.

———. "Two Theories of Modernity." *Public Culture* 11, no. 1 (1999).

Tharu, Susie. "Tracing Savitri's Pedigree." *Recasting Women*, ed. Kumkum Sangari and Sudesh Vaid. New Brunswick: Rutgers University Press, 1990.

Toulmin, Stephen. *Cosmopolis: The Hidden Agenda of Modernity*. New York: Free Press, 1990.

Trautmann, Thomas. *Aryans and British India*. Berkeley: University of California Press, 1997.

Veyne, Paul. *Writing History*, trans. Mina Moore-Rinvolueri. Middletown, Conn.: Wesleyan University Press, 1984.

Viswanathan, Gauri. *Masks of Conquest: Literary Study and British Rule in India*. New York: Columbia University Press, 1989.

Waghorne, Joanne P., and Norman Cutler, eds. *Gods of Flesh, Gods of Stone: The Embodiment of Divinity in India*. Chambersburg, Penn.: Anima 1985.

Walsh, Judith. "The Virtuous Wife and the Well-Ordered Home: The Re-conceptualization of Bengali Women and Their Worlds." *Mind, Body and Society: Life and Mentality in Colonial Bengal*, ed. Rajat Kanta Ray. Calcutta: Oxford University Press, 1995.

Warnke, Georgia. *Gadamer: Hermeneutics, Tradition and Reason*. Stanford: Stanford University Press, 1987.

Weber, Max. "Objectivity in Social Science and Social Policy." *The Methodology of the Social Sciences: Max Weber*, ed. Edward Shils and Henry Finch. New York: Free Press, 1949.

Winch, Peter. *The Idea of a Social Science*, 2nd edn. London: Routledge, 1998.

Wittgenstein, Ludwig. *Remarks on Frazer's Golden Bough*, ed. Rush Rhees, trans. A. C. Miles. Atlantic Highlands, N.J.: Humanities, 1979.

Wood, Ananda K. *Knowledge before Printing and After: The Indian Tradition in Changing Kerala*. Delhi: Oxford University Press, 1985.

Young, Richard Fox. *Resistant Hinduism*. Vienna: De Nobili Research Library, 1981.

Zammito, John H. *Kant, Herder, and the Birth of Anthropology*. Chicago: University of Chicago Press, 2002.

Zastoupil, Lynn, and Martin Moir, eds. *The Great Indian Education Debate: Documents Relating to the Orientalist-Anglicist Controversy, 1781–1843*. Richmond: Curzon, 1999.

Žižek, Slavoj. "Is There a Cause of the Subject?" *Supposing the Subject*, ed. Joan Copjec. London: Verso, 1994.

Index

Sanjay Seth is a reader in politics at La Trobe University, Melbourne. He is also a professor of politics at Goldsmiths College, University of London.

Library of Congress Cataloging-in-Publication Data
Seth, Sanjay, 1961–
Subject lessons : the Western education of colonial India / Sanjay Seth.
p. cm. – (Politics, history, and culture)
Includes bibliographical references and index.
ISBN 978-0-8223-4086-7 (cloth : alk. paper)
ISBN 978-0-8223-4105-5 (pbk. : alk. paper)
1. Education – India – Western influences – History – 19th century. 2. Education
and state – India – History – 19th century. 3. Nationalism and education – India –
History – 20th century. I. Title.
LA1151.S4115 2007
379.54'09034 – dc22

2007004104

Printed in Great Britain
by Amazon